The world's first atomic bomb explodes in the New Mexico desert on July 16, 1945.

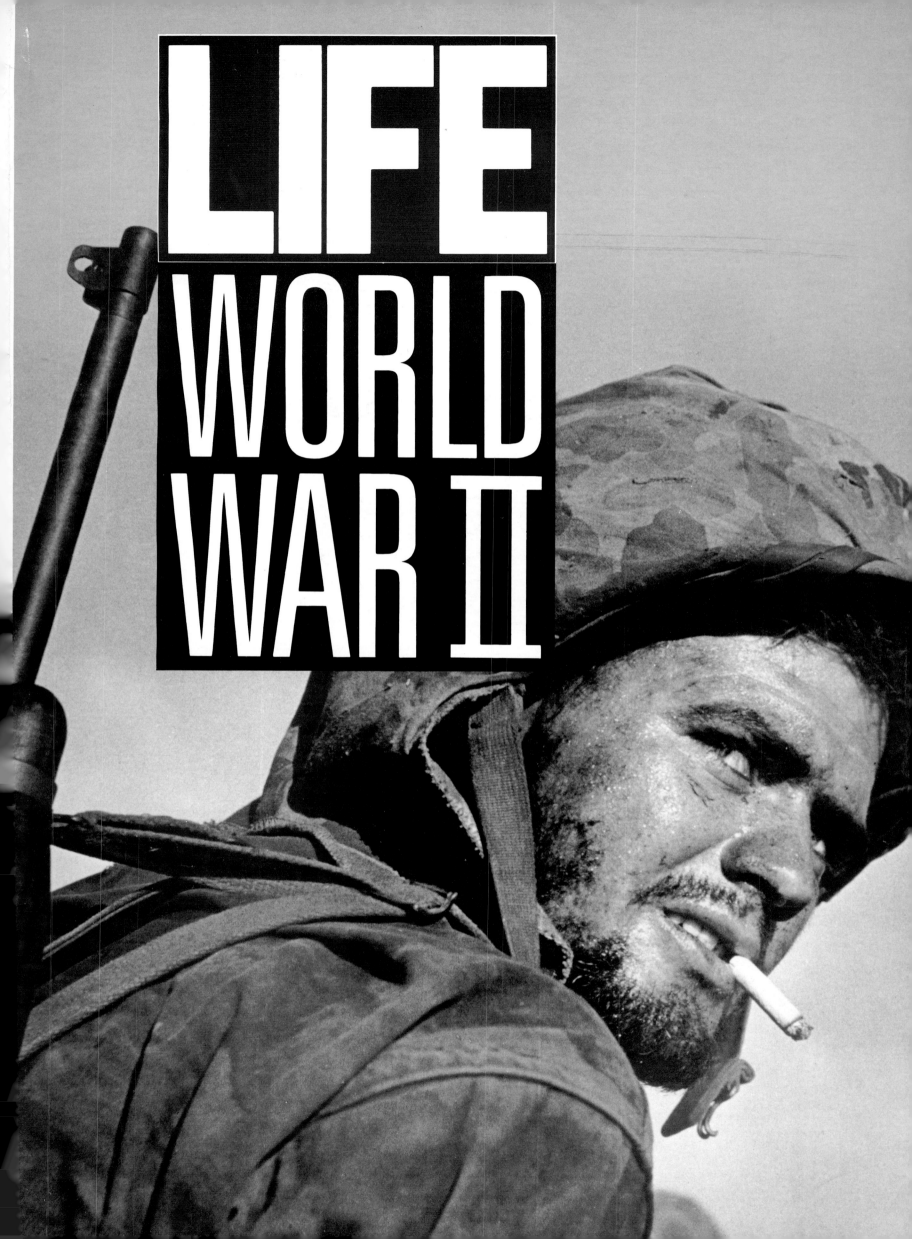

LIFE
WORLD
WAR II

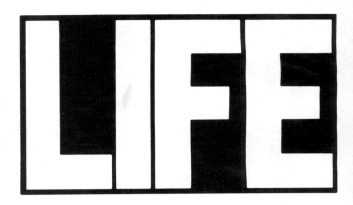

Published simultaneously in Canada by Little, Brown and Company (Canada) Limited

FIRST EDITION

Library of Congress Catalog Card No. 90-053296

PRINTED IN THE UNITED STATES OF AMERICA

WORLD WAR II

Edited by **Philip B. Kunhardt Jr.**

CONTENTS

Written by **Frank K. Kappler**
Design and Production: **Gene Light**
Editorial Coordinator: **Gedeon de Margitay**
Copy Editor: **Ricki Tarlow**
Research: **Elsie B. Washington**
Picture Research: **Gretchen Wessels**

Little, Brown and Company
BOSTON   TORONTO   LONDON

INTRODUCTION

When World War II broke out, LIFE was not quite three years old. Henry Luce, its founder, had not planned his big, exciting, picture weekly as a war magazine, but it soon became one, and for the next six years it brought the very look and smell and sound of combat into the American living room with speed and detail and force. It was not long before LIFE had become a national institution even though some people found it hard to look at the heart-wrenching pictures.

In the beginning LIFE's reporters and photographers had no experience in covering battle; most of the word men had a magazine or newspaper background or were tyro generalists, fresh out of school. And as for the picture takers, one had an architecture background, another glamourized movie stars and most were "little camera" specialists, adept at candidly capturing the American scene. Bob Capa was an exception, having risked his life for memorable pictures of the Spanish Civil War. These, and many more like them who would rapidly be hired, were the men (and some women too) who would soon be accompanying convoys stalked by U-boats, flying bombing missions, riding tanks in the desert, landing on Pacific atolls, jumping with paratroop-

ers into enemy territory and, like the warriors they covered, just trying to survive—all to send the truth, or as close to the truth as they could come, back home. Some were wounded or captured. A few were killed.

Later, several would become famous—Teddy White and John Hersey as prizewinning writers and, to name but a handful of the dozens of much-heralded photographers, Margaret Bourke-White, Carl Mydans, W. Eugene Smith, George Silk and, of course, Capa. When the war was done, most went back to what they had been doing before. But none would forget what each separately had gone through in the process of contributing to an extraordinary record of a world gone mad. And what they recorded and described, along with the thousands of pictures the magazine published that were taken by armed service combat photographers and from foreign sources, made LIFE mandatory reading during the war and the most successful and admired publication of its time.

In 1950, with the fighting still fresh and the wounds not yet healed, LIFE published a large-size picture history of World War II, which was basically a compilation of the magazine's extraordinary battle coverage. In a preface Henry Luce stated the book's case:

"Wars do settle some things, but wars are more than military action. This book is strictly a book of military history. It is therefore not a complete history of the war. It does not deal with the vast complex of political and social forces which precede and follow wars and are indeed intertwined with every battle . . . The military war . . . came to a successful conclusion for us in September 1945 with the final destruction of our enemies' capacity to resist our will. It then took its place on the great scroll of history as a completed entity. It was the greatest feat of arms ever accomplished on this planet. This book devotes itself to the recording of that tremendous feat. In large sweep or in fine detail, it is a ghastly, grisly story, but also one of high inspiration, of vast self-sacrifice, of a will-to-die for freedom."

Those very words can be repeated here to preface this new LIFE book. For, half a century and 175 million new Americans later, with the time come for the world to scrutinize the great conflict once again, it seems only fitting that LIFE publish a newly conceived and updated picture history of this war of all wars. First of all, the presentation of photographs has changed radically over the decades. Picture power, juxtaposition and surprise have superseded covering all the bases, making LIFE's long out-of-print 1950 work seem antique and no longer compelling. Secondly, and more important, new material and points of view have surfaced in the intervening years, much of it from LIFE's own pages, for the magazine has continued to be drawn to the subject of its first great crusade. Memoirs, newly discovered pictures and reassessments have constantly appeared, and entire special issues of the magazine have been devoted to this never-endingly fascinating subject.

Therefore, to make the military story of the war through its pictures as comprehensive as possible today, LIFE here has drawn upon not only its own resources and those of the American government and its World War II allies but on the archives of our former enemies as well. Along with the hundreds of professional camera wielders, the amateur photographer is now well represented too—Russian partisan, Polish resister, SS trooper, Japanese crewman, even a prisoner-of-war ingeniously resorting to X-ray film to record the sad sight before him *(page 274).*

Some pictures were made without an eye behind the camera; for example, the strips taken by purely mechanical, trigger-activated fighter-pilot's gun cameras or through the periscopes of submarines. Many of the important war negatives have had something less than archival care—a few were even buried, submerged, frozen or left to rot. When negatives were impossible to obtain, a number of the old prints from which we have made our reproductions we found cracked, torn, stained, mottled and blurred. How, for instance, did any film emulsion survive the atomic explosions at Hiroshima and Nagasaki to record so graphically the tragic scenes of the immediate aftermath that appear on pages 352-353 and 416 to 421?

This book is designed to tell the story of the war in the simplest, most direct and dramatic terms possible. Its sequence is chronological; it is divided into the war's seven years. Except for "The Seeds of War" at the beginning, "The War's Statistics" at the end and various spreads throughout— my contributions—the original text for this book was written by WW II expert Frank Kappler, for many years a distinguished LIFE writer and editor who saw action in the war in the Aleutians and in Italy as a sergeant in the 10th Mountain Division. His essays at the beginning of the chapters sum up in bold strokes the course of the war during those given 12 months. Immediately following each essay is a military calendar of the year, leaving the pictures that follow free of the necessity for tight, chronological order and for being all-inclusive.

In each of the seven chapters devoted to the war years are sections describing the American home front. Flocks of contemporary LIFE pictures are used to show what the war changed in the U.S. and what went on pretty much as usual. Even though this book does not attempt to tell the detailed story of LIFE's own involvement in the coverage of the conflict, particularly pertinent passages from original reports, editorials and correspondent files are occasionally included.

A word on the choice of pictures. Some will be new even to most WW II aficionados. But the great classics of the war have not been omitted because of overfamiliarity. Instead we have tried to use them in fresh and provocative ways. The 10 great pictures that end the book, for instance, illustrate the statistics that the war left behind, and in so doing they force cold, hard numbers to come alive and demand attention.

Today's editors of LIFE dedicate this book to yesterday's gallant journalists who reported World War II with such skill and bravery and devotion.

Philip B. Kunhardt Jr.
Editor

THE SEE

May 7, 1919. At this very moment, as military aides strain for a glimpse into the conference room at Versailles, the Allies' peace terms are being handed to the humiliated Germans.

On November 11, 1918, bells rang out all over Europe heralding peace. Soldiers on both sides climbed from their trenches and exchanged greetings. People embraced everywhere and a few even made love on the doorstoops of Europe to confirm the "war to end all war" was really over and life was still intact. Along with 30,000,000 casualties, World War I had effectively sabotaged the development of a European order for civilization, but, in addition, the very Peace that ended the carnage had, ironically, sown the seeds for an even greater and more widespread harvest of death and destruction—World War II. In the name of Peace the Allies remapped much of Europe in hope of getting rid of the territorial quarrels and the blood feuds that had led to WW I. Instead, Woodrow Wilson's idealistic dream of new countries and new boundaries based on common language and ethnic origin spawned only new minorities, new bitterness. Back from war, the Germans would not admit defeat and seethed under impossibly high reparations imposed by the Allies. Inflation ravaged the already tottering German economy as paper marks were carted to banks by the wheelbarrow, at the worst of the crisis 2½ million of them to the dollar. Class struggles swept the Continent as the old social orders began to break down. Dictators rose to power on promises, bombast and fear. Millions died by the sword, millions more from famine. The U.S. retreated into itself and hid from the bleak world, unwilling to face the fact that the crumbling of the European order threatened America as well. A worldwide depression ushered in the '30s. Totalitarian aggression was the order of the day. In the Pacific, Japan invaded Manchuria and then China itself. In Africa, Italy attacked Ethiopia. In Spain civil war broke out. Germany violated the Versailles peace treaty by fashioning a once-again-mighty army and reoccupying the Rhineland. The foundations of European order were rapidly crumbling. The fear of war only made war more inevitable as out-of-date diplomats knuckled under instead of standing up to new aggressions.

As the decade of the '30s spun toward its close amid upheaval and discord and confusion and alarm, the world suddenly found itself on the threshold of a true global war. So advanced now was mankind in the technology of killing that the next six years would see the loss of more than 50 million lives.

In 1917 the severely beaten Russians made a separate peace with Germany allowing them to stop killing foreigners and get on with the business of killing one another. The Czar's armies had disintegrated into a mutinous mob and for the next five years civil war raged, the death toll of which exceeded that of the world war the Russians had just quit. Torture, rape and atrocity became a way of life, but man was not the only killer as famine and disease joined in the slaughter. After a rapid succession of ever more radical governments, the Communist Party took over with Vladimir Ilyich Lenin its chief. This new form of political organization, which abolished religion and private ownership, seized control of the country's working-class revolution and started constructing a fearsome one-party military state. Typical of the impulsive, random fighting that swept Russia during the civil war is this 1917 Petrograd scene showing a crowd of Bolshevik sympathizers being cut down and dispersed by pro-czarist machine-gun fire. Another great wave of killing took place in the 1930s as a new leader, Joseph Stalin, made sure of his control by exterminating 8 million citizens and sending tens of millions more to forced labor camps.

Other new forces at work in Europe included the fascism of Benito Mussolini in a victorious yet frustrated Italy that had been denied the spoils and the Nazism of Adolf Hitler in a destitute Germany that had been forced to wallow in guilt. Both men had artfully taken power, the Duce in the early 1920s and the little Austrian drifter a decade later. Setting themselves up as old-time monarchs, each used his personal magnetism to hypnotize his people. Both were unscrupulous bullies who demanded absolute loyalty and were adept at getting rid of their enemies. Each despised communism. Hitler's hates included democracies in general and Jews in particular. With propaganda machines loudly proclaiming their messages of hope and fear, with radio harangues and dramatic orchestrated appearances, each became not only the leader of his government but the government itself. It did not take long for the demonic, introspective Führer to surpass his bombastic friend to the south in both cruelty and achievement. Having revived the German economy through a program of public works, secret rearmament and complete control of labor, Hitler used his Storm Troopers to arrest, confiscate and exterminate freely. He burned books in his campaign against the intellect, and in his initial step to rid the world of Jews he barred them from public office, teaching, journalism and sexual contact with Aryans. On the whole, the German people were enchanted. Revived and suddenly on the rise, few of them seemed much concerned over the brutal dictatorship behind it all.

Japan had been one of the Allies in World War I but the peace had brought her none of the land or raw materials her 80 million citizens so needed. How unfair and wrong, Japan felt, that the riches of the East—in particular rubber, tin and oil—were in the hands of the Western colonial powers. The 1930s, called the "dark valley" by the Japanese, were years filled with poverty, violence and political upheaval as the Imperial Army gained control of the government. In 1935 Japanese troops, hardened by four years of conquest in Manchuria, went clambering over the Great Wall and down into Peking. By autumn of '38 the warriors of the Rising Sun had taken half of China and killed 2 million in the process, including 100,000 civilians during the Rape of Nanking when Chinese were burned alive, butchered, raped and tied together in clumps for bayonet practice. The massacre failed in its intent—surrender by the Chinese—and instead prompted the U.S. to tighten its embargo on war materials. Admiration for Hitler's bold steps and mounting frustration with America led Tokyo to prepare for war, creating sights such as the one here, showing Emperor Hirohito inspecting the capital's defenses, dwarfed by outlandish ear-trumpet listening devices eventually to be put out of business by radar.

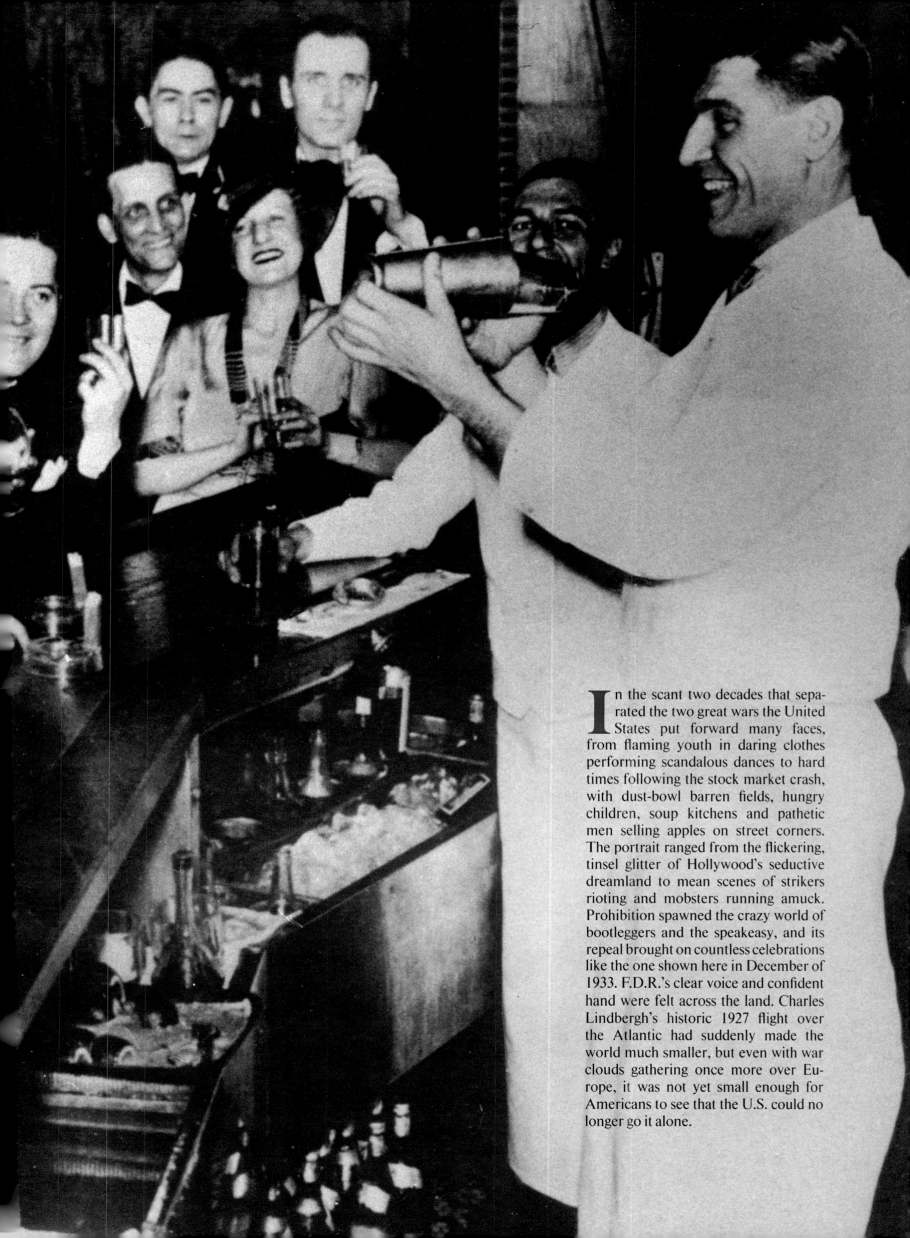

In the scant two decades that separated the two great wars the United States put forward many faces, from flaming youth in daring clothes performing scandalous dances to hard times following the stock market crash, with dust-bowl barren fields, hungry children, soup kitchens and pathetic men selling apples on street corners. The portrait ranged from the flickering, tinsel glitter of Hollywood's seductive dreamland to mean scenes of strikers rioting and mobsters running amuck. Prohibition spawned the crazy world of bootleggers and the speakeasy, and its repeal brought on countless celebrations like the one shown here in December of 1933. F.D.R.'s clear voice and confident hand were felt across the land. Charles Lindbergh's historic 1927 flight over the Atlantic had suddenly made the world much smaller, but even with war clouds gathering once more over Europe, it was not yet small enough for Americans to see that the U.S. could no longer go it alone.

After coming to power in 1933, Hitler gave lip service to Germany's treaty restrictions on arms but the war-game jalopies made to look like tanks by the addition of tin sides and wood guns *(above)* were soon replaced by the real thing. A new type of warfare was emerging as Hitler rebuilt the German army, and where better to test it and its weapons than in the Spanish rebellion near by at which he was an invited participant. The Luftwaffe and its bombing techniques proved deadly in the cause of the stubborn, power-hungry Spanish general, Francisco Franco. The revolution against the faction-ridden Republican government lasted three years and cost 600,000 lives, one of which was immortalized by a young photographer named Robert Capa who caught this Loyalist soldier at the split second of his death. Italy helped out to the tune of 50,000 troops and more than 700 planes, while simultaneously Mussolini was outraging most of the world by his unprovoked invasion of Ethiopia and by doing so holding up to ridicule the do-nothing League of Nations. "It is us today," Ethiopia's leader, Haile Selassie, prophetically told the League in a specially called session. "It will be you tomorrow."

Hitler did nothing less than captivate the German soul. Here at the 1937 Harvest Day festival, one of his carefully orchestrated outdoor spectacles designed to make enormous audiences proud of their country, the chief event is happening—the arrival of the Führer. With shrewd political instincts, a flair for the symbolic and a superb sense of timing he rekindled love of Fatherland while at the same time planting seeds of hate that would work in his behalf. Wagnerian music, goose-stepping troops, that hooked cross—the swastika—the Nazi eagle, Luftwaffe flyovers and a billion booming *Sieg Heils* not only recalled the Germanic tribal past but also heralded a mystical Third Reich future. To produce the diabolical master race that Hitler envisioned, two things had to happen—the breeding of perfect human specimens and the extermination of everyone imperfect. For the first, the government set up a chain of maternity homes and exhorted "biologically flawless" young women to carry out their "sacred duty" and mate with SS men. Many new mothers were so caught up in patriotic fervor that they chose to stare at a picture of Hitler while giving birth to their "parcels" in lieu of anesthetic. To accomplish the second, disposal techniques were already being used to rid Germany of its sick, retarded and insane. They were easy to adapt to the much larger problem of the country's gypsies, homosexuals and other "inferior stock," in particular Jews who, in Hitler's eyes, were to blame for everything. Pretty soon an irrational, petty hatred in the heart of a former Austrian house painter was causing the death of a people.

After only three years in power, Hitler was itching to move. In 1936 he defied the Versailles treaty and sent his newly revitalized army into the Rhineland, the sensitive demilitarized zone that bordered on French soil. Both Britain and France were shocked, and threatened intervention but in the end did nothing, having talked themselves into believing Germany was really only invading itself. Two years later Hitler gambled again, sent his army into Austria and proceeded to annex his homeland by means of a subsequent plebiscite. Again he had read the West's irresolution correctly. In October 1938, Nazi troops occupied the Sudetenland, a frontier region of Czechoslovakia, with the announced purpose of freeing the Germans there. As so graphically depicted here, the welcome provided the invaders was so enthusiastic that troopers had to hold back Sudeten Germans with a belt-to-belt chain of arms. The greeting elsewhere in the country, however, was something less than jubilant as Hitler again broke his promises and continued to feed on Czechoslovakia. A few months later, in early 1939, when the Germans entered Prague unopposed, they were met with angry tears, shaking fists and despair. Having deceitfully bullied his way to more strategic frontiers by joining Austria and Czechoslovakia to Germany, Hitler left little doubt that he was more than willing to plunge the whole of Europe into another war.

With the memory of the First World War's horror still fresh, peace was all Britain and France yearned for, and after Neville Chamberlain eagerly set off to meet with Hitler at Munich in September of 1938 *(left, second from right)*, it looked as if the Allies might yet keep it. PEACE was the message London newsboys ran through the streets upon the Prime Minister's return—"peace for our time" he told his fellow countrymen, having just paid Hitler's price and participated in the dismemberment of Czechoslovakia. Appeasement was not quite yet a dirty word. To the West it still meant negotiation, it meant wise men working things out. Hardly anyone, least of all the Prime Minister, though, seemed to realize the enormity of the consequences of renouncing former pledges of protection and giving in to Hitler. And too few seemed to take in the fact that the "wise man" on the other side of the table was instead a lying, treacherous, ruthless megalomaniac bent on a new world order by force, who would now allot the frail peace less than a year.

1939 WAR

Suddenly the air was hostile territory. As the Spaniards had done before them, the rest of Europe craned their necks and scanned the skies. First Poles (above) and soon Britishers (opposite page), here children picking hops in a field, assumed the strange new posture. No one, from Scandinavia to the Mediterranean, was immune—including Germans.

September dawned on Poland with skies split by Hitler's screaming Stukas and with earth shuddering under the tread of his panzers. Within hours the very names of these engines of Blitzkrieg (lightning war) were as frightening to the dazed and dying Poles as the machines themselves. The terrifying German weapons trumpeted a new kind of warfare. The Stuka (dive bomber), equipped with sirens that heightened its horror and led its prey to nickname it "shrieking vulture," dropped from skies darkened by waves of high-level bombers, precisely coordinated with panzer (literally, armor) divisions below. Surprise put much of the blitz in Blitzkrieg; its essential fifth weapon was that it was undeclared. And to complete the new nomenclature, this was total war, waged against both the military and the civilian population.

Surprise and the fabrication of a pretext for invasion took a lot of planning, much of it not taught in the war colleges of Western nations. On Thursday, August 31, twelve of 13 convicted German

BEGINS

criminals from a concentration camp at Oranienburg, near the Polish border, were ordered to don Polish military uniforms, which had been procured by Heinrich Himmler, chief of Hitler's SS (the Nazis' own armed force of protection squads). Suited up, the ex-convicts were injected with a fatal drug, taken to a wood 10 miles from the border and shot. Their bodies were arranged to make it appear that they had been advancing into Germany.

Later the same day SS Major Alfred Naujocks and five other SS men, in civilian clothes, hustled the remaining prisoner to the nearby town of Gleiwitz, where they took over the radio station. One of them, speaking in Polish, broadcast an announcement that Poland was attacking Germany and pleaded for Poles to rally to the colors. After a simulated scuffle with station personnel that included shots in front of

1939

A New Terror Called Total War

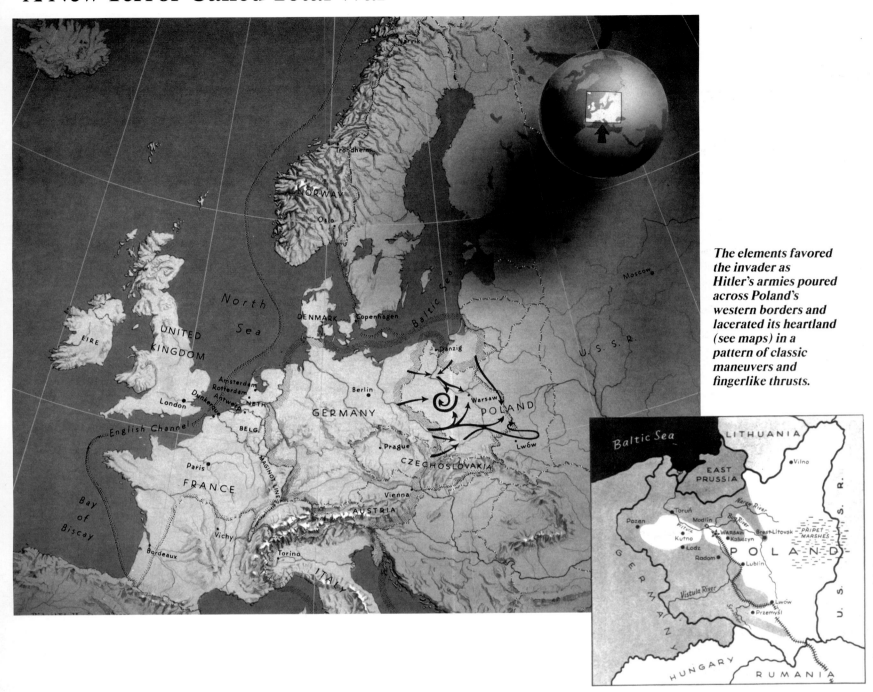

The elements favored the invader as Hitler's armies poured across Poland's western borders and lacerated its heartland (see maps) in a pattern of classic maneuvers and fingerlike thrusts.

the open microphone, the ex-con "invader" was killed and his body left on the studio floor. At 10 a.m. Friday, when the war was five hours and 15 minutes old, the Führer, addressing the Reichstag in Berlin, cited the Gleiwitz radio drama as an instance of Polish aggression and announced that he had thrown all the Reich's might against the aggressor.

For the real invasion, the Luftwaffe needed daylight. Its formations took off into the dim streak of light on the eastern horizon that signaled dawn. The armored columns of the Wehrmacht (German armed forces) were already lumbering east along Poland's western approaches. The battleship *Schleswig-Holstein*, a World War I relic turned training vessel, which had steamed into Danzig (today's Gdansk) a few days earlier on what Ber-

lin called a courtesy visit, zeroed in on the harbor fortress of Westerplatte. At 4:45 a.m., before the German tanks and infantry splintered the blue and white customs barriers on the Polish border and before the Luftwaffe's first bombs fell, one of the old warship's 11-inch guns fired the shot that reverberated around the world for the next six years.

Aided immensely by what the Poles came to call "Hitler weather"—sunny and dry, perfect for advancing tanks and strikes from the air—the heavy bombers destroyed most of the Polish air force on the ground, eliminated its fuel dumps, blew up trains, rail lines and stations full of mobilizing soldiers, and set cities afire. Stukas dived on terrified troops in the front lines, hit supply depots and strafed fleeing civilians, clotting roads with pedestrians and small vehicles and making them impassable to Poland's

ground forces, which pitted outmoded cavalry against the panzers. The combined German forces of 1.516 million men were supported by 2,000 planes and 1,700 tanks. Poland's entire armed forces comprised 935 aircraft, many obsolete, and 500 tanks; its army's 1.75 million men included largely unmobilized reserves. No wonder that within 24 hours the Luftwaffe controlled the Polish skies and the panzers had knifed through the astonished Polish army with dazzling speed.

On Sunday, September 3, Britain and France declared war on Germany to protest the attack and to fulfill a pledge. When the next day dawned without attack by the Germans on either country, Britons and Frenchmen dubbed the conflict a phony war, and sat down behind their navy and their

Maginot Line respectively in what came to be known as the *Sitzkrieg*.

By September 14 the Wehrmacht, right on schedule, had surrounded a Warsaw largely pounded into rubble. Under a truce flag, the Germans demanded unconditional surrender. But instead of giving up, Warsavians started fortifying their city.

Into the night children alongside adults, chauffeured aristocrats shoulder to shoulder with office workers dug trenches in parks and vacant lots and erected street barricades of furniture and cars; trolley cars were tipped across intersections. When panzers jumped off for the attack, they were stopped in their tracks, often by civilians who set them afire with burning rags. Infantrymen who had mowed down the Polish army in the field were pinned down by snipers in every house. Every 30 seconds Radio Warsaw broadcast a few bars of Chopin's fiery *Polonaise in A-Flat* to tell the world Poland still lived.

The infuriated German High Command resumed its pulverization tactics, bombing everything previously unleveled, destroying reservoirs and burning residential areas.

On September 17, the desperate Polish troops on the eastern front suffered a lethal blow and Europe underwent a face change that was to redefine central and eastern European societies. With no more war declaration than Hitler had made, Stalin suddenly sent waves of troops across Poland's largely undefended eastern frontier. It was the implementation of a pact that the previously unreconcilable leaders of the world's two greatest military powers had arrived at on August 23, just a week before the invasion. It guaranteed Hitler a free hand in the east (and a secure rear in operations against the West) and gave Stalin spheres of influence in eastern Poland, in Finland, in the Baltic states of Latvia, Estonia and Lithuania, and in southeastern Europe from Czechoslovakia to the Black Sea. In Warsaw the gallant resistance continued. But food ran out—as one described the scene, famished Poles "cut off pieces of flesh as soon as a horse fell, leaving only the skeleton"—and on September 28 Radio Warsaw replaced the *Polonaise* with a dirge.

Already Nazi policy was taking shape, largely unnoted by the rest of the world. The Führer had warned his generals that there would be no room for humanitarian scruples in Poland. But some old-line Wehrmacht officers were amazed and outraged when an SS private and a military policeman, dissatisfied with the performance of a work detail of 50 Polish Jews they were overseeing, herded them into a synagogue and killed them all. (Although the pair were court-martialed, neither served a day in prison.) The generals who disapproved of such tactics soon learned to look the other way. Astonished and disapproving, these professional soldiers were made aware that Jews and Polish intellectuals, clergy and nobility—all groups that might provide leaders for a resistance—were to be the objects of "housecleaning," a term for physical extermination that demonstrated the Nazis' genius for euphemism.

Amid the confusion and doubts on both sides of the Atlantic, one thing was starkly clear. Poland, the buffer state, was no more, and without that keystone the entire European order, the elaborate patchwork so laboriously crafted at Versailles just 20 years earlier, had fallen to pieces. Western Europe overnight had lost the leadership of the world.

As Hitler's speech announcing war against Poland roared from the radio, a Berlin taxi driver, a garage attendant and a spit-shined civilian saluted.

CHRONOLOGY 1939

January

10
● *Chamberlain meets with Mussolini in Rome*

12
● *Roosevelt's rearmament program: $552 million*

20
● *No nation will impose sanctions on Japan*

24
● *Germany's solution to "Jewish problem" sped up*

26
● *Barcelona falls*

February

10
● *Japanese occupy Hainan Island*

15
● *Hungary premier forced to resign because of Jewish blood*

19
● *Trade agreement between Poland and Soviets*

24
● *British and French naval maneuvers in Mediterranean*

27
● *British and French recognize Franco government*

March

15
● *German troops cross Czech frontier*

28
● *Madrid falls to Franco's forces*

31
● *British and French pledge support to Poland*

April

7
● *Italians occupy Albania*

20
● *Hitler's 50th birthday*

26
● *English conscription announced*

May

22
● *"Pact of Steel" signed, creating Axis*

June

■ **War in Europe**   ■ **War in Asia**   ■ **U.S.A.**

July	August	September	October	November	December
25 • *British aircraft train over France*	**23** • *Soviet-German nonaggression pact* **25** • *Anglo-Polish treaty: intervention if invaded*	**1** • *Germany invades Poland* **3** • *Britain and France declare war on Germany* • *Battle of the Atlantic begins with sinking of Athenia* **9** • *First British units embark for France* **16** • *British convoys begin in Atlantic* **17** • *Soviets invade East Poland* **27** • *Warsaw surrenders* • *U-boat sinks British carrier Courageous* **29** • *Soviets and Germans partition Poland* **30** • *Polish government in exile set up in Paris*	**6** • *Hitler appeals for peace* **10** • *Soviets enter Lithuania, Latvia and Estonia* **12** • *Britain rejects Hitler's peace proposal* **14** • *U-boat sinks British battleship Royal Oak*	**30** • *Soviets invade Finland*	**7** • *Soviets halted at Mannerheim Line* **13** • *Battle of the River Plate* **14** • *Soviets expelled from League of Nations* **17** • *Germany's Atlantic raider Graf Spee scuttled at Montevideo, Uruguay* **28** • *Meat rationing in Britain* **29** • *Russians driven back by Finns* **31** • *All quiet on the Western Front*

1939 *Blitzkrieg!*

Panzers race across blitzed Polish terrain. Their infantry, going all-out to keep up with them, sometimes covered 30 miles a day.

1939

The Gates of Poland Fall Beneath a Lightning Strike

Hitler, adept in realpolitik and a master of symbolism, made sure that both his Polish victims and the rest of the world saw the terrible punishment packed in the lightning war his air and land forces had worked out in Spain. On Day One, panzers converged on Warsaw. Five days later the Luftwaffe, its mission to destroy the city utterly, was systematically doing so with wave after wave of high-level bombers and echelons of dive-bombing Stukas.

By dawn's early light, at H Hour of invasion day, Nazi troops, starting off the hostilities with a symbolic act, lean into tanks' work, breaking a wooden border barrier.

Digging In Against an Army of Technicians

The efficiency of the German engineers, called the Pioneers in the military, was demonstrated in the infantry's speed marches. Here motorized troops cross a wooden bridge that had been blown up by retreating defenders as Pioneers who rebuilt it look on with satisfaction.

Residents of a Polish farm village not yet under fire appear undisturbed by a string of reconnaissance motorcyclists, one even grinning at the photographer.

As the Germans approach their city, Warsaw residents dig some of the 13 miles of trenches that will serve as antiaircraft gun emplacements, tank traps and shelters for the battle just ahead.

1939

The Cavalry Is Slaughtered by the Most Modern of War Machines

In a scene so out-of-the-past that it astounded the invaders, white-gloved officers and pure-white steeds of Poland's crack Pomorske Cavalry Brigade charge across open fields straight into the fire of General Heinz Guderian's XIX Armored Corps tanks.

In Warsaw's outskirts after a week of Blitzkrieg, an infantryman of a motorized unit (left) reconnoiters for the drive into the city's heart. Next, panzers and infantry drive through a suburb wheeling up a howitzer to blast the inner city. The Luftwaffe had not yet started reducing

The carnage was much more frightful than it ever was in battles of yore, particularly for the horses. Murderous fire from the tanks tore apart the mounts as well as their saber- and lance-wielding riders. Some of the cavalry believed the Nazi tanks were of cardboard.

the capital to rubble. After three weeks of war, a sea of prisoners (right) was all that remained of Poland's army. Cutting off entire armies en route to Warsaw, the Germans captured some 700,000; some 200,000 who fled east were taken by the Red Army.

1939
Even the Hangmen Have Wheels

In occupied Warsaw, civilians who dared to resist their conquerors swing from a portable gallows, which was rolled down the city's streets, the Nazis' new wrinkle in the weaponry of realpolitik.

39

1939
Captivity and Death as the Purge Begins

Jews herded near a railroad station by the SS, Hitler's elite security force, wait nervously to learn their fate.

Three Polish civilians are executed before a mound of earth by a firing squad of German military police. Death was punishment for sabotage, violating Nazi racial laws, helping friends escape from jail or stealing German food parcels.

On a Warsaw street Jews walk on the cobbles (sidewalks were verboten),
with the new sign of their shame, the yellow star, in target position on their
backs. The SS was under orders to segregate and deport or shoot them.

Poles executed with their hands tied behind their backs await burial by prisoner compatriots.
Many were shot simply for being Poles: the Germans proclaimed 100 Poles would be executed for
every German civilian killed, 10 for every one with a weapon.

1939
Hitler Bestrides a Land of Tears and Corpses

Visiting Poland to see for himself the site of his victory and to mull the war's next phase, Hitler walks, in perfect step and identical attitude, with his Foreign Minister, Joachim von Ribbentrop, along a muddy road past the pilot engine that always preceded his train.

In a potato field strafed by the Luftwaffe, a young girl mourns her sister, one of three women in a group of neighbors and their children who were killed by machine-gun bullets as they dug their crop.

43

1939
England Prepares for War

Although England, lulled by Neville Chamberlain's "peace for our time," was accused of sleeping while Hitler moved toward war, the nation acted swiftly when the time came. Sandbags at hand, civil defense and other volunteers sprang to protect the things they loved. Nowhere was this more apparent than in the case of children. The day the bombs fell, their gas masks were ready, their parents knew what to pack. From September 1st to

Little Londoners, clutching their kits and gas masks and wearing tags bearing their names and addresses, await evacuation to the country.

Queen Elizabeth inspects air-raid precautions at Vincent Square Infants Hospital.

King George, inspecting a munitions plant, peers down a new antiaircraft gun.

A mandolin-playing medic corporal leads an ad hoc Royal Army Medical Corps chorus in the current hit, "We're Gonna Hang Out the Washing on the Siegfried Line."

3rd, 650,000 youngsters from four to 16 were evacuated from London. By train and bus they were taken, by parents and teachers, westward to rural safety.

The stained-glass windows of Canterbury Cathedral are removed for safekeeping. The church, the object of several Luftwaffe reprisal raids, suffered no direct hits.

Much of England's great art was secretly stored for the duration in the heart of a mountain in Wales, cared for by a staff of 30.

Russian Surprise: A New Ally for Hitler

Yule shoppers in Helsinki run for cover as Soviet bombers appear the day before Christmas. Stalin's war against the Finns started with a massive November 30 bombing that brutalized the beautiful capital but failed to break its morale.

In Helsinki's Toolo residential suburb, people unable to find shelter from the bombs crowd against a wall.

In the Kremlin, Stalin dictates a note to his chief of staff, General Boris Shaposhnikov.

In September Hitler had got himself a powerful ally when Russia stepped in to help subdue the Poles. Now, for the Reds, Finland seemed like another easy mark. But for six weeks and more of bitter struggle in Finland's Arctic and subarctic winter, Stalin's legions were frustrated, on the frozen ground and in the mostly sunless skies.

The Western world gloated and cheered as white-clad Finns skilled in a unique kind of deep-frozen guerrilla warfare glided out of snow-steeped forests, often in the sub-zero night, and sliced apart Russian forces three times their size, at one time cutting off two divisions and killing 5,000. Buoyed by their forces' over-snow successes, Hel-

sinki and other cities refused to break under heavy bombing. The glory was not to last. Even before spring came to the rescue of the Red Army, Soviet reinforcements, including ski troops who proved worthy of their gallant enemy, pushed the Finns back to their fortresslike Mannerheim Line and their defeat was in sight.

In a forest north of the Arctic Circle, in the depth of winter, Finnish ski troopers with reindeer-drawn supplies patrol against the thus-far hapless Russians.

A Finnish ski patrol in white camouflage combat attire glides through a snow-whitened village. The building at left is a hat shop.

An elderly Helsinkian who survived the savage bombing flees from still-falling ruins as the planes depart.

1939
Blitz Fails to Daunt the Doughty Finns

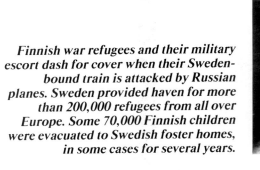

Finnish war refugees and their military escort dash for cover when their Sweden-bound train is attacked by Russian planes. Sweden provided haven for more than 200,000 refugees from all over Europe. Some 70,000 Finnish children were evacuated to Swedish foster homes, in some cases for several years.

A dog team mushes across Finland's winter landscape with a war casualty bundled up on a typical Finnish sledge. Often dogs pulled wounded who were simply laid on a pair of skis.

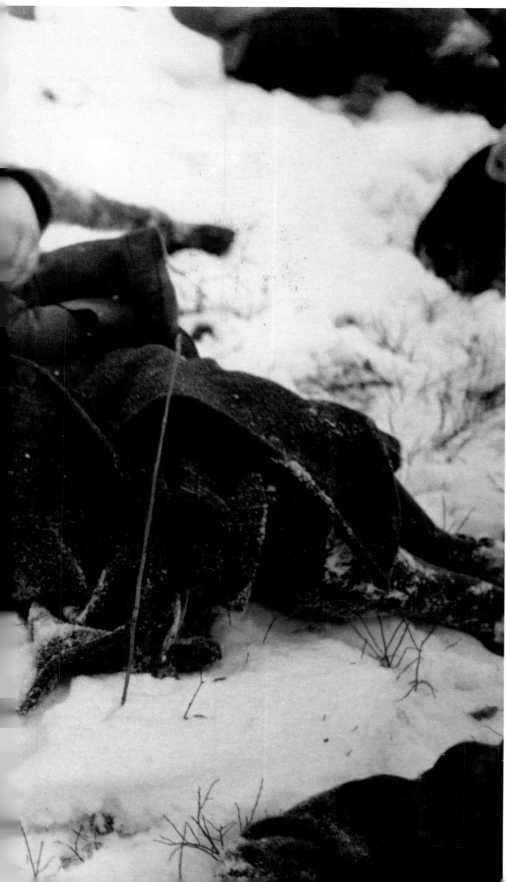

Fear widens the eyes of young Finns as Soviet bombers drop their hateful eggs on the fishing and farming village of Tammisaari. LIFE photographer Carl Mydans, who covered the whole of the Russo-Finnish war, detailed the fear-filled lives of the 800 noncombatants who remained behind when the other 3,000 villagers left for service or safety. Old men, mothers and children, they spent the four hours of daylight in the birch and fir forests, huddled around bonfires, eating cold food, playing games and shrinking into the snow when the bombers came.

What Should the U.S. Do?

One way LIFE covered the start of the war was to show how vast the Atlantic Ocean still was by detailing humdrum day-to-day U.S. events while death stalked Europe. The article ended:

If the First World War seemed incredible, the second seemed doubly so. There was in it some element of a grisly masquerade; its actions had a childishly imitative quality and its protagonists viewed from a distance were like characters playing in a nightmare some game of which they knew the rules but not the purpose.

Many things that were going on before the First World War continued to go on during it; and many things that started during the War continued to go on after it. There was however a deep change in the way that people experienced all things—a change expressed most simply by the fact that since 1917 "before the War" and "after the War" have been familiar phrases, all over the world. When Europe went to war again last week, these phrases became suddenly meaningless. Like a grandfather's clock marking the hours, the guns in Poland and along the Rhine, sounded a new interval of time in this century. Superficially, nothing in the U.S. changed much except the prices of stock, the prices of food, the number of people who listened to the radio. Actually, everything was changed.

Whatever its effect upon the U.S. imagination, World War No. 2 seemed sure, like World War No. 1 to mark the end of an epoch. And the trivial aspects of that epoch—the sun over Kansas cattle, Dewey in Plattsburg, Good Humor trucks on the summer roads—acquired suddenly a strange importance. Against the background of war, they emerged sharp and impressive, like a conversation prolonged in the theater after the rising of the curtain or like a familiar landscape made clear by lightning in the summer night.

Yankees star Joe DiMaggio kisses movie starlet Dorothy Arnold, his bride, after their San Francisco wedding.

Modeling beachwear, Rita Hayworth adjusts the zipper of her suit to let more sun in.

Clustered before the tube as Americans will soon be doing in their homes, Radio Corporation of America executives watch TV, soon to make its commercial debut.

University of Kansas coeds keep house in a low-cost co-op dorm while waiting to become wives, mothers and homemakers.

F.D.R. shows off two grandsons, Franklin III and John Boettiger Jr., at a Christmas party.

WHAT AMERICA THINKS ABOUT THE WAR...

Who do you want to win the War?

Allies **83%**

Germany **1%**

Neither Side—or don't know . . **16%**

What should the U. S. do?

Fight with Allies now **3%**

Fight with Allies if they are losing **13.5%**

Send supplies to Allies but not Germany **20%**

Sell to both sides cash and carry . **29%**

No aid to either **25%**

Help Germany . . . **1/10 of 1%**

Don't know and others . . . **9%**

FOR DETAILS OF THIS NEW FORTUNE POLL SEE OPPOSITE PAGE

27

LIFE illustrated a story on the opinion survey of its sister publication Fortune three weeks after Hitler launched his Blitzkrieg. It indicated Americans weren't ready to put their money where their mouth was.

Armies Play, Plot and Wait

American Legionnaires, convening in Chicago at the height of the neutrality/ intervention controversy, hoist chorus girls as usual. In convention sessions they voted to leave the issue up to President and Congress.

On the other side of the world, Vice Admiral Koshiro Oikawa, commander of Japan's China Seas fleet, maps plans with his staff aboard his flagship.

In a photograph that has become an icon of what France called la drôle de guerre (the wei war)—the phony war in the U.S.—a poilu sits guard on the German border while behi him France, hopeful that the Maginot Line will hold off le Blitz, awaits Hitler's next mo

Stalin's war plan, unlike Hitler's, started ignominiously. Having secured his Baltic flank by turning its three states into little Soviet republics, he invaded "brave little Finland," as the former Russian grand duchy was invariably called by the Western press. His strategic objective was its deep-frozen Karelian Isthmus, a narrow strip of land between Lake Ladoga and the Gulf of Finland that joined Finland to Russia only 20 miles from Leningrad. He needed it, he claimed, to defend the U.S.S.R. from brave little Finland. (The dictator, seeking to acquire it the easy way, said, "We can't move Leningrad, so we must move the border." The Finnish negotiators were not amused.)

Stalin's mighty Red Army machine sputtered and stalled in the northern winter, beset not only by the severest one in 50 years, with temperatures reaching −50° F, but also by Finnish ski troops, who were trained and equipped

1940 THE FIGH

to fight in the frozen forest. Ski-borne white-clad wraiths glided out of the piney cover with rifles and artillery, plus the antitank weapon the Finns had invented, the "Molotov cocktail" (a kerosene and potassium chlorate blend in a bottle with a detonator in its neck that, hurled by an expert infantryman, burst into flame as it smashed against the steel of the turret).

The neighboring Scandinavian states reiterated their neutrality (though Swedish, Norwegian and Danish volunteers joined the Finnish ranks), and the Allies and Germans were preoccupied with the *Sitzkrieg* on their Maginot and Siegfried Lines. The Finns, outnumbered three to one, smashed the attackers, annihilating one Russian army and part of another.

The cheering stopped, however, when the Russian invaders, supported by intensive air bombardment of Finn-

Pope Pius XII, arms outflung, concludes a special Mass, in the first year of his papacy, with a fervent plea to God to "restore honor and concord among nations."

TING SPREADS

As the German navy's undersea war against the Allies' Atlantic shipping intensifies, a torpedoed British freighter goes down stern first.

1940

Suddenly the Phony War Was Real

ish cities and reinforced by their own well-trained ski troops, pushed back the supposedly invincible Mannerheim Line. The 88-mile-long string of concrete pillboxes, protected by minefields and boulder or timber tank stoppers and linked by a network of trenches, was named for Finland's World War I hero, Field Marshal Gustaf Mannerheim, who had been called from retirement in 1931 to gird his nation against Russia. On March 12 Finland surrendered, having held out 105 days against 45 Russian divisions.

Then, suddenly, the phony war was real. On the morning of April 9, German columns, heading for the Danish Royal Palace, usurped the traffic lanes of Copenhageners bicycling to work. At the same time in Norway, Hitler admirers organized by turncoat Norwegian Major Vidkun Quisling seized government buildings and communications stations throughout that country. Denmark fell in four hours. The Norway thrust indicated that Hitler and Britain's First Lord of the Admiralty, Winston Churchill, thought alike strategically. It gave the British an excuse to put into effect an old pet plan of Churchill's: invading Norway to forge a supply route to Finland and to seize the Norwegian sources of Germany's iron ore. But for Britain it was a case of too little and too late.

The awesomely efficient Germans, after making the war's first amphibious landings at Oslo, Narvik and other coastal cities, had seized all the best airfields. They blasted the airstrips and supply bases of the Allies (the British had been joined by French forces) after their belated landing at Narvik, and strafed their unprotected columns, making the Allied mission impossible.

On May 10, the Germans, without missing a beat in their victorious Norwegian campaign, dropped out of the dawn sky on Holland and Belgium. Paratroops, some in Dutch uniforms, fanned out through cities bombed by the Luftwaffe, and gliders landed more of the Wehrmacht on the Belgian side of the Albert Canal. Over seized key bridges, the Germans poured across the Ardennes Forest into France and crossed the Meuse at Sedan, the northern end of the Maginot Line *(map, far*

right). The Allied forces to the west, in Flanders, were outflanked. With Rotterdam blitzed to rubble, Holland surrendered May 14. By the time Belgium followed suit two weeks later, on May 28, the British, cut off from the French, their air shield riddled, were trudging along refugee-clogged roads toward burning Dunkirk, their last, slim hope of escape.

Three days before the invasion, the British Parliament, fed up with defeats in Norway, had turned on the peace-in-our-time Prime Minister. One M.P., echoing Oliver Cromwell, had cried out to Neville Chamberlain, "Depart, I say, and let us have done with you. In the name of God—go!" The government had fallen and the King had asked Churchill to take over. Even as the gliders and chutes dotted the Lowlands skies, the new P.M. was telling Commons, in his maiden speech, "I have nothing to offer but blood, toil, tears and sweat." Learning to his amazement that there were no reserves available to reinforce his cut-off

troops, he set the Admiralty to rounding up all available bottoms, from warships, transports and ferries to fishing smacks and pleasure craft, in the forlorn hope some few thousands might be snatched from the teeth of the German armor.

On May 26 Operation Dynamo began. In 10 days, naval and civilian skippers, threading their vessels through minefields under incessant bombing and shelling, brought 336,427 British and French troops across the Channel to safety. The "miracle of Dunkirk" turned Germany's military victory into the worst possible omen for Hitler and the plans he had made for Operation Sea Lion, the invasion of England. It heartened the dispirited British people and imbued them, of all parties and classes, with a common purpose.

Having failed to land a knockout blow on Britain at the Channel, Hitler now decided to put first things first and

As apparently unending columns of Canadian soldiers march down a street in New Westminster, British Columbia, headed for points unknown, a small boy breaks loose from his mother in the crowd to say goodbye to his father.

go after, in his own words, England's "continental soldier, France." Often heralded as the best army in the world, the French forces soon turned out to be anything but. In the fighting in Belgium and northern France they had already lost 370,000 men and most of their medium tanks. By an error in command they had also left an unprotected gap to their south. Morale in the ranks was low, leadership was aged and tactics defense-minded and outdated. The invincible fortifications of the Maginot Line had already been outflanked. Even the German generals could not believe their good fortune. The fall of France was unthinkable, not only to Frenchmen but to most of the rest of the world. True, the fierce German panzers had taken Poland in no time. But France was something else again. Still, as normal life continued in Paris with theaters alight and shops filled, the Nazis were closing in, 139 divisions strong. With dive-bombers softening up the paths of the

onrushing tanks, the Germans simply overwhelmed the hapless French as their swift armor raced forward, outflanked and cut off the molasses-slow forces. In a matter of days the breakthrough achieved had become a rout as French soldiers and civilians fled together in panic. On June 14 the Nazis entered Paris unopposed and the shocked and shamed Parisians were treated to the sight of Nazi troops goose-stepping on the Champs-Elysées.

Only days before, Mussolini had allied Italy with Germany—on this day, President Roosevelt said, "the hand that held the dagger has struck it into the back of its neighbor"— and extended the war southward by bombing Britain's Mediterranean fortress at Malta. The British raided Libya, the keystone of Mussolini's African empire, and bombed the Italian base at Tobruk. Il Duce, even though he faced a desert war with Britain, launched in-

vasions of both Egypt and Greece. France's new premier, the collaborationist Marshal Henri Pétain, signed armistices with Germany and Italy, moved the government south to Vichy and banned Jews from civil service, management, press and radio. In London, General Charles de Gaulle announced the birth of a Free French army.

If Hitler was to fulfill his dream, to be the first since 1066 to conquer the sceptered isle of the fellow Aryans he had long admired, he must start by destroying the RAF. Throughout August, as "invasion fever" gripped Britain and the public, schools, homes and workplaces rehearsed for that grim event, waves of German bombers, flying at more than 10,000 feet, blasted bases of the Fighter Command, along with shipping and coastal ports. But the Blitzkrieg scenario did not unfold as usual. Dedicated and skilled young RAF pilots (average age 23), flying the improved Hurricane and brand-new Spitfire fighters, rose to shoot down the scourge of European skies in a two-for-one ratio that shocked Luftwaffe chief Hermann Göring.

Scenting victory even as the sky battle was reaching its height, Churchill, on August 20, hailed the airmen as saviors, telling Commons, "Never in the field of human conflict was so much owed by so many to so few." Then Göring, at the critical juncture, when despite his loss ratio he might in a fortnight more have won the air war, switched his attacks from RAF airfields to London and civilian targets. By mid-October the daytime skies of southern England were clear of German planes and by winter there was no doubt that Hitler had lost the Battle of Britain.

Equal in portent were several events far from the European theater. Japan, in the fourth year of its war with China, entered Indonesia to block aid for its enemy (Vichy had ceded Nippon France's bases on Vietnam's Gulf of Tonkin) and formally joined the Rome-Berlin Axis.

In the U.S. the first number was drawn in the nation's first peacetime draft. Third-term President F.D.R., calling America the "arsenal of democracy," told the nation that to save civilization it must produce more shipments to the Allies of guns, planes, ships, "more of everything."

After a busy winter and spring of invasion, Germany had scrawled its military graffiti over the war maps of Europe from the northernmost regions of the Scandinavian peninsula to the border of the Iberian one.

CHRONOLOGY 1940

January	February	March	April	May	June
8 • *Major Finn victory at Suomussalmi* • *British food rationing starts* **24** • *British renew pledge to support Belgium* **26** • *U.S.-Japanese trade treaty expires*	**9** • *U.S. special envoy Sumner Welles seeks peace in Europe* **11** • *Intense fighting between Finns and Russians* **13** • *Soviets penetrate Mannerheim Line* **21** • *Germans start building Auschwitz* **28** • *Finns retreat at Viipuri*	**12** • *Finns surrender* **18** • *Mussolini agrees to join war* **30** • *Japan sets up puppet government in Nanking, China*	**2** • *U.S. fleet leaves coast, heads west* **4** • *Churchill gets overall defense charge* **9** • *Germany invades Norway and Denmark* **10** • *Battles of Narvik start off Norway coast* **14** • *Allies land at Narvik and near Trondheim* **20** • *50,000 Allied troops advance on Germans in Norway* **24** • *Allies repulsed in Norway*	**1** • *Britain starts to evacuate Norway* • *Antiwar coalition in U.S.* **7** • *Roosevelt orders fleet to stay in Hawaiian waters* **10** • *Nazis invade Holland, Belgium, Luxembourg* • *Churchill becomes Britain's Prime Minister* • *First British air raid on Germany* **12** • *Germany invades France* **13** • *1,500 German and French tanks clash in Belgium* **14** • *Holland surrenders* • *Germans take Sedan* **15** • *Breakthrough at the Meuse* **21** • *Germans reach English Channel* • *Allies trapped at Dunkirk* **23** • *Germans capture Boulogne* **26** • *Evacuation of Dunkirk begins* **28** • *Belgium surrenders*	**1** • *U.S. launches first new battleship since 1921* **3** • *Dunkirk evacuation completed* • *Paris hit by 200 German planes* • *German assault on Maginot Line* • *Norway sues for peace* • *U.S. offers surplus arms to Allies* **5** • *Germans launch Aisne offensive* **10** • *Italy declares war on Britain and France* **11** • *Italian planes raid Malta* • *Norway surrenders* • *British bomb Tobruk* • *Paris declared open city* • *RAF bombs Italy* • *U.S. orders up 22 new warships* **14** • *Paris falls* **15** • *Soviets begin to occupy Lithuania, Latvia, Estonia* **18** • *Heavy bombing of England begins* • *De Gaulle broadcasts for Free French from London* **21** • *France surrenders* **25** • *Japan occupies French Indochina ports* **28** • *Italy invades Egypt* • *Willkie nominated for President by Republicans* **29** • *Russia invades Rumania*

■ **War in Europe**   ■ **War in Asia**   ■ **U.S.A.**

July	August	September	October	November	December
1 • *French government moves to Vichy* **3** • *British destroy French fleet in Algerian ports* **6** • *Triumphant return from field for Hitler* **9** • *British and Italians clash off Calabria* **10** • *Channel dogfight begins Battle of Britain* **16** • *Nazi invasion of England (Operation Sea Lion) set for Sept. 15* **18** • *F.D.R. nominated by Democrats for third term* **21** • *Hitler directs German army to plan invasion of Russia* **22** • *British reject Nazi peace proposal* **24** • *Italy blasts British bases in Egypt, Palestine* **25** • *U.S. embargo on strategic materials to Japan* **29** • *Spectacular air battle over Channel*	**5** • *Hitler approves Operation Sea Lion* • *Italy invades British Somaliland* **6** • *British exit leaves Japan in control of Shanghai* **24** • *Air attacks on London begin* **25** • *British bomb Berlin*	**2** • *France must pay 400 million francs a day for being occupied* **3** • *D Day for invasion of England now Sept. 21* • *50 antiquated U.S. ships leased to Britain* **7** • *London blitz begins* **9** • *U.S. destroyers begin operating in North Atlantic* **11** • *Buckingham Palace hit* **13** • *Italy invades Egypt* • *Japanese Zeros win big over Chungking* **15** • *The decisive day of the Battle of Britain* **16** • *U.S. selective service act passed* **17** • *Hitler postpones Operation Sea Lion "indefinitely"* **24** • *French bomb British at Gibraltar* **25** • *U.S. breaks Japanese secret code* **27** • *Japan joins Axis* **30** • *Germans decide Battle of Britain is lost*	**3** • *English troops land at Malta* **7** • *Germans enter Rumania* **8** • *U.S. citizens advised to leave Far East* **10** • *St. Paul's Cathedral hit* **16** • *Total of 16,400,000 men register for U.S. draft* **18** • *Vichy bans Jews from civil service, press* **23** • *Hitler and Franco meet* **27** • *Free French occupy Gabon* **28** • *Italy invades Greece* **29** • *British land in Crete* • *First draft number is drawn in U.S.*	**3** • *British troops arrive in Greece* **4** • *Spain seizes Tangier* **5** • *F.D.R. elected to third term* **8** • *Italy suffers major defeat in Greece* **10** • *Neville Chamberlain dies* **11** • *British inflict heavy losses on Italian fleet at Taranto* **14** • *Coventry destroyed in worst bombing so far* **20** • *Hungary joins Axis* • *Heavy fighting in China* **21** • *Greeks overwhelm Italians at Kovitza* **23** • *Rumania joins Axis* **26** • *Herding Warsaw Jews behind eight-foot ghetto wall begins* **27** • *Sea Battle of Scandinavia* **29** • *Germany completes plan for invasion of Russia*	**1** • *Greeks enter Albania, force Italians back* **8** • *Italy requests German intervention in Greece* **9** • *British counteroffensive in Egypt* • *Japan states war with U.S. "not inevitable"* **11** • *Italians routed in western Egypt* **16** • *Huge Mannheim bombing raid by British* **17** • *F.D.R. suggests direct arms aid to Britain* • *English push into Libya* **20-24** • *Heavy bombing of Liverpool* **28** • *Japanese use charcoal in cars to conserve fuel* **29** • *F.D.R.'s Arsenal of Democracy Fireside Chat* • *Heavy incendiary raid on London*

59

The dawn quiet of a village in the vicinity of Amsterdam's Schipol Airport is shattered by the first bombs of Hitler's blitz on Holland.

"Former naval person" Winston Churchill, upped from the Admiralty to Prime Minister on the very morning that Hitler's new blitz began, emerges from 10 Downing Street to helm the ship of state.

With the ringing declaration that "The fight beginning today decides the fate of the German nation for the next thousand years!" Hitler hurled his divisions against tiny Holland and Belgium after seven months of phony war lull. If the Dutch were great hydrologists, the Nazis were equally expert military technologists. When the defenders flooded their canals the Germans built makeshift bridges wherever possible or paddled across in rubber boats. At one bridge fifth columnists (the term for the enemy's traitorous sympathizers was coined in 1936 when four columns of rebels marched on Madrid) disconnected the wires before the span could be dynamited. The Luftwaffe knocked out all but 12 planes of the Dutch air fleet on the invasion's second day and the Dutch surrendered on the fourth. Belgium, clinging to neutrality, had refused to integrate its defense with that of the Dutch or the French. It quit two weeks later.

Paratroops and Infantry Riddle the Dutch Defense

German paratroopers hit the silk over bomb-softened Holland. Berlin said its purpose was to protect the Low Countries from an Allied invasion.

German infantrymen invade the border city of Maastricht, crossing the Meuse River on planks laid across rubber boats and scaling the ruins of a blown bridge.

1940

German Assault Troops Devour Western Europe

Pushing along into Belgium, German shock troops paddle across the Albert Canal under heavy protective fire as an explosion blasts the rocky face of Fort Eben Emael.

Using yet another means of attack on the Albert Canal line, Wehrmacht raiders dart out from beneath railroad cars. Eben Emael, considered impregnable, was taken in less than an hour by glider troops.

Lugging their rubber boat through Kanne, the Germans bypass a demolished canal bridge. The Belgians had laid charges to blow up the span and two others covered by the fort's guns.

Deposited by glider to within 20 yards of their targets, the invaders, behind a flamethrower, approach an Eben Emael bunker. They dropped specially prepared explosives down gun turrets, which spread gas throughout.

60,000 Square Miles of Norway Has Already Fallen

Invading thawing Norway, German troops strain in mud to emplace a field gun.

The invaders dash into what remains of a town after half an hour's bombardment by the Luftwaffe.

A bicycle patrol, surprised by sniper fire, takes cover behind its maneuverable two-man M-1 tank.

British naval attackers of Narvik survey the results of their shelling of the fjord's mouth.

In the Air and on the Ground It's Deutschland Uber Alles

Seen from a German bomber strafing Allied trucks, smoke puffs from near-misses on a tree-lined Belgian road.

Screened by mortar-laid smoke, Germans scramble up a rocky slope to rush an Allied bunker in Belgium.

Dunkirk: A Third of a Million Battered Allies Are Driven into the Sea

In a doleful queue, British units clinging to formation by units form a huge "S" on Dunkirk's broad beach.

Operation Dynamo, which turned the humiliating rout in Flanders into the Miracle of Dunkirk, began a full 10 days before its official D Day, May 26. For 10 days Churchill's old stamping grounds, the Admiralty, had been rounding up all available boats against the appalling probability that a third of a million Allied troops would otherwise be pushed into the sea. It scraped together 36 transports, 30 ferryboats and a ragtag collection of coastal vessels, including private pleasure craft. On the day Dynamo went into operation, 40 Dutch *schuits,* or scouts, that had fled to Britain were manned by Royal Navy crews. Since Dunkirk was the last possible port from

which the men could be evacuated, Churchill ordered the small garrison at Calais to fight to the death. The RAF threw an umbrella overhead as the troops swarmed over the sands and out onto the Dunkirk piers. Of the motley fleet, destroyers had the most heroic role. Their limited deck space jampacked with soldiers, they raced across the strait to Dover, guns firing incessantly to protect unarmed rescue vessels as well as themselves. But much more carrying capacity was required. Large ships lay outside the harbor while smaller boats ferried men to them. When it became clear that small craft were effective, professional and amateur sailors manned anything that floated and

joined the action. But more than the enemy had to be overcome. Only three days into the lift, the Calais garrison surrendered. The next day King Leopold delivered Belgium's armies to the Nazis. Nonetheless, the perimeter held, chiefly because everyone on the water and overhead did a superb job. Although an estimated 2,000 men, 243 craft and most of the British army's equipment were lost at sea, by June 4, when Dynamo officially ended, the RAF had shot down 159 German aircraft, the Royal Navy and the few French naval units had accounted for two thirds of those brought to safety, and 336,427 Allied soldiers, including 123,095 French, had been rescued to fight again.

A phalanx of tin-hatted Tommies, still clutching their weapons, wait on the beach for the vessels of Operation Dynamo to carry them home across the English Channel. In the background is a bombed and beached ship.

Evacuated Allied troops gaze back at smoking Dunkirk, set afire by German incendiary bombs and their own demolition experts.

German Dive-Bombers Hasten the Allied Exodus

Hundreds of thousands of tons of arms and supplies are abandoned by the Allies, who crowd the Dunkirk beaches, on the run whenever the Stukas attack.

'Wars Are Not Won by Evacuations, but There Was a Victory Inside This

Evacuated French soldiers and marines are treated to hot tea at a British haven.

Safe in England, French troops jammed on fishing boats prepare to disembark.

British soldiers awaiting their turn for rescue on an improvised pier of lorries driven into the sea register varied emotions as one of their buddies snaps a historic picture.

Disguised as a panic-stricken refugee at Dunkirk, this Belgian girl has just been found guilty of Fifth Column treason. Minutes after this picture was taken she was executed by French marines headed by the corporal in the helmet.

In the U.S. It's Business As Usual

As Hitler's legions marched across the map of Europe, Americans, behind their ocean barrier, reacted in various ways. It became popular later with editors and amateur sociologists to bear down heavily on the foolishness and fripperies that many pursued, some determinedly, while the Old World was falling apart. (LIFE could not resist loading its article on "What Americans Said and Did as Nazis Triumphed" with the pictures like

Katharine Hepburn poses on the lawn of her family home in Hartford, Connecticut, with her sisters Marion and Peggy (standing).

Flying Alligators, an association of private plane owners, initiate a member by making her walk barefoot and blindfolded over a live alligator. She is unaware that its jaws are bound.

Mickey Rooney hops on the lap of Mrs. John Hay "Liz" Whitney, who was expected soon to appear in a Gene Autry movie.

Aquatic showgirls of Billy Rose's Aquacade, hit of the New York World's Fair, swim, dive and float in the finale as land-locked chorus girls rim the watery stage.

Unknown Montgomery Clift made his first appearance in LIFE in the Broadway production of Robert Sherwood's anti-Nazi play, There Shall Be No Night.

A new champion wrestler, who billed himself as The Angel, scared opponents and spectators alike with his most unangelic looks.

Replication of a meal eaten by Eleanor Roosevelt makes a graphic point. It was precisely what an individual on relief was served.

the ones shown below.) Fraternal orders and private enterprises did stage ridiculous stunts and college students did sunbathe as usual.

But despite the appearance of frivolities, Americans were also seriously debating isolationism vs. intervention; playwrights wrote dramas about the effect of the war on moral values. And some of those students left their books and the beaches to drive ambulances in Europe.

Republican hopeful Robert A. Taft, a shy President's son said to dislike dancing, takes a turn around the floor with Mrs. Taft for the benefit of photographers.

Vivien Leigh, Gone With the Wind's Scarlett O'Hara, places her Best Actress Oscar on the mantel in her Beverly Hills home following the Academy Awards dinner.

UCLA students, some of them with books, find their backs to the wall as an early spring drives them to the beach at Santa Monica.

Henry Ford inspects a P-40 fighter with more than passing interest. He had stated publicly that, once geared up, he could make 1,000 planes a day.

Wearing caps modeled on the Nazis', candidates for America's own Fifth Column, U.S.-born members of the German-American Bund, perch in a tree at Camp Siegfried, Long Island, where they pledged loyalty to Hitler.

Suddenly a symbol of America's defense and not of boys playing soldier, a West Virginia National Guardsman takes part in a maneuver. F.D.R. had just asked Congress to let him call up parts of the Guard to help protect the nation.

1940

LIFE's Editor Sounds a Warning

After a month in Europe just before Dunkirk, Henry Luce returned with this message for his fellow Americans.

America is now confronted with a greater challenge to its survival as a land of liberty than any it has had to face in 80 years . . . the American way of life is bitterly opposed by mighty and ruthless military nations. Nothing will stop them—not money or cajolery or friendship—nothing but superior force . . . Certain stupefying events have happened in Europe. And we realize we have to take action . . .

First we have to arm ourselves . . . That is a colossal job. And second we have to make up our minds what we are willing to fight for. That for us, as for all free peoples, is an even harder job . . . In the end the great decision has to be made in the heart and in the private conscience . . . I have made my decision . . . What I am willing to fight for is, of course, America but not America as a geological mass, not for its mountains and plains and rivers, greatly though I love them and much though they have concerned me. The America I want to fight for is the America of freedom and justice, the

America that has stood throughout the world for the hope of progress in the democratic way of life and for faith in the ultimate brotherhood of man. America belongs to us, the lucky 130,000,000 people who are living here today. But America does not belong entirely to us. A little of America belongs to every man and woman everywhere who has had faith in democracy and hope in a world of peace and justice. We the living who control the destiny of America today are the heirs of a great inheritance from men who lived and from men who died to make men free. What they meant by

America is what I would wish to mean by America. And for that America I am willing to fight. For I know that America, the America we love, has small chance of surviving the tyranny and chaos which everywhere advances unless those who love America make it plain that they are willing and ready to . . . take their stand at Armageddon.

Seen over the horizon from the heights of Honolulu, the carefree searchlights of the largest number of warships ever docked in Pearl Harbor fill the sky with a network of light.

Even as his generals and admirals brutalize the Chinese and threaten all the western Pacific with a Japan-dominated Greater Far Eastern Co-Prosperity Sphere, Emperor Hirohito takes his troops' salute outside the Imperial Palace in Tokyo.

War Minister Hideki Tojo, Foreign Minister Yosuke Matsuoka (second from right) and other Japanese officials join German and Italian representatives in toasting the pact that officially made Japan a member of the Axis.

Bemedaled Hirohito reviews his fleet on the mythical 2,600th birthday of his family.

Direct Hits on the Nazis' Road to Paris

In a rare sequence of
combat action, a house
in Sarreguemines stands
exposed to German
artillery fire, a
high-explosive shell hits
just under the eaves,
and a growing cloud of
powder smoke mixes
with the gray dust
of pulverized concrete.

The crew of a self-propelled howitzer helping to clear the way of the Wehrmacht across France fires point-blank at the railroad station in Hangest, held by the French.

1940
The Unthinkable: Hitler Struts on French Soil

Fulfilling one of his greatest dreams of glory, Adolf Hitler, conqueror of Paris, walks with his retinue on the heights of Montmartre. The Führer, whose thirst for revenge over World War I was no secret, staged the surrender of France in the old railroad car at Compiègne where Germany had surrendered in 1918. When he learned that France was ready to capitulate he couldn't resist raising his right foot in an exultant stamp that became famous as a "dance of joy" through the official motion picture of the signing (at right). It was not until some years later that the world learned that a Canadian editor had doctored the movie frames to turn Hitler's single stamp into the Dictator's Stomp.

83

1940
Two 'Little Corporals' Meet in Paris and France Mourns

The sightseeing conqueror of France looks down on Napoleon Bonaparte's marble tomb in Les Invalides.

His country's grief distorts the face of a Marseillais watching the flags of France's lost regiments being shipped to Africa.

bers Are Leveling Chungking

At the same time that Hitler is dealing out destruction in Europe, Chungking, capital of Free China, virtually disappears in the smoke of a Japanese air raid. The punishment of China, which Japan was trying to make a vassal, had been going on since 1937.

In a section of England's bristling antiaircraft defenses during the height of the bombing, four guns fire simultaneously at Luftwaffe night bombers. When LIFE first published the picture of this little victim of the bombing, it said, "Margaret Curtis, 2, is about to die." Two years later the magazine learned that Margaret had survived.

1940
Ingenuity and Skill Fend Off the Thirsty Luftwaffe

In a four-picture sequence made by an RAF fighter's combat camera, a German plane, caught from behind by another British fighter, is hit in the tail. Under heavy fire, pieces fly off, and finally it explodes in flames. During this phase of the war, the Hurricane was the RAF's main weapon; the Allied world's favorite, the faster, higher-flying Spitfire, was still in more limited production.

Myriads of balloons trailing their deadly cables convert the English landscape into a steel jungle for low-flying Luftwaffe pilots. As many as 2,300 hovered over the island at one time.

Contrary to Britishers' invasion fears, the Battle of Britain turned out to be a war of night-and-day bombing and strafing by Hermann Göring's Luftwaffe and encirclement by U-boats, as depicted above in an above-the-battle map from an unusual angle, looking south and east, as from Greenland. Dogfights between fighter planes, the mano a mano of warfare in the skies, were but one leg of the triad of defense against the Luftwaffe. The others were antiaircraft guns and a forest of barrage balloons dangling long steel cables.

Hitler's ambivalence about the British, his hesitation to launch the invasion of the "nation of shopkeepers," resulted in a drawn-out war against the island's civilians. Axis propaganda offices made the most of it by calling it a "war of nerves." Virginio Gayda, Mussolini's Goebbels, told Italians not to expect a lightning attack on England. Berlin, even as German troops, guns and warships were massing at night along the Channel, predicted a long, hard fight. The constant bombing by the Luftwaffe produced much damage and many casualties, but it also brought forth prodigious defenses and stiffened British morale as the bad news from the Continent never had.

On Land as Well, Defenders of the Empire, All

Members of the Anti-Aircraft Defenses watch on the chalk cliffs of the Channel for German planes. Churchill had told his people, "Hitler knows he will have to break us in this island or lose the war."

To hide installations and confuse enemy planes, smoke billows from burning oil spread on the Channel waters through pipes laid by British engineers.

WAAFs at Fighter Command Headquarters near London, using long magnetic rods in the manner of croupiers in a casino, move markers representing Luftwaffe and RAF squadrons.

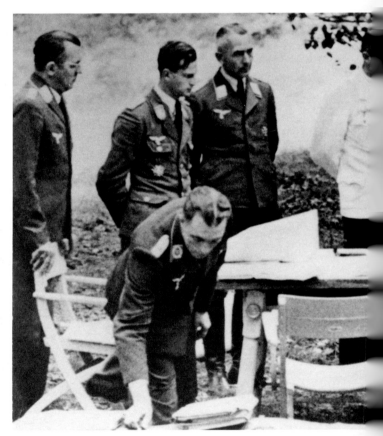

Children in a London school practice taking shelter under their desks in case of a German bombing.

The guns of "Seaforts" far out in the Thames estuary stand ready to shoot down German mine-laying planes.

Employing the revolutionary new technology of "radiolocation," a radar station scans the sky for low-flying planes. It could sense attackers at 30 miles.

Shirt-sleeved Luftwaffe chief Hermann Göring studies the war on Britain with aides at his estate near Berlin.

Westminster Abbey's sacristan, the Rev. Jocelyn Henry Temple Perkins, 70, learns to present arms in defense of Britain.

Civilians in Grayford, Kent, train to shoot Nazi paratroopers by popping at clay pigeons with 70-year-old Swiss rifles.

The hoses of a fireboat on the Thames and firefighters ashore pour arcs of water on a blaze at an East End brewery hit by incendiary bombs.

Sifting Rubble for the Wounded Becomes a Round-the-Clock Occupation

*All that remains of St. Michael's Cathedral in Coventry, from whose spire this photograph
was taken, is a Gothic-framed pile of rubble. The provost, the Rev. Richard T. Howard, and
four assistants extinguished 10 firebombs before one set the roof aflame.*

Rescuers extricate a woman from the basement of her bomb-shattered house after 18 hours of digging.
More than 50,000 "incidents" kept Londoners digging—to find and disarm buried land mines, clear streets
for firefighters and repair gas pipes and telephone cables as well as rescue their neighbors.

1940
The P.M. Presides over a Land of Troglodytes

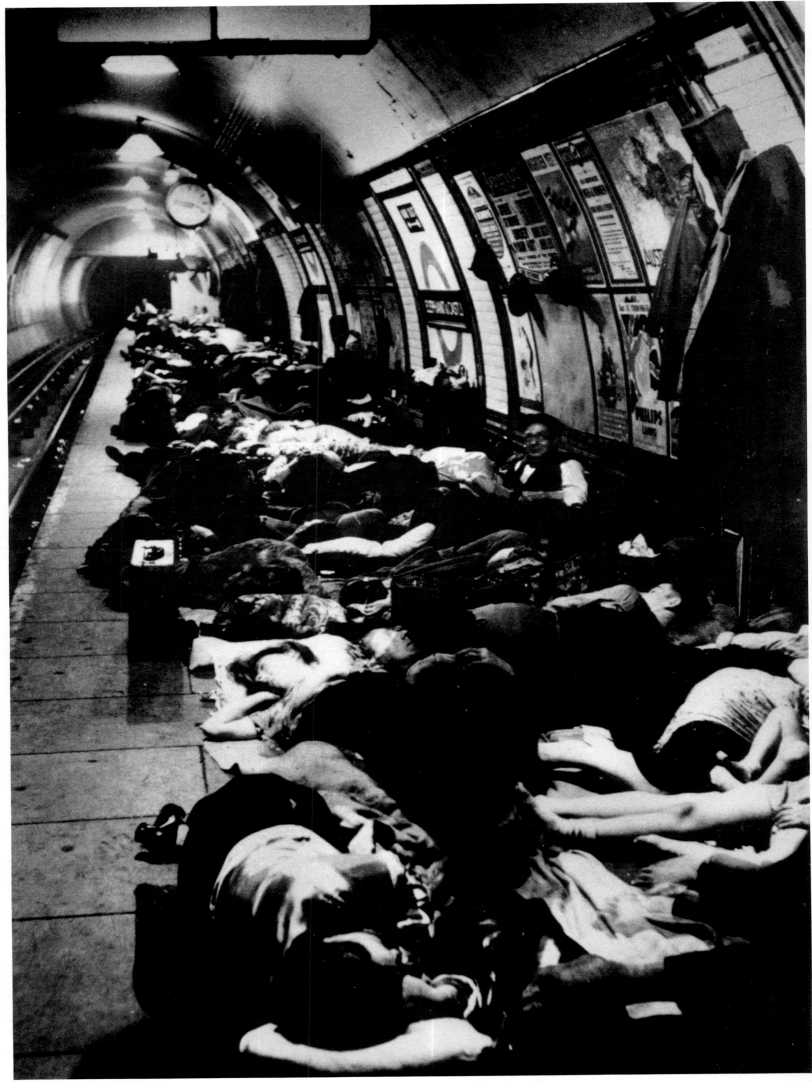

Londoners bed down in an underground station south of the Thames at the height of the bombing.

The Prime Minister relaxes on a bench and peruses a paper for some good news.

1940

London Endures a Christmas Dickens Never Envisaged

On the war's first blacked-out Christmas, Westminster Hospital nurses carrying lanterns and singing carols pass between tightly packed rows of beds of the war's wounded.

Youngsters evacuated to a rural area rush to a brief reunion at the railroad station with their parents, who came out from the city on one of the "cheap day" special trips arranged by the government.

Seen through a rift in the pall of smoke London's walled City, the great dome of St. P Cathedral, which had been rebuilt by Christopher W after the Great Fire of 1666, stands intact almost serene amid the gutted buildings hit by Gern bombers in an all-out raid three days before the New Y

1940

Across the Sea, the U.S. Watches and Waits

The first Yank RAF officer killed in action, Hurricane pilot William Meade Lindsley Fiske, 29, captain of the 1932 U.S. Olympic bobsled team, is borne, wrapped in U.S. and British flags, by his British buddies to his grave at Boxgrove, England.

Rita Hayworth stands up under the 30-pound weight of an 80,000-pearl (102 of them genuine) I. Magnin dress she is to wear to a party for the benefit of War Relief charities.

In Callander, Ontario, the Dionne quints—(from left) Cécile, Yvonne, Marie, Annette and Emilie—dress up for their first Communion.

A Nisei—U.S.-born of Japanese ancestry—who graduated from the University of California agricultural school tends his flowers in a Los Angeles County field before West Coast Japanese-Americans were removed from their homes to the interior.

Lana Turner smiles from an autographed pin-up picture that LIFE published in a special issue on the Navy. The magazine, throwing a party for the men of the battleship Idaho, asked them what movie star they wanted as guest of honor. They voted Lana.

Laundryman Yuen Chong Chan, the first name picked in the New York City draft lottery, practices in an Eighth Avenue shooting gallery. A step ahead of history, he said he'd shoot Japanese.

Aquabelles of Billy Rose's San Francisco Fair Aquacade, turn in their bathing suits to the wardrobe mistress after the final performance.

The Republican presidential nominee, Wendell L. Willkie, a business executive with views on the war not greatly different from President Roosevelt's, rides into Elwood, Indiana, to open his vigorous but futile campaign to deny F.D.R. a third term.

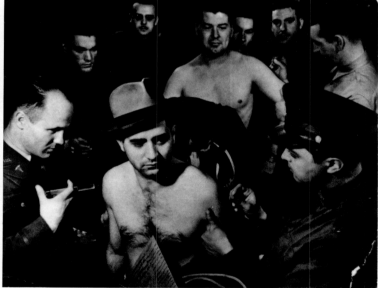

At Fort Dix, New Jersey, GIs refrain, at the photographer's request, from yelling "Watch the needle!" as draftee Sam Arcadipan gets a typhoid injection and smallpox vaccination simultaneously.

F.D.R. writes his name for history as voter No. 292 in the registration book at his polling place in Hyde Park, New York.

1941 TRIUMPH

As winter turned to spring, Adolf Hitler, the grand strategist who had made himself the master of continental Europe, had a right to Napoleonic feelings. He had misjudged the British people, but even after he toned down his dream of invasion his navy kept slashing at their lifeline. Germany's state-of-the-art dreadnoughts and speedy 10,000-ton "pocket battleships" on the surface of the Atlantic and U-boats below took such a toll of British shipping that Churchill, in March, had proclaimed a "Battle of the Atlantic." Even after planes from the carrier *Ark Royal* ended the surface war by sinking the 42,000-ton supership *Bismarck* (in retaliation for its sinking Britain's pride, the battleship *Hood*), the U-boats continued it beneath the sea.

The German leader also felt, as he pondered what next, that he could handle the ally who increasingly was adding to his problems rather than relieving him of them. While black-shirted modern Romans greeted Mussolini with cadenced cries of "Duce! Duce!" every time he postured on his Palazzo Venezia balcony, his vaunted empire in North Africa was being eroded by British tanks. (The British, after all, had invented tank warfare in the conflict Hitler still smoldered about.) And back in the birthplace of western civilization ragged Greek mountaineers were thrashing his foot-dragging legions. Hitler's other ally, Stalin, sought to make Soviet satellites of the Balkan countries that the Führer's emissaries had turned into Axis bases against possible Red treachery.

Hitler was thus forced to deploy his forces in many directions not of his own choosing. In February the Afrika Korps, a panzer division and a motorized division trained in desert fighting, landed in Tripoli. Their intent was to reverse the pastings that the British and Australians,

S FOR THE AXIS

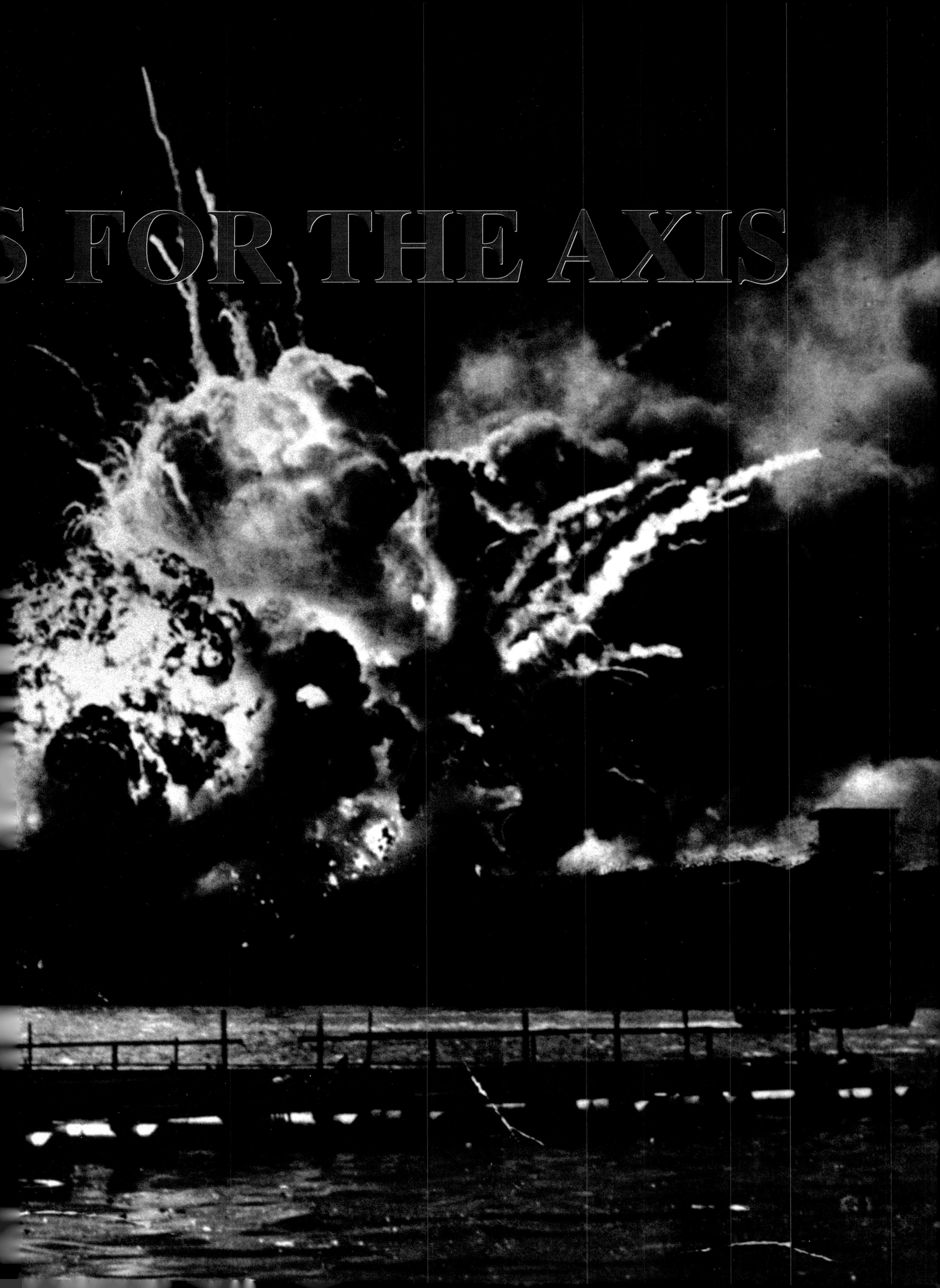

'The Biggest Battle in the History of the World'

The arrows of Hitler's war show the grand plan of his Drang nach Osten, *or drive to the east. Those*

under the command of Field Marshal Archibald Wavell, and Free French forces in the south were handing to Marshal Rodolfo Graziani's Italians in Libya. (Other British forces were ousting the Italians from the Sudan and Haile Selassie's Ethiopia.) Then the Yugoslav army, furious that Premier Dragisha Cvetovich had signed a pact with the Axis, threw him out, replaced him with General Dusan Simovitch and enthroned Peter II. This forced Hitler's hand. In April his troops started weaving through the tortuous Balkan valleys into Greece and Yugoslavia. They were in Yugoslavia too speedily for the British to aid the defense, and they took the capital, Belgrade, within a week and a half. (A fiery Communist, Joseph Broz Tito, vowed he would fight to the end.) When, in accordance with a long-standing alliance, Churchill sent 53,000 troops to Greece, the Wehrmacht outflanked them and pushed them into the sea. The Balkans and Greece were Hitler's, after just three weeks of combat.

When he slanted the arrows of his war maps toward the Middle East, Hitler was perforce following a traditional plan of German general staffs in quest of empire. But like Napoleon and the Teutonic Knights before him, the Führer felt that the road to glory and plenty—and, best of all, *Lebensraum*—lay to his east, across the Ukrainian wheat fields toward Moscow. His resolve was supported by his second great miscalculation. The Red Army's poor performance in its initial battles with Finland had imbued him with disdain for Stalin's military power. On the second day of summer, June 22—two days behind Napoleon's 1812 timetable—he launched Operation Barbarossa, the invasion of the Soviet Union.

Proclaiming that turning on his partner was a move to avert a "stab in the back" (he had evidently liked President Roosevelt's line about Italy and France), he flung 121 divisions and 3,000 planes against the world's largest army—7.15 million including reserves, 350,000 more than his own. It was called "the biggest battle in the history of the world," and was fought along a 2,000-mile front from the Arctic to the Black Sea. Although Stalin had been warned by Roosevelt and Churchill, among others, that such an attack was coming, his generals were caught off guard.

Hitler proposed to destroy the Red Army within a month, and in the opening days the war photographs were dreadfully familiar: they looked like the conquest of Poland, Holland and France all over again. Division after division, army after army was wiped out as the Wehrmacht executed a series of giant pincer movements around towns and cities. Whole Soviet republics were blitzed into terror and confusion by the Luftwaffe and motorized artillery. Bombed-out peasants fled along country roads, civilians cowered in city streets, children huddled in dugouts.

But this was not Poland, and this was not the Polish army. Nor was it the same army the Finns had pushed around in Karelia. These men had been trained to fight as individuals; they were skilled at guerrilla warfare. To most of them this was Mother Russia.

The Soviets immediately established the last-ditch principle of the "scorched earth." Nothing in the path of the enemy—no structure, no crop, no piece of equipment—was left undestroyed. And by their brutal treatment of the people in that path the Nazis lost the one essential of success in guerrilla warfare, a local populace that could be cajoled or forced into providing food or shelter when supply lines were outrun. Even the peasants of the Soviet-leery Ukraine and the newly Sovietized Baltic satellites were vengeful beyond reconciliation.

Hitler's early-knockout plan was based on destroying Russian morale by swiftly sacking Moscow, Leningrad and

Hitler confers with Mussolini the roles of their 19 meeting reversed: Hit

in Greece indicate the Axis invasion path from Bulgaria as well as from the boot of Italy.

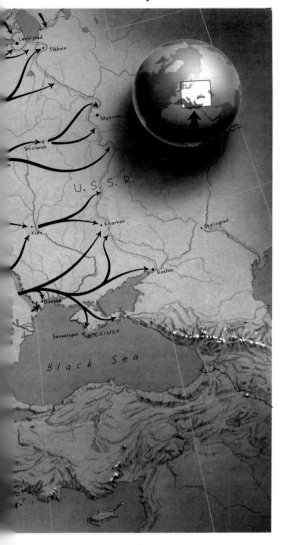

...longer the shabby junior ...rtner but the new Napoleon ...ride the Western world.

Kiev, Mother Russia's heart and soul. Its way blasted clear by the Luftwaffe, the Wehrmacht won victory after victory along the northern and central parts of the "Stalin Line" as it ground toward Leningrad and fought across the vast Pripet marshes on Napoleon's old route to Moscow. But Smolensk, the historic gateway to the capital on the upper Dnieper river, proved a tough nut to crack. The Red Army mounted fierce counterattacks there that stalled the Germans and crimped Hitler's psychological-warfare plan. From that sector south, in the Ukraine, which the Germans had to traverse to reach Kiev, Rostov and the Black Sea, the resistance was fiercest, although Leningrad, once surrounded, proved so hard to penetrate that Berlin announced it would starve the city to death. Mechanized might ultimately prevailed in the central and southern reaches, however; Smolensk fell, but the going eastward was painfully slow and costly in lives, and the idea of early victory glimmered and died. Despite a steady advance on bomb-battered Moscow that threw Muscovites into panic and caused Stalin to declare a state of siege, early cold blew in, all the way south to the Black Sea, by the time the Nazis took Odessa in October. It was not long before Moscow's defenders were reinforced by the old ally who had saved them from Napoleon, General Winter.

Soon after Hitler shattered his partnership with Stalin, two meetings within a fortnight in the West marked the start of a mightier one, which would by year's end become the fully fledged alliance of the Big Three. On July 28 and 31, presidential aide Harry Hopkins, F.D.R.'s "eyes and ears," met with Stalin in the Kremlin to assess Russia's war effort and to ask what they needed. (The answer he took back: a colossal war plan and a $1 billion shopping list of matériel.) On August 14 the President and Prime Minister Churchill met aboard the U.S. cruiser *Augusta* off

Newfoundland's secluded port of Argentia for the first of a series of one-on-one talks. At the end, they issued a joint declaration, called the Atlantic Charter, that summarized the common goals of their people. The two invited Stalin to make it a trio and he accepted promptly.

Roosevelt kept his eye all the while on the other ocean, whose Asian rim was inflamed by Japan's deepening war with China. The invasion of Indochina and the Malay peninsula were also part of her newly launched expansionist war for hegemony in a "Greater Far Eastern Co-Prosperity Sphere." Roosevelt nationalized the Philippine army under General Douglas MacArthur and had Secretary of State Cordell Hull warn Tokyo to leave the Pacific open to U.S. shipping.

Then, in rapid succession: Fumimaro Konoye resigned; Emperor Hirohito appointed his war minister, General Hideki Tojo, Premier; Tojo blasted U.S.-British "exploitation" of Asians; and Ambassador Kichisaburo Nomura started a series of talks with the U.S. State Department. Subsequently, after Ambassador Grew in Tokyo warned Washington of a possible attack on U.S. installations, the President appealed personally to Hirohito to avert war.

On Sunday, December 7, as a church bell rang across the water at Pearl Harbor for 8 a.m. Mass, a torpedo from one of more than 350 Japanese planes launched from six carriers hit the battleship *Oklahoma*. In the ensuing, precisely orchestrated surprise attack, the *Oklahoma* and five more battleships, plus 16 other warships, were sunk, 164 planes were burned up, and 2,008 sailors, 218 soldiers, 109 Marines and 68 civilians were killed. Congress declared war on Japan immediately and days later added Germany and Italy. On the radio, F.D.R., calling December 7 "a date which will live in infamy," told Americans to prepare for a long war "in which we will gain the inevitable triumph, so help us God."

CHRONOLOGY 1941

January	February	March	April	May	June
1 • *Britain pounds Bardia on Egyptian frontier* **5** • *Bardia falls* • *Savage Axis bombing of Malta begins* **6** • *Thai troops attack Cambodia* **10** • *Soviet-German economic agreement signed* • *Lend-Lease bill introduced* **15** • *Axis punishing British fleet in Mediterranean* **19** • *British invade Eritrea* **20** • *Hitler and Mussolini meet in Berlin* • *F.D.R. is inaugurated* **21** • *Japan warns U.S. not to interfere in its territory* **22** • *Tobruk falls to British* **27** • *Rumors of a Japanese attack on Pearl Harbor received by U.S.* **30** • *British take Derna, Libya*	**6** • *British take Benghazi* **7** • *Italians badly beaten in Libya* **8** • *Germany and Bulgaria in pact* **9** • *English pound Genoa* **10** • *British invade Italian Somaliland* **12** • *Rommel arrives Tripoli* **16** • *British mine Singapore waters* **28** • *End of Greek counteroffensive*	**1** • *Bulgaria joins Axis* • *U.S. starts guarding convoys* **5** • *Hitler tells Japan to enter war* • *British enter Ethiopia* **11** • *F.D.R. signs Lend-Lease bill, Allies start getting arms* **16** • *Italians repulsed by Greeks* • *British enter Ethiopia* • *Hitler predicts war over in one year* **20** • *U.S. warns Russia of coming Nazi attack* **21** • *U.S. lifts Soviet arms ban* **24** • *Rommel starts major offensive in Libya* **27** • *Yugoslavia revolution* **28** • *Battle of Cape Matapan, the southernmost point of Greece—serious naval defeat for Italians*	**3** • *Rommel captures Benghazi* • *Premier Paul Teleki commits suicide to avoid submitting to Hungary's entry into war* **4** • *F.D.R. opens ports to British* **6** • *Germany invades Yugoslavia and Greece* **11** • *Siege of Tobruk begins* **12** • *Hungary enters war* **13** • *Reds and Japanese sign non-aggression pact* • *Germans take Belgrade* **14** • *Rommel repulsed at Tobruk* **17** • *Surrender of Yugoslav army* **21** • *Japanese occupy Foochow* **22** • *Greek army surrenders* **23** • *Lindbergh appeasement speech* **27** • *Germans take Athens* **28** • *British evacuate Greece*	**2** • *Iraqi revolt against British* **5** • *Japan suspects U.S. has broken its code* • *Haile Selassie back in Addis Ababa* **6** • *Stalin becomes Soviet premier* **9** • *Nazi wave of terror in Poland* • *German secret code captured on U-boat* **10** • *Rudolph Hess parachutes into Scotland* **13** • *Martin Bormann replaces Hess* **20** • *German airborne assault on Crete* **24** *British battle cruiser Hood sunk by Bismarck* **26** • *British concede defeat in Crete* **27** • *British sink Bismarck* • *U.S. claims national emergency* **31** • *Iraqi revolt collapses*	**1** • *British complete evacuation of Crete* **7** • *Japanese raids on Chungking begin* **8** • *British and Free French invade Syria* **11** • *German troops mass on Soviet border* **15** • *British counteroffensive at Tobruk* **22** • *Germany invades Russia* **24** • *In two days 2,000 Soviet planes destroyed* **26** • *Finland declares war on Soviet Union* **27** • *Hungary declares war on Soviets*

■ **War in Europe**   ■ **War in Asia**   ■ **U.S.A.**

July	August	September	October	November	December
1 • Germans take Riga **2** • 7,000 Jews murdered at Lvov **3** • Germans say Russian war will be over in month • Japanese call up 1 million for military service **4** • Tito's Partisans announced **5** • Germans reach Dnieper River **7** • U.S. enters Iceland to forestall Nazis **10** • Finland attacks Russia • Stalin makes himself commander in chief of Soviet forces **12** • Cease-fire in Syria **16** • Germans take Smolensk **17** • Franco: "The Allies have lost" **21** • Japanese occupy bases in French Indochina **23** • Germans bomb Moscow **26** • F.D.R. nationalizes Filipino troops under MacArthur • U.S. stops all trade with Japan **27** • Hitler slows drive on Moscow in favor of Ukraine and Leningrad	**5** • Germans take Smolensk **12** • Germans push to Black Sea, surround Odessa • Petain commits Vichy to Nazi new order **14** • F.D.R. and Churchill issue Atlantic Charter off Newfoundland **15** • Germans break through in Ukraine **21** • Battle of Kiev begins **25** • England and Russia invade Iran • Hitler and Mussolini meet in East Prussia **26** • Great Dam on Dnieper blown up by retreating Russians **28** • Hostilities cease in Iran **29** • Hitler and Mussolini meet in Berlin	**3** • Germans use "poison gas" for extermination **4** • Siege of Leningrad begins **5** • Children under 12 evacuated from Moscow **6** • German Jews ordered to wear yellow star • Hirohito told by warlords defeat of U.S. impossible **7** • Britain and Russia occupy Tehran **8** • Biggest raid on Berlin yet • Germans lay siege to Leningrad **9** • Franco sends division to help attack Leningrad **11** • F.D.R. orders Navy to fire on Axis raiders **12** • Early snow along Russian front **19** • Germans capture Kiev **24** • British try to supply besieged Malta **27** • First U.S. Liberty ship launched • 100,000 Japanese trapped by Chinese at Changsha **29** • In two days SS massacre 34,000 Jews at Babi Yar ravine	**1** • Chinese repulse Japanese at Changla **2** • Gestapo begins destroying synagogues of Paris **5** • Counterattacks by Reds in Ukraine start **8** • Heavy rains turn Russian front into quagmire **11** • 2,000 Japanese-Americans to be moved from West Coast **12** • Germans take Bryansk **13** • Germans take Vyazma **15** • Germans take Kalinin **16** • Half a million citizens complete defenses of Moscow • Soviet government moved out of Moscow • U.S. destroyer torpedoed off Iceland • Germans take Odessa **17** • Tojo becomes prime minister of Japan **20** • Siege of Moscow begins **27** • Russian counterattack at Moscow **29** • Manstein's offensive in Crimea begins **30** • Nine-month-long siege of Sevastopol begins	**3** • Ambassador Grew cables warning of imminent Japanese attack **8** • Germans push into Crimea **9** • British annihilate Italian convoys south of Taranto **13** • U.S. Neutrality Act revised • Germans take Sevastopol • Germans approach Moscow in coldest winter in 140 years **14** • Russians airlift supplies to Leningrad **16** • Germans capture Kerch **18** • British begin second western desert offensive **20** • U.S.-Japanese negotiations begin in Washington **22** • Germans seize Rostov **23** • Rommel repulses British in the desert • Japanese strike force given mission: Pearl Harbor **24** • Germans take Kharkov **26** • Japanese strike force heads for Hawaii **27** • U.S. Pacific units put on "war warning" • Conquest of Italian East Africa complete • Germans 19 miles from Moscow **29** • In bitter cold Reds recapture Rostov	**1** • Tojo rejects U.S. Pacific proposals as "fantastic" **5** • Germans stopped just outside Moscow **6** • Counteroffensive begins as Reds strike with 100 divisions • F.D.R. appeals directly to Emperor to avoid war • Hitler issues Night and Fog decree for Jewish elimination • F.D.R. approves research funds for A-bomb **7** • Japanese attack U.S. at Pearl Harbor **7-8** • Malaya, Thailand, Singapore, Hong Kong, Guam, Wake, Manila also under attack **8** • U.S. declares war on Japan • Bloodbath in Riga, Latvia, claims lives of 27,000 Jews **11** • U.S. declares war on Germany and Italy **16** • Germans in retreat along entire eastern front **19** • Hitler assumes personal command of German army **22** • Japanese launch major attack on Philippines • German execution squad murders 32,000 Jews in Lithuania **26** • Manila declared open city **29** • Japanese attack Corregidor

Rape of Russia

June 22, the day after the summer solstice, the longest day of the year, was to the Soviet people a date of infamy as deep-dyed and unforgettable as December 7, two weeks before the shortest, was to be to Americans. On that day Adolf Hitler turned the land of the world's largest army from his partner to his enemy. The operation, intended to crush that enemy within a month, was code-named Barbarossa. The Italian for Redbeard, this was the appellation of Frederick I, the redheaded 12th century Holy Roman emperor, but for the Western world it had self-descriptive overtones: it sounded "barbarous." And barbarous Barbarossa was. The idea was to replicate the shattering of Poland on a vastly larger scale. All the means, all the methods, of Blitzkrieg and psychological warfare were in place.

A "lesson" for the local citizenry, Russians suspected of fighting as partisans hang from gallows erected by the SS.

The bombers, the Stukas, the panzers punished cities, villages, farms. Death squads of the SS, well supplied with rifles and gibbets, roamed the countryside killing people suspected of being partisans, and, more important, showing citizens what would happen to them if they lifted a finger to help in their own defense. In less than three weeks the Wehrmacht was in Leningrad province, closing in on the city whose capture would make it possible to supply its forces by sea, and had captured Minsk, the key rail junction for Moscow. But as hatred for the invader mounted, the going got slower and costlier. Leningrad settled in for a siege that would last a year and a half. And the brutalized citizenry of all the rest of Russia torched their own towns, scorched their earth, fled to fight elsewhere, or died.

A Lvov rape victim screams as a woman tries to comfort her. Such rapes were routinely committed in the streets.

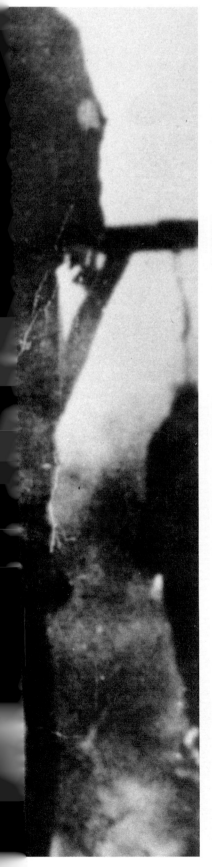

1941
Barbarossa Begins

*German invasion troops, in the gray of the summer dawn,
cross an undefended bridge on the Russian border.*

A Russian mother kisses her son goodbye as he leaves with his Red Army buddies for somewhere on the vast front.

At high noon Sunday, June 22, Muscovites listen in silence to Foreign Minister Vyacheslav Molotov's announcement, over a street-corner public-address system, of the invasion of their country by their erstwhile military ally. Not long afterward they were to find their voice and raise it in the anthem (below), which moved tough soldiers to tears and was to become their most popular patriotic song of the war.

The Sacred War

Arise, vast Land, in awesome might!
For mortal combat gird
Against the evil powers of night,
The fascist hordes accursed!
Let storms of indignation rage
And righteous wrath outpour!
This is a sacred war we wage,
A people's sacred war.

1941

Hatred Pours from Every House

*Panzer troops leap from their armored troop carrier to
finish off Red Army sharpshooters in a farmhouse.*

1941
Steel, Lead, Fire and Vodka

The moment of truth arrives for Russian and German armor on a road the panzers thought they had conquered. A column of Red Army heavy tanks suddenly appears over the horizon. In the foreground is a German "tank chaser"—a big gun on tractors—that had blasted other Red tanks while those now approaching hid in nearby woods.

Wehrmacht riflemen advancing on a Russian sniper take concealment behind a ramshackle fence.

Germans attacking Vitebsk take a lunch break of field rations and captured vodka, houses they torched blazing behind them.

The all too familiar sight of children huddled in mixed terror and curiosity recurs as the Luftwaffe blasts Moscow.

A Moscow Rerun of Last Summer's London

Antiaircraft fire patterns the sky over Red Square as seven German parachute flares, dropping evenly, silhouette the Kremlin. Families, mostly mothers and children (inset), turn in on cots in Moscow's Mayakovsky metro station. Serving as air-raid shelters was the roughest treatment the showplace underground stations had received since they opened in 1935.

1941
Vast Landscape of Refugees, Prisoners and Corpses

A Nazi sentry stands guard over Red Army prisoners of war herded into a compound at Porkhov.

Ukrainians embittered at Nazi cruelties join the Red Army in retreat before the all-engulfing waves of the Wehrmacht.

Jewish survivors of the German conquest of the Crimea, searching for missing relatives when the Red Army recaptured the peninsula's eastern tip, come upon early evidence of Nazi atrocities, bodies of Jews murdered by Einsatzgruppen. These were special forces that followed the Wehrmacht with the express mission of executing all Jews left alive.

As the Wehrmacht cuts a swath through Belorussia, the SS deploys its chief instrument of information and education, the street gallows.

With the Nazi push into Yugoslavia and Greece, the Mediterranean, living up to its name, became the center of an entirely separate major war. The British were already fighting the Italians in North Africa.

When the Yugoslav army kicked out their pro-Axis premier, the warfare that flared in southern Europe was more than a minor diversion to eastward-looking Hitler. A theater of operations as vast as European Russia and even more varied in terrain taxed every branch of his military forces. Besides sending the Wehrmacht through rough Balkan terrain to Belgrade, he had to end the embarrassing pasting his ally Mussolini had been receiving from the Greek army since his October invasion of the equally rugged Hellenic peninsula. Across the Mediterranean, his desert forces had their hands full fighting back the British, who were out to terminate Mussolini's African empire. When the Wehrmacht did conquer the Yugoslavs, British forces that had come to their aid were evacuated from the east coast to the Greek island of Crete, to which the Greek government had also fled. His airborne troops gave the Führer a spectacular victory in capturing the island in history's first invasion without conventional infantry. But it was a Pyrrhic victory: losses were so heavy that Hitler told General Kurt Student, their commander, "The day of parachute troops is over." Within a fortnight the Royal Navy started removing the 15,000 British troops (out of 30,000) who survived the Battle of Crete.

Heavy German armor pushing through snowy Balkan valleys is reminiscent of Hannibal's elephants crossing the Alps. Here tanks from satellite Bulgaria stream toward Yugoslavia's capital.

BATTLEFRONTS: *Swastikas on the Acropolis, Parachutes over Crete*

German parachutists land on Crete's rocky slopes i
completely airborne invasion. Although Germany had u.
paratroops in its conquest of northern Europe, they k
always been a sort of spearhead for regular infan

*With the Parthenon as a backdrop, German soldiers raise
the flag of the Third Reich over the Acropolis, after
the Greek army, exhausted by a year's fighting in Albania,
surrendered in the mountains. It took a week more for
the panzers, battling tough British rearguard action, to push
through the narrow passes at Thermopylae and Olympus,
after their Alpenjaeger seized the guardian peaks,
planting the swastika atop Mount Olympus in the process.*

The coast of conquered France provided the German navy an array of bases from which to prey on Britain's ocean lifeline. It did this with increasing success, with the time-tested vessels of naval warfare: huge dreadnoughts such as the new 42,000-ton supership *Bismarck*, submarines and surface raiders disguised as civilian ships, in the image of German World War I hero Count Felix von Luckner's *Sea Wolf*. When the new wrinkle, 10,000-ton pocket battleships, took to sea, British losses became even worse. The Admiralty devised new escort techniques and ever larger convoys; it constantly altered convoy routes, but still the losses were at an unacceptable level. The U.S. Senate voted to arm merchant ships and the U.S. Navy instituted an Atlantic Air Patrol in which PBYs, Consolidated patrol bombers, kept an eye on convoys. When the sinking of the *Bismarck* ended the surface war, Germany's still-swelling U-boat fleet protracted the Battle of the Atlantic until the summer of 1944.

The 4,983-ton freighter Lehigh, *two U.S. flags painted on her side, sinks in the South Atlantic 75 miles northwest of Freetown, Sierra Leone, the victim of a U-boat's torpedo. The first picture in the series was taken by the ship's second engineer from the U-boat, which took him and other crew aboard. In it the* Lehigh's *last two lifeboats wait for three men who went back aboard to rig an emergency radio, one of whom is still atop the rear mast. In the rest of the series, taken by one of the three, the freighter sinks slowly, one of her painted flags disappears, her bow rears up, becomes vertical and finally, in a thunder of foam, plunges from sight.*

Killer U-boats

Ropes from the British cruiser Dorsetshire are clutched by half-drowned survivors of the enemy Bismarck, sunk two miles away. Word that German planes were approaching caused the Dorsetshire to leave before its rescue mission was complete. It steamed off, dropping rafts behind.

A merchant fleet flotilla heads east across sub-infested Atlantic waters under the watchful eye of the U.S. Navy's Atlantic Air Patrol, from one of whose PBYs this picture was taken.

This unnerving sight, the sudden emergence of a submarine knifing out of the chop and waves, was exactly what neither Axis nor Allied surface ships cared to see.

Having Taken It During the Blitz, Britain Dishes It Out in the Air

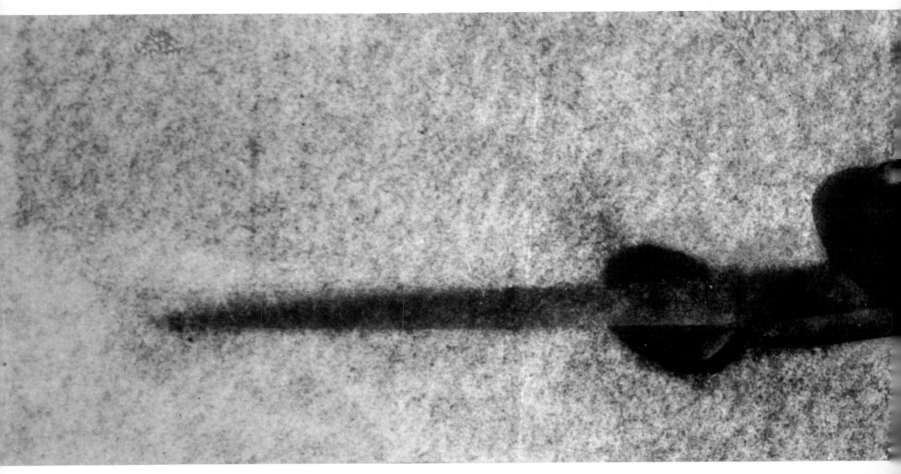

Five British bombs fall toward the Knapsack power station north of Cologne.

RAF fighter pilots relax at night in the lounge of the Officers' Mess.

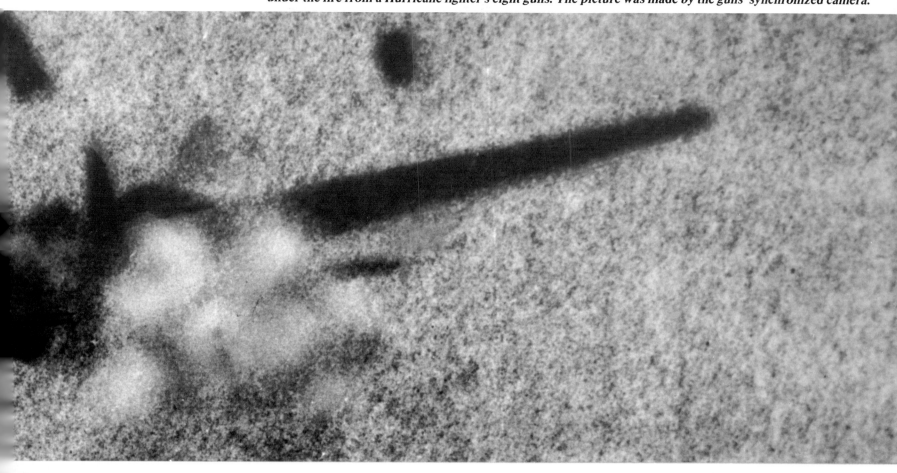

A German Heinkel III bomber attacking a small secret airfield during the Battle of Britain starts to break up under the fire from a Hurricane fighter's eight guns. The picture was made by the guns' synchronized camera.

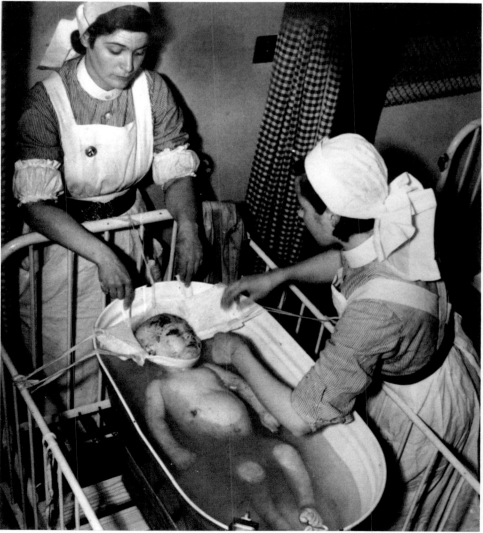

Terry Stone, 18 months old, burned over 60 percent of his body by the Luftwaffe bomb that killed his mother and 11 more of his family, lies in a life-saving saline bath in a London hospital. He lived to walk again.

1941

For England, Always the Fear of Invasion

Seen at Dunkirk by the cameras of the RAF Bomber Command as invasion jitters seized Britain, some of the 3,000 barges that the Germans collected at "invasion ports" across the Channel provide a good target. The RAF smashed 1 million deadweight tons of the barges in a three-week onslaught.

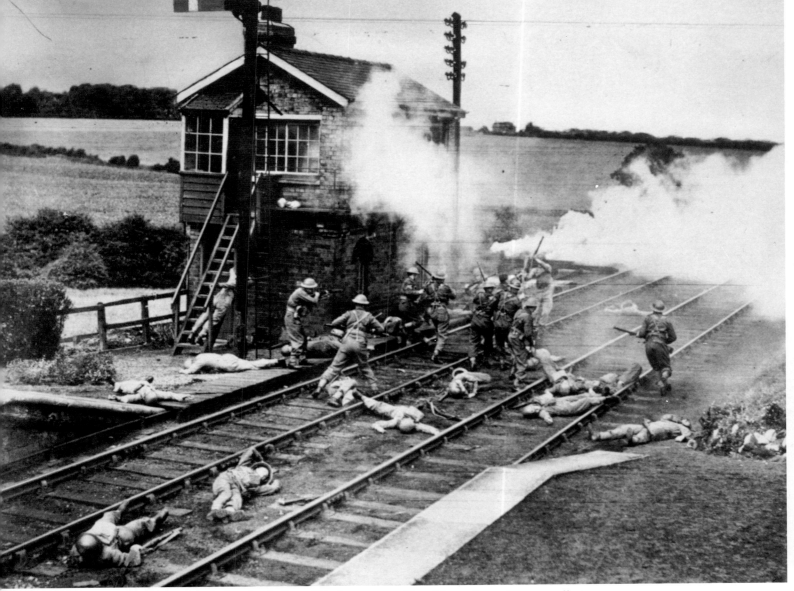

A different kind of make-believe fills the countryside with smoke and "corpses" as the British Home Guard stages a rehearsal of invasion by German parachutists.

Drawings for LIFE depict a landing by a German invasion force on the Channel coast of Britain, based on "the best military likelihoods." The Luftwaffe (center left) clearly has won control of the air as men and tanks are disgorged on the beach and troop transports fly in to captured airfields. At left, the inevitable panzer charge has a different look in pastoral England.

Carrying rehearsal realism to the extreme, the possibility of collaborationists is faced when a "fifth columnist" disguised as a nanny draws a gun on a Home Guard sentry suspicious of her empty carriage.

1941
Wartime Summer a World Apart

While across the Channel the Wehrmacht waffles, women war workers take the British sun on invasion-ready beaches.

Simultaneously, Chungking civilians crushed in a tunnel shelter during a Japanese air raid lie where they were dumped by frantic rescuers. These two pictures were published in the same 1941 issue of LIFE a page apart.

Hideki Tojo, Japan's war minister turned premier, smiles his Greater Far Eastern Co-Prosperity smile.

When Harry Hopkins, F.D.R.'s "eyes and ears," reached Moscow on July 30, he found LIFE photographer Margaret Bourke-White already there. Hopkins' mission: to smell out the resolution and ability of the Soviet war effort. After their second meeting within the Kremlin, Stalin allowed Bourke-White to photograph them. "His mustache and hair have a kind of chewed up, straw-like look," Bourke-White wrote of Stalin. "He looks like a completely strong person, immobile and unemotional." Hopkins' evaluation of Russia's determination gained the Reds a billion dollars worth of U.S. aid.

Nos. 2 and 3 of Hitler's war machine (each thought he was No. 2), Joseph Goebbels, who spread the propaganda, and Marshal Hermann Göring, who spread the bombs, confer at a dress parade when both their services were at the peak of their power.

President Roosevelt and Prime Minister Churchill raise their voices in "Onward, Christian Soldiers" at a service aboard H.M.S. Prince of Wales in Argentia Bay, Newfoundland. It was the first of 10 historic meetings of the two.

Hitler and Mussolini meet on the Russian front. The August meeting was their twelfth, and since both dictators had their hands full it lasted five "fervid" days, as Mussolini put it.

Still Slowed by Isolationists, the U.S. Is Becoming Democracy's Great Ars

If by invading Russia Hitler had turned his partner into his enemy, he had at the same time effectively galvanized the U.S. against him. His underestimation of both was to be his undoing. His biggest minus, in the case of the latter, was the effect the invasion had on the course of isolationism in the U.S. Barbarossa made the war worldwide, and one glance at a U.S.-centered map of the globe *(right)* and the great circle routes from both coasts to the enemies of Hitlerism showed clearly that a separate future for the New World was but a dream. Isolationism had been set back in the earlier debates, but many patriotic Americans kept hoping there was still a chance to avoid spilling American blood and treasure, as had been done in World War I without achieving peace. Barbarossa dealt the fatal blow to that hope.

The first step was obvious. All forces fighting Hitler must be backed up with American supplies. Cash-and-carry went out the window. Once it was established that the polite fiction of Lend-Lease meant that the U.S. taxpayer would pay all the bills, industry's throttle was pushed wide open. Ships, planes, tanks, guns were produced in record time. War production greatly exceeded the pace of World War I. In a fireside chat F.D.R. coined the term Arsenal of Democracy. Long before the year's end the U.S. had made that more than a metaphor.

The battleship Indiana, *on the ways at Newport News, Virginia, nears launching, shortly after her sister ship* North Carolina.

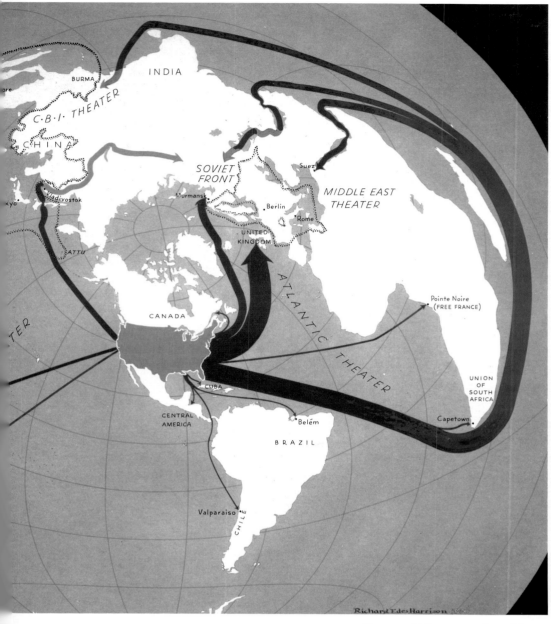

Above, a U.S. centered world map shows the many Allied centers now supplied by the U.S. and the routes by which American arms and war necessities reach their varied destinations.

A new Garbo, ornately gowned and bejeweled, dances a rumba with Bob Alton, a dance director who taught her the number for her yet unfinished film, Two Faced Woman. *Two year earlier she and MGM anticipated alliance with Russia, making the comedy* Ninotchka, *in which she played a Soviet apparatchik.*

The first U.S. Gold Star mother, Mrs. Jennie Dobnika, of Cleveland, holds the pictures of her three Navy sons, Frank (left), John (right) and Louis, killed in action when the destroyer Kearny was hit by a Nazi torpedo west of Iceland.

1941
And War Moves Ever Closer

The first U.S. troops to embark for foreign soil, GIs board the former liner America (itself a former German liner interned during World War I) to guard the Newfoundland naval base leased from Britain under F.D.R.'s bases-for-destroyers deal.

The year's hottest new star prospect, Howard Hughes's find, Jane Russell, 20, rests on a stack of corn tassels during shooting of her first film, Hughes's The Outlaw.

The familiar swing, the familiar crack and Joe DiMaggio sends Cleveland pitcher Al Milnar's pitch rocketing past him for a record-setting hit. The Yankee outfielder had now batted safely in 56 consecutive games.

In a TV first, CBS broadcasts a bowl of flowers in full color.

A phalanx of "Mothers' Crusade" isolationists kneels before the Capitol and prays for the defeat of the Lend-Lease bill.

In a San Francisco
restaurant,
Ingrid Bergman,
interrupting a
ski vacation, discusses
with Ernest Hemingway
the prospect of
playing Maria, the
heroine of his
novel of the Spanish
Civil War, For Whom
the Bell Tolls.

In his maiden speech as a member of the
isolationist America First Committee,
in Chicago, flier-hero Charles A.
Lindbergh, impressed with the quality of
the Luftwaffe, tells the nation that
Britain is losing the war and the U.S. will
be unsuccessful if it intervenes.

Latin-American diplomats and family members listen as
President Roosevelt, from the East Room of the White
House, broadcasts an appeal for all-American unity.

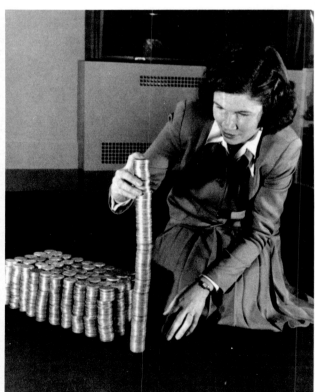

A housewife, identified by LIFE
merely as an average reader of the
magazine, stacks her husband's
$2,500 income, in silver dollars, and
finds that to buy what cost her that
in 1939 she needs 186 more.

Saburo Kurusu, flown dramatically
to Washington as Hirohito's
special envoy, and Ambassador
Kichisaburo Nomura wait at
the State Department, in apparent
high spirits, for talks with
F.D.R. and Secretary of State
Cordell Hull about how to reduce
tension between the U.S. and Japan.

Body Language

Daring dread punishment by the SS, a young Dutchman walks down an Amsterdam street, naked save for a fedora and shoes, to protest clothes rationing by the occupying Germans.

Rita Hayworth, about to star with Fred Astaire in You'll Never Get Rich, *poses for LIFE photographer Robert Landry who creates a classic pin-up for the growing population of GIs.*

In the dawn of December 7, crewmen on the flight deck of a Japanese carrier northwest of Pearl Harbor prepare to release fighter planes revving up for the surprise attack on the U.S. naval base.

Mounted troops of the Red Army cross snow-covered fields near Moscow as the climactic battle for the capital looms.

1941
Russian Scenes Evoke Images of Past Wars

Moscow civilians, mostly women and old men, wield picks and shovels to carve an immense tank trap out of the earth to halt the panzers advancing on the capital.

With fixed bayonets, regular infantry troops of the Red Army wade through snow to attack Germans in a village on Moscow's outskirts.

...rging right out of Russia's ...ist past, saber-wielding Cossacks ...p to Moscow's defense.

149

1941
The Carefully Plotted Infamy at Pearl Harbor

For the entire year, Japan had been plotting the attack on Pearl Harbor, and for the entire year Pearl Harbor, and Washington, had been aware of the possibility of war with Japan. But by September, when Tokyo perfected the plan of the sneak attack, the U.S. had dropped its guard. Both war machines, ironically, presumed that war between them would be unprofitable. Admiral Yamamoto felt that after the first crippling blow he could command the Pacific for six months to a year, but he wasn't sure about a second year. But when the last, exhaustively researched detail of the attack was in place, hot-headed army leaders were in control in Tokyo and they told Yamamoto to get on with the operation. It came, that cloudy Sunday morning, from six carriers, which had steamed during the night to within 275 miles of the big base. There were no transports, no ground troops, since no invasion was contemplated. The transports were carrying troops to Malaya, Siam, the Philippines, Guam and Wake Island. The carriers got up-to-the-minute reconnaissance from midget submarines up close to the harbor. It was the crew of one of these who were the first casualties of the attack. An hour before the first torpedo hit the *Oklahoma*, the destroyer *Ward* sank the sub. The *Ward*'s warning message to command headquarters was flubbed along the chain of communication: an Army radar operator's report was laughed off by his superior officer. And, for the U.S., World War II was on.

One of the first wave of planes takes off from a carrier, to the "Banzai!" of officers and crew.

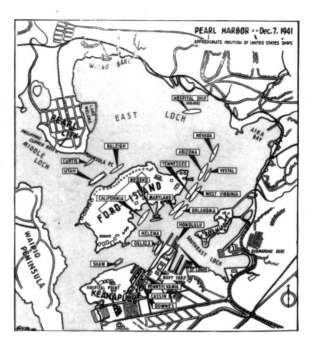

Just as they looked in the final version of the operation mockup, the raid's principal target, the dreadnought kingpins of the Pacific Fleet, are neatly arrayed around Ford Island in this map of Pearl Harbor.

On a painstakingly detailed model of Pearl Harbor back in Tokyo, used to familiarize attack pilots with their targets, Japanese technicians emplace replicas of U.S. warships at their moorings in Pearl Harbor.

Attacking planes zoom off as a geyser rises from direct hit on the battleship Oklahoma.

Tracks of the killer torpedoes are visible as waves spread from the stricken warships.

1941

'This is the day of wrath. It is also the day of hope.'

After Pearl Harbor LIFE flew the American flag on its cover and inside the magazine the editor editorialized in his own, unique form of flag-waving. Luce considered himself not only a spokesman for the country but also its conscience. Often at odds with F.D.R., he felt that the administration had been slow in preparing the nation for the war he was convinced was inevitable. Now that its beginning had arrived, here was Luce's chance to both chide the country and inspire it.

By Henry R. Luce

This is the day of wrath. The disaster that befell America on December 7, 1941 was an episode. But it was also a sign. It was a sign of all the weakness and wrongness of American life in recent years. The thousand-odd dead at Pearl Harbor that first day were not merely the victims of Japanese treachery. They were victims also of a weak and faltering America that had lost its way and failed the world in leadership.

On Oahu's eastern coast, a sailor runs for cover past flaming wreckage at the Kaneohe Bay Naval Air Station, hit by dive bombers that had already blasted Pearl Harbor and Hickam Field.

A Navy launch rescues a man who leaped overboard when a torpedo hit the battleship West Virginia, *which is sinking beside the* **Tennessee.**

We have come to the end, now, of as pusillanimous an epoch as there ever was in the history of a great people: the twenty years of American history between 1921 and 1941. It is not even possible to call these years tragic, for tragedy implies at least the dignity of fate. And there was no dignity in these years, and nothing of fate that we did not bring upon ourselves. The epoch that is closing was much less tragic than it was shameful.

The President says we have learned a lesson. Some people think he means that

we have learned that the Japanese (as now constituted) are a treacherous and dangerous people. But if that is the only lesson we have learned, then God knows what agonies we shall have to undergo before we learn the lessons we have got to learn.

We will learn. Every American, not excepting Mr. Roosevelt, now faces the deepest necessity of his life—the necessity of learning that he must find a spiritual rebirth or lose his soul alive. "Still stands Thine ancient sacrifice, an humble and a contrite heart." It is not enough

for us at home to say: "Okay, lets go!" as if we could forget the past by one easy act of renunciation . . .

What then do we lack? In this first hour of common counsel in an aroused nation, it is necessary to concentrate first on two things. We lack good organization. And we lack unity.

We are fortunate that we have done what we have done, that many ships are on the ways, that great factories are built and being built, that we have trained fliers and soldiers and sailors. But the fact is that we haven't done enough—nor

Luce—continued

done this vast job well enough. And the principal reason is that the organization of our war-effort has not been good. It has been poor . . .

And what about unity? Are we united? Are we resolved? We all say the same hearty, manly-sounding things. What, then, makes our brave words sound a trifle hollow, and our rage carry a slight suggestion of impotence?

What we lack, still, is a brave acceptance of our terrible reality. We demand victory, but the price of it, in risk, hardship, pain, adventure, is not yet clear to us. The high resolve is yet to come to us that it would be better to leave America

a heap of smoking stones than surrender it to the mechanized medievalism which is the Mikado or to the anti-Christ which is Hitler.

This lack of resolve is not surprising. The actual destruction of the American nation by a force outside has seemed fantastic. But it is not fantastic now. It could happen. And America will never win this war against the forces of evil until Americans in every walk of life are gripped at the throat by the realization that we can lose the war. For three years we have been losing it. When we realize that—then, only then, our own righteous fury will be unloosed.

We must cultivate that realization, and all the resolves that go with it. For the day is not coming; the day is come. It is the day we have all dreaded, yet known in our secret hearts it was our inescapable duty to meet when the world attack on freedom finally came home to us.

This is the day of wrath. It is also the day of hope. For this is the day that Churchill described to the people of Britain in their own blackest hour: the day when "the New World, with all its power and might, steps forth to the rescue and the liberation of the old." Now at last the issue is inexorably joined: either our ideals as free men shall dominate in this century, or the pitiless bayonets of our enemies will.

We have lost something of our power and might. But now at last our battleground is the whole world. The whole world is now our battle-stake. What we have temporarily lost in might we will gain forever in vision and resolve.

For this hour America was made. Uniquely among the nations, America was created out of the hopes of mankind and dedicated to the fulfillment of those hopes. It is for this reason that we accept only two alternatives—either to die in the smoking ruins of a totally destroyed America or else to justify forever the faith of our fathers and the hopes of mankind.

Years ago Woodrow Wilson begged us not to "break the great heart of the world." We go forth now from a half-beleaguered continent to join hands with all men everywhere and by our character and our deeds to write with them the happy and triumphant songs of a new world . . .

Sailors standing stunned amid the ruins of the Naval Air Station on Ford Island watch the explosion of the battleship Arizona.

'... *Either to die in the smoking ruins* ...'

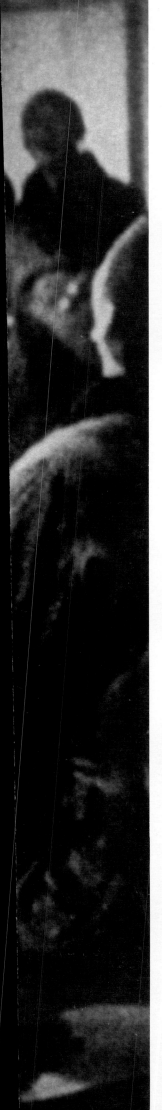

As their carrier heads for the Pearl Harbor attack, Japanese pilots laugh over a radio broadcast from Honolulu, underscoring how unaware Hawaii is of the approaching danger. This captured picture is a frame from a wartime Japanese propaganda film.

The Oklahoma's keel plates and one of her screws jut from the waters of Pearl Harbor. She was one of the ships Navy Secretary Frank Knox said could be repaired. Below: the Arizona rests on the bottom, her draft just sufficient to keep the guns of her forward top turret above the surface.

In Drydock No. 1 the destroyer Cassin rests on another destroyer, the Downes, in front of the other occupant of the drydock, the battleship Pennsylvania, whose damage was relatively light. Bombs that passed through the Cassin exploded on the bottom; flooding the dock to put out the fire floated the destroyer off her keel blocks.

1942 THE DES

PERATE YEAR

Grinning Japanese infantrymen herd exhausted Corregidor defenders upon their surrender after four months' bitter battle.

The more the dazed and furious Americans thought about it, the bleaker the future looked. The predatory pounce on Pearl Harbor was as almost as faultless in its strategy as it was in its execution. The U.S., with its Pacific fleet virtually wiped out, was a "paper tiger," helpless to counter Tokyo's master plan. That plan was based on the conventional wisdom that naval power depended on fixed bases, and that fighting ships were nearly helpless against land-based planes. The islands scattered throughout the Pacific provided airstrip stepping-stones to the limits of the empire Japan's war planners envisaged—an empire they euphemistically called the Greater East Asia Co-Prosperity Sphere. Their plan was to sweep south into the Malay Peninsula and the Indonesian archipelago. Sitting on that huge reservoir of raw materials, they could balance an immensely expanded economy while repulsing any counterattack the Allies could mount across that vastness. Any "bridge of ships" by the U.S. and Britain would be insufficient to supply expeditionary forces 10,000 miles from their bases.

The plan looked unbeatable, and for the first five months after Pearl Harbor Japan owned the Pacific. Even before all of Pearl's dead were buried the Japanese were landing on Wake, the first of two stepping-stones between Hawaii and the Philippines. Then came the second, Guam, and while the Imperial Navy was softening up the Philippines for invasion, Hong Kong and Singapore fell. Japanese infantry double-timed into Bangkok, taking Thailand without firing a shot. Burma was lost, cutting off land access to China.

As U.S. mortification over the capture of Manila turned to agony over the bloody fighting and torture of the defenders on the Bataan Peninsula, all of Indonesia and New Guinea were overrun. Java was captured after the British navy and what was left of the U.S. Navy lost the Battle of the Java Sea. Australia was bombed at Rabaul, and Nipponese planes wrecked Al-

Now It Is Truly a World War

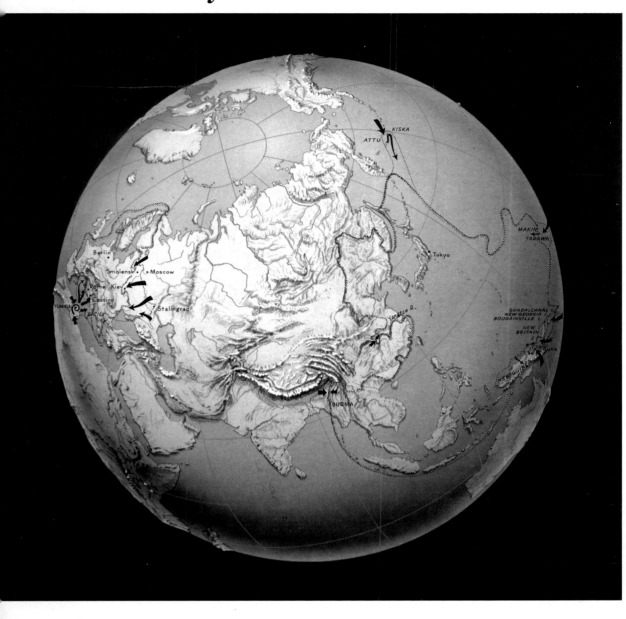

The real nature of Japan's "Co-Prosperity Sphere" is apparent on a global map. Pearl Harbor was strategically a diversion. Co-prosperity meant conquest.

lied shipping at Darwin. In mid-April a flight of B-25 Billy Mitchell bombers commanded by General James Doolittle managed to take off from the carrier *Hornet* 600 miles off the Japanese coast and bomb Tokyo and other Japanese cities. Japan lost more face than war matériel as a result of this tour de force, but it gave Americans, who had looked in vain for some victory, somewhere, their first chance to give one small cheer.

The news from across the Atlantic was not a great deal better. U-boats were still taking an appalling toll among the convoys carrying the slowly increasing war supplies the Arsenal of Democracy was producing. Churchill and F.D.R. had previously agreed that naval strength could not be diverted to the Pacific from the war against Hitler. The Luftwaffe continued to punish British cities, causing the RAF to widen its focus from bombing military objectives exclusively to entire German cities. The Russians were struggling to defend their scorched and frozen earth, and

General Erwin Rommel's Afrika Korps was savagely contesting the British tanks for North Africa's dusty terrain.

But amid all the depressing headlines—PACIFIC ISLANDS CAPTURED, ATLANTIC CONVOY SHIPS SUNK, BURMA SUPPLY ROUTES TO CHINA SEVERED, WEHRMACHT IN CAUCASUS OFFENSIVE—glimmers of hope appeared, almost unnoticed at the time.

Hitler's old nightmare had come true: he was fighting on two fronts. He could not much longer supply both his "Desert Fox" General Rommel and his legions in the heart of Mother Russia. Leningrad, encircled since autumn, experienced its first summer of siege still unstarved.

Even in the earliest naval horror stories from the Pacific lay subtle auguries of a better time. His Majesty's battleship *Prince of Wales* and battle cruiser *Repulse* were sunk, in the defense of Singapore, by Japanese bombers and torpedo planes, the first significant evidence of the change in naval warfare that General Billy Mitchell had predicted in 1920. The

dreadnought was no longer queen of the fleet; floating gun platforms would not henceforth decide naval engagements. And it was the battleships and cruisers that reposed in Pearl Harbor's mud: all three aircraft carriers had been away on maneuvers on December 7. The new era was adumbrated off the New Guinea coast in May. The Japanese grand plan to seal off Australia called for the capture of Port Moresby, on the New Guinea side of the Coral Sea (Operation Mo), and Tulagi, capital of the Solomon Islands, on the east. Phase Two, the taking of Midway and the western Aleutians, would complete Admiral of the Combined Fleet Isoroku Yamamoto's projected operation to eliminate what was left of the U.S. Pacific Fleet.

Aided by the Allied cryptographers, who had broken the Japanese code, Admiral Chester W. Nimitz, Commander in Chief of the Pacific Fleet (CINCPAC) decided to fight at both places. In the Battle of the Coral Sea, Rear Admiral Frank Jack Fletcher's carrier force crippled the giant carriers *Zuikaku* and *Shokaku* so badly they couldn't make it to Midway. The U.S. lost its big carrier *Lexington*, and the *Yorktown* was hit. The battle was a standoff, but Port Moresby was saved. It was the first naval battle in history in which no surface ship engaged another. A month later, off Midway, the westernmost U.S. naval base, which the Japanese had skirted in their initial island-hopping, the U.S. Navy really gave Yamamoto a pasting. The Japanese lost carriers and planes in numbers that they were never able to make up. From Midway on, although the islands were many and bloody on the road back, the offensive in the Pacific was the Allies'.

One week into August, on opposite sides of the earth, two epic struggles commenced simultaneously. They raged simultaneously, spilling unprecedented amounts of blood as they continued unabated through the rest of the year and a month into the next, when they ended simultaneously. As August 7 dawned on the Solomon Islands, U.S. Marines off the jungle island of Guadalcanal took to their landing craft for the first invasion. It was to become a three-year saga of gore-drenched island-hopping to roll back the Japanese empire all the way to its home isles. The same day, on Russia's burned and cratered southeastern front the Wehrmacht launched a pincer movement intended to cut off Stalingrad and capture the industrial city of half a million within a week or two.

Neither campaign followed its expected timetable. The Japanese bombed "Guadal" by day and, by means of destroyer transport that the Americans called the Tokyo Express, they reinforced their jungle-trained troops by night. A three-day naval battle off Guadalcanal in October cost the U.S. two carriers, and the fighting in the insect- and snake-infested jungle grew even more savage. When the Japanese evacuated the island, at the end of January, they left 24,000 dead, to the U.S.'s 1,752.

On Stalingrad's outskirts, the combined forces of the Sixth Army and the Fourth Panzer Army were stopped in their tracks repeatedly by depleted Red Army divisions. As weeks turned to months, starting in mid-September, there was hand-to-hand fighting in the city, street by street, then house by house; finally, gains were being measured by yards. In November the reinforced Russians surrounded the city and the freezing Wehrmacht was reduced to eating its own horses. At the end, the last day of January, more than 90,000 Germans had died of cold and starvation; 100,000 more had died in the fighting in the previous three weeks alone.

In Africa, too, the Axis momentum was slowing. General Bernard Law Montgomery whipped Rommel at El Alamein, the Allies recaptured Tobruk, and, with General Eisenhower supervising from a tunnel across the Mediterranean under the Rock of Gibraltar, F.D.R.'s pet Operation Torch caught the Germans napping and put American and British troops ashore on the beaches at Casablanca, Algiers and Oran. As usual, Churchill provided historians the textbook description for the year: "It is not even the beginning of the end," he opined. "But it is, perhaps, the end of the beginning."

On two sides of the globe the Axis' seemingly ineluctable progress is slowed, particularly by two titanic battles, at Guadalcanal and at Stalingrad.

CHRONOLOGY 1942

January	February	March	April	May	June
1 • *United Nations conceived at Washington conference* **2** • British and South Africans recapture Bardia • Corregidor under daily attack **4** • Japanese bomb Rabaul for first time **7** • *U.S. budget earmarks $53 billion for war* • Chinese victorious at Changsha • MacArthur completes withdrawal to Bataan **11** • Japanese invade Borneo **11-17** • British eliminate last Axis strongholds in Egypt **15** • German U-boats start sinking ships off east coast of U.S. **16** • Japanese penetrate Allied center on Bataan **21** • Rommel turns Afrika Korps around and pushes British east **23** • Japan invades New Britain, New Ireland, Dutch Borneo and Solomons **25** • Thailand declares war on Britain and U.S. **26** • Rabaul falls to Japan • *Against protest U.S. troops arrive in Ulster* • Japanese third landing on southwest Bataan	**1** • USS Enterprise and Yorktown strike Marshall and Gilbert Islands **8** • Battle for Singapore begins **13** • Third Japanese landing on Bataan repulsed • Hitler finally kills Operation Sea Lion for good • Stalemate in Western Desert **15** • Singapore surrenders after a week of siege • U.S. fleet pounds Japanese bases in Gilberts and Marshalls **18** • Japanese land on Bali **19** • Japanese carrier raid on Darwin, Australia **20** • *F.D.R. authorizes internment of West Coast Japanese-Americans* **23** • *Japanese bombs fall on California oil fields* **24** • Soviets encircle Germany's 16th Army at Staraya Russa • USS Enterprise hits Wake Island **27-28** • Battle of Java Sea **28** • Japanese land on Java	*This month German losses reach 1.5 million* **1** • Chinese troops under Stilwell enter Burma to help British • Renewed Soviet offensive in Crimea **7** • British evacuate Rangoon • Japanese land on New Guinea **8** • Allies surrender on Java **9** • Dutch surrender Netherland East Indies **11** • MacArthur leaves Philippines: "I shall return" **13** • Japanese land on Bougainville, Solomons **17** • Nazis start deporting Poles to Belsen • MacArthur arrives in Australia, Commander Southwest Pacific Theater **20** • General Wainwright in command of Philippines **26** • Nazis start deporting Jews to Auschwitz **27** • British commando raid on U-boat base Saint-Nazaire	**1** • Japanese fleet in Indian Ocean and Bay of Bengal strikes Ceylon, driven out by RAF **3** • Japanese break through on Bataan • B-17s blast Japanese fleet off Burma • Japanese bomb Mandalay **8** • Japanese land Admiralty Islands **9** • Bataan surrenders, Japanese bomb Corregidor **18** • Japanese cut off Burma supply routes to China • Doolittle's bombers attack Tokyo • Hitler pushes Pierre Laval on Petain as Vichy premier **24** • Air war continues over Britain, Exeter bombed **26** • *Blackout in New England begins* **27** • Gandhi objects to the stationing of U.S. troops in India **28** • *OPA freezes prices of all living-cost items* **29** • Japanese capture head of Burma Road	**1** • British evacuate Mandalay **4-9** • Battle of the Coral Sea, first Japanese setback **5** • British land on Madagascar and take Vichy naval bases **6** • Corregidor surrenders **8** • Germans begin Kerch offensive • Japanese navy battered in Coral Sea, Lexington sunk **10** • Malta offensive by Axis over **12** • Red offensive at Kharkov • *U-boat sinks U.S. cargo ship off New Orleans* **15** • British retreat from Burma to India • *F.D.R. creates Women's Auxiliary Army Corps* **19** • Reds driven from Kerch **20** • General Stilwell reaches Imphal in India • *U.S. admits first black recruits* **27** • Rommel orders another German offensive in Western Desert **30** • RAF's first thousand plane raid—on Cologne	**4-6** • Battle of Midway: Japan loses supremacy at sea **7** • Battle of Sevastopol begins **10** • In retaliation for assassination of Hitler's "hangman," Germans wipe out Czech town of Lidice **13** • U.S. bombers strike Rumanian oil fields • Rommel defeats British tank force in Libya • Japanese take Attu in Aleutians **18-21** • *Second Washington conference* **21** • Rommel captures Tobruk • Japanese take Kiska in Aleutians • *Axis shells hit Oregon coast* **24** • Eisenhower made commander in chief of all U.S. forces in Europe **26** • Churchill, F.D.R. agree on Second Front in Europe • *German saboteurs off U-boats seized on L.I. and Florida beaches* **27** • Red planes, tanks decimate Nazis crossing Don River **28** • Germans launch summer offensive at Kursk **30** • Rommel stopped at El Alamein

■ **War in Europe**   ■ **War in Asia**   ■ **U.S.A.**

July	August	September	October	November	December
1 • *Germans take Sevastopol, fighting in streets*	**7** • *Marines land on Guadalcanal in Solomons* • *Germans' Sixth Army traps Russians at Don River, clears way to Stalingrad*	*By this month U-boats have sunk 5 million tons of Allied shipping in the Atlantic*	*By this month Leningrad has been under siege a full year*	**1** • *Germans halted in heart of Stalingrad*	**4** • *Germans force Allies out of Tebourba in Tunisia*
2 • *British attack El Alamein*	**8-9** • *Naval battle of Savo Island in Solomons*	*Toll of Nazi executions in occupied Europe reaches 207,373*	**1** • *British push Axis forces from El Alamein positions*	**2** • *Aussies take Kokoda in Papua*	**9** • *Aussies take Gona in New Guinea*
4 • *First U.S. air raid on Germans (over Netherlands)*	**11** • *Germans advance on Stalingrad*	**1** • *RAF blasts Afrika Korps*	**10** • *U.S. blasts Japanese supply base at Rabaul*	**4** • *Montgomery pursues Rommel at El Alamein*	**11** • *Montgomery attacks El Agheila*
7 • *Rommel repulsed, abandons Egypt offensive*	**12** • *First Moscow conference, to discuss Second Front*	**3** • *Germans reach outskirts of Stalingrad proper*	**16** • *Large Japanese force lands on Guadalcanal*	**5** • *Vichy France surrenders on Madagascar*	**13** • *Rommel retreats from El Agheila*
14 • *13,000 Paris Jews locked in Velodrome* • *Ike and De Gaulle meet in London*	**13** • *Montgomery takes charge of British Eighth Army in Egypt*	**6** • *Germans take Novorossisk*	**18** • *Admiral "Bull" Halsey put in charge of South Pacific Theater*	**6** • *German advance halted in Caucasus*	**20** • *Japanese planes from Burma hit Calcutta for first time*
23 • *Japanese invade East New Guinea*	**17** • *First U.S. air raid on France hits Rouen* • *Japanese attack on Guadalcanal*	**7** • *Rommel repulsed at Alam Halfa* • *Red Army hurls back Stalingrad attackers northwest of city*	**22-24** • *Aussies take Goodenough Island*	**7-8** • *Finally a big Allied invasion in North Africa*	**24** • *Admiral Darlan assassinated in Algiers*
24 • *Italians hit Yugoslavian rebels*	**19** • *Dieppe raid fails, Second Front set back*	**12-14** • *Battle of Lunga Ridge on Guadalcanal*	**23** • *Battle of El Alamein begins*	**10** • *Hitler orders Operation Attila (occupation of Vichy France)*	**28** • *Street fighting in Stalingrad* • *Heavy fighting continues on Guadalcanal*
25 • *Germans take Rostov and cross Don*	**22-25** • *Naval battle of eastern Solomons*	**16** • *Germans slowed in outskirts of Stalingrad* • *Japanese halted 30 miles from Port Moresby*	**23-26** • *Japanese offensive on Guadalcanal repulsed*	**11** • *Germans and Italians overrun "unoccupied" France*	**31** • *Germans in full retreat at Stalingrad*
	23 • *German tanks stab at Stalingrad*	**17** • *Fierce fighting in Caucasus*	**24** • *Ike directs big task force to North Africa*	**12-15** • *Naval battle of Guadalcanal*	
	26 • *Reds bomb Berlin*	**18** • *Nazis kill 116 in Paris for attacks on their troops*	**26** • *Naval battle of Santa Cruz Islands*	**13** • *Allies recapture Tobruk*	
	27 • *Rotterdam blasted by Allies*	**20** • *Germans take Terek in center of Caucasus*		**18** • *Selective Service extended to 18-year-olds*	
	30 • *Week-long battle of Alam Halfa begins*	**22** • *British attack Japanese Line in Burma* • *Germans now at center of Stalingrad but Soviets hold on*		**20** • *British take Benghazi*	
		25 • *U.S. War Labor Board orders equal pay for women*		**22** • *Massive Red counteroffensive at Stalingrad*	
		27 • *Aussies drive Japanese back in New Guinea*		**27** • *French scuttle fleet at Toulon*	
				29 • *Coffee rationing begins in U.S.*	

In China, after a Japanese officer bloodied his sword (left) and left a prisoner dying, an infantryman finished the job (below) with the form he acquired in basic training.

The attack on Pearl Harbor seemed monstrous to the U.S., but it was simply the efficient use of the modern machines of war compared with what Japan was doing to its Asian neighbors. The bombing of city after city in China over more than four years had produced unimaginable carnage. Now the removal of the U.S. fleet turned the Japanese infantry loose on all of Southeast Asia. Even as the dreadnought hulls lay smoking at Pearl, there was simultaneous bombing of the step-ping-stone islands of Wake and Guam. Almost immediately thereafter the softening-up blasting of the Philippines presaged the vicious hand-to-hand combat to come in the bloody march to the oil-rich Dutch East Indies and the establishment of the Greater Asian Co-Prosperity Sphere. Soon after the Japanese took Luzon and Manila and wrested Hong Kong from its British garrison, the British pulled out of Singapore. Tojo's men, stepping up their long siege of the for-

In the streets of Singapore a Malayan mother (center) wails as she views the body of her dead child. Another woman screams in pain as she grasps her wounded leg.

tress island, took it after two weeks of particularly bloody battle. This gave Japan absolute control over the Malay Peninsula, all the way down to the Strait of Malacca, just 65 miles from Sumatra's rich oil fields. From conquered Thailand, its land forces crossed the mountainous border into that other jewel of Britain's empire, Burma, and after four months of spilling that normally peaceful people's blood, seized their capital, Rangoon, cutting off the Allies' overland supply route to China.

1942
The Surrenders That Haunted America

A T-shirted Japanese colonel arranges Bataan's surrender with Major General King (center).

U.S. troops, ravaged by their 28-day besiegement, march off Corregidor to cruel internment, passing fresh Japanese troops on their way to battle.

The depleted condition of the Pacific fleet—which could not be reinforced because of the Navy's commitments in the Atlantic—foreordained the tragic end of the epic of the Philippines. General MacArthur declared Manila an open city before he left for Australia. His Luzon troops—18,000 U.S. Army and 2,500 Navy and Marines plus 8,000 Philippine Scouts and 60,000 poorly equipped Philippine Army troops— withdrew to the Bataan peninsula and the island fortress of Corregidor, where they began a heroic defense that made those names a rallying cry for the U.S. The Bataan forces were down to one-third rations when the Japanese began a final push on April 3. Although Major General Jonathan Wainwright, MacArthur's successor, forbade it, Major General Edward King surrendered his starving forces on April 9. Then began the Death March out of Bataan that was to become legendary for its cruelty. Along the line of march and later within the prison camp, the weak, the halt, the stragglers were shot or bayoneted to death and often Americans, at bayonet point, were forced to bury their buddies alive (overleaf). The invaders brought their big guns to shell Corregidor, which continued to hold out, until, the night of May 5, they started their landings on the island. Two days later Wainwright surrendered Corregidor's 10,000 and they were removed to Bataan to suffer the same savage fate as their predecessors.

The traumatic loss of the Philippines is traced on a map of the main islands. First the enemy bombed airfields near Manila, destroying half of their 123 combat aircraft. Next they destroyed the Cavite naval base. Landing forces closed in on Manila from the north and the southeast and defending forces withdrew to Bataan and Corregidor.

Japanese infantrymen with a flamethrower attack a Corregidor pillbox. All three pictures were taken by Japanese photographers.

March of Death for Bataan's Defenders

The survivors of Bataan arrive at Clark Field. By the end of their 65-mile march, more than one in every 10 who began it were dead.

While on the march, regular cleanup squads of Japanese followed at the rear to dispose of the prisoners who fell out. A Death March prisoner described his ordeal in LIFE.

The first time it happened, I didn't know what was up. An enlisted man had keeled over—he had been stumbling for hours—and the Japs dragged him out of the line to a ditch about a hundred yards from the road. I was taken out of the line and escorted to where the Japs had placed this unconscious man in the ditch. One of the Japs handed me a shovel. Another jammed a bayonet into my side and gave an order in Japanese. A Jap grabbed the shovel out of my hands and demonstrated by throwing a few shovelsful of earth on the unconscious soldier. Then he handed me the shovel. God! ... It doesn't help to tell myself that the soldier, and others later, were already more dead than alive ... The worst time was once when a burial victim with about six inches of earth over him suddenly regained consciousness and clawed his way out until he was almost sitting upright. Then I learned to what lengths a man will go ... to hang onto his own life. The bayonets began to prod me in the side and I was forced to bash the soldier over the head with the shovel and then finish burying him."

Marchers bearing disabled buddies who had escaped execution approach their dusty destination, the prison enclosure at Camp O'Donnell.

Prisoners, their hands tied behind their backs and gaunt from starvation and lack of water, get a moment's respite. Beatings of the slow or recalcitrant continued during these intervals.

A Break in the Clouds of America's Gloom

The task force's B-25s are readied on the Hornet's *flight deck.*

The No. 1 plane, Doolittle's, takes off on its daring mission.

On a Chinese peak inevitable rubberneckers swarm over Doolittle's plane. The leader and his crew had bailed out safely.

Colonel Jimmy Doolittle's morale-boosting mission was a spectacular success because it was meticulously planned. The twin-engine Billy Mitchells were never made to be carrier based. But after their pilots had taken intensive training in short takeoffs 16 B-25s were loaded onto the *Hornet*, flagship of a special task force under Vice Admiral William F. (Bull) Halsey. The planes were to be launched within 500 nautical miles of Japan, and only into wind sufficient to make their short takeoffs possible. After they had dropped their bombs they were to fly 1,100 miles farther and land in China. But on April 18 the force was spotted by picket boats 650 miles off Japan. Immediately the *Hornet* headed full speed into a providential light wind and the planes took off. After the bombing the fliers ran into foul weather and had to crash-land or bail out. Of 80 fliers 71 survived. Three were executed. The U.S. went wild over Doolittle. Congress voted him the Medal of Honor and the President promoted him to general. When newsmen pressed F.D.R. to reveal where the raid was launched from he grinned and replied, "Shangri-La," recalling James Hilton's novel *Lost Horizon* and providing a name for a future aircraft carrier.

The Yokosuka naval base appears beneath the starboard prop of one of the raiders. Several of its installations, including a drydock, were demolished.

Lieutenant Robert Hite, one of eight raiders captured in China, is brought to Tokyo.

Chinese soldiers escort fliers in a village near which they crash-landed.

F.D.R. pins the Medal of Honor on Doolittle, already wearing his Brigadier General star, as Air Force chief Henry H. (Hap) Arnold looks on.

1942
A Naval Battle Historic in More Ways than One

During the historic battle the Lexington, *her magazines set afire by a torpedo hit, is fatally wracked by explosions, one of which blows one of her planes off her stern.*

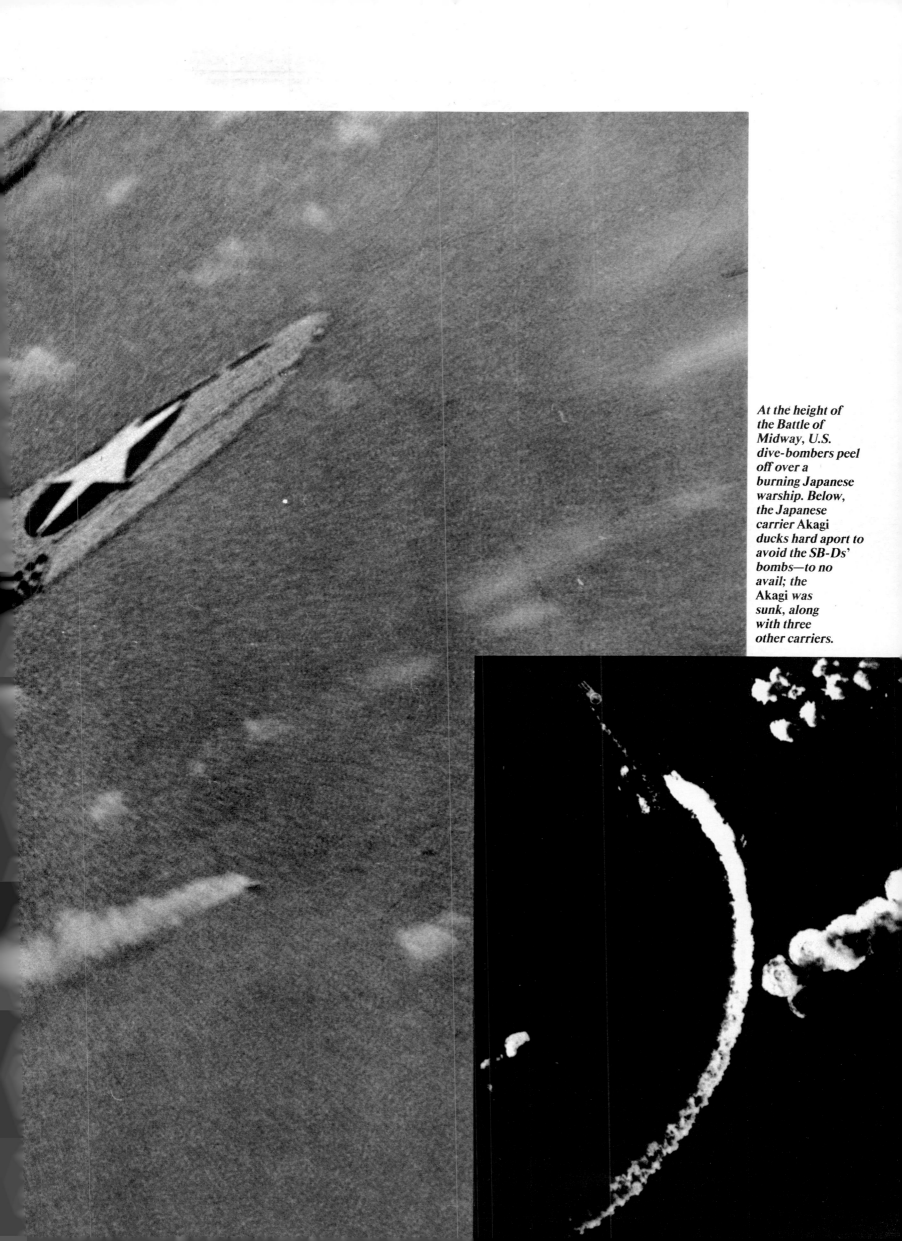

At the height of the Battle of Midway, U.S. dive-bombers peel off over a burning Japanese warship. Below, the Japanese carrier Akagi ducks hard aport to avoid the SB-Ds' bombs—to no avail; the Akagi was sunk, along with three other carriers.

A draft board hears a hardship plea. The facial expressions were perhaps typical of draft boards all over, but this one was literally from Missouri.

Recruits in civvies march with overnight bags to the railroad station in Macon, Georgia, on their way to the Navy training station in Norfolk, Virginia.

A three-star flag in a window tells the world that three members of this family —usually but not always men—are in the service of their country.

Florida recruits take an aptitude test in a Miami Beach movie theater.

1942
Images from the Home Front

In July 1942 LIFE published the fifth of Stephen Vincent Benet's "Dear Adolf" letters. This series of dramatic poems written for radio by one of the country's foremost poets was highly acclaimed across the land. Benet's latest war effort began:

Dear Adolf—this is me—one American soldier. My dogtag's number's in the millions—my draft number came out of the hat in every State in the Union. I'm from Janesville and Little Rock, Monroe City and Nashua. I'm from Blue Eye, Missouri, and the sidewalks of New York. I'm from the Green Mountains and the big sky-hooting plains, from the roll of the prairie and the rocks of Marblehead, from the little towns where a dog can go to sleep in the middle of Main Street, and the nickel-plated suburbs and the cities that stick their skyscrapers into the sky. I used to be a carpenter and a school teacher and a soda jerker and a mechanic. I used to be a hackie and a farm hand and a legman and a bookkeeper—the son of a guy with money and the son of a guy with none. But I'm a soldier now. Four and a half million of us by the end of this year ... We weren't picked out for our looks or our Aryan names. We weren't picked out to heil heels or to chew up small countries that never did us any harm ... Sure, we let you get away with a lot. We sat around and argued, over here, while you were cooking with gas. But that's all over ...

Shortly after the bombing of Pearl Harbor, sandbags heaped high cover the front of the telephone company in San Francisco.

Well worth the price and well suited to the war economy is this tennis outfit, right out of the Sears catalogue and worn by a Sears model.

Detroit police tussle with a rioter during an explosion of racial violence after white defense workers cordoned off a housing project intended for blacks.

Boy Scouts, turning their motto, Be Prepared, into a war cry, lead a Stevens Point, Wisconsin, procession of trucks bearing old tires for recycling.

HERE'S OUR ANSWER PRESIDENT ROOSEVELT

Sailors from the Kaneohe Naval Air Station place leis on the graves of buddies killed in the December 7 bombing.

The Australian nurse Sister Eliz Kenny demonstrates in polio-r Little Rock, Arkansas, her controv method of combating the fright disease with hot-water-soaked cloths and passive exe

Chomping a trademark cigar, Price Administrator Leon Henderson pedals a Victory Bike (meaning save gasoline).

A Coast Guard lifeboat escorts San Francisco crab fishermen fearful of Japanese submarines.

Pearl Harbor widows, enlisted by the U.S. government, report for work at a West Coast aircraft plant.

An air-raid warden lights up under a street lamp, the only place striking a match was permitted during a blackout.

A woman at a lathe at the Alameda, California, Naval Air Station wears proper garb: heavy shoes, slack suit and bandanna.

Conover model Peggy Lloyd wears cloth-saving cuffless tapered slacks approved under War Production Board standards.

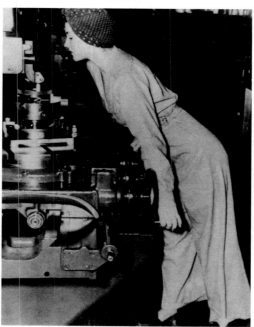

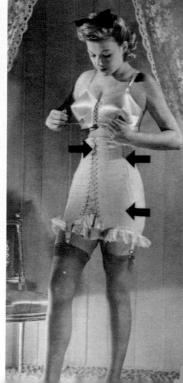

A model shows how to lace a corset now that elastic and zippers have "gone to war," as the WPB's jettisoning of amenities was put to consumers.

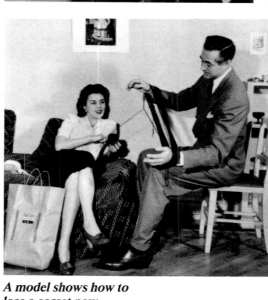

A "lonely wife" keeps a prospective "wolf" at bay in a LIFE article on a popular book of advice for women whose husbands are in the service.

179

Production Lines Hum at the Ever Growing Arsenal

The first major Navy vessel built on the Great Lakes, the 1,500-ton submarine Peto, is launched, sidewise, into a Lake Michigan basin at Manitowoc, Wisconsin.

Twenty-eight-ton tanks mass-produced in the manner of automobiles move through assembly lines at the Chrysler-operated Detroit Tank Arsenal. A year earlier the site of the huge plant had been an exurban cow pasture.

Vought Corsairs, folding-wing Navy fighters, take shape on a Stratford, Connecticut, assembly line. At this point the plant had turned out more than 6,000 of them.

1942
About as Close as Danger Came

The first German missile of the war to land on Western Hemisphere soil, an 18-foot torpedo from a U-boat off the Dutch Caribbean island of Aruba, is eyed by Dutch and American officers. It later exploded, killing four men.

The American tanker R.P. Resor, part of a convoy, goes down in a billow of smoke after being torpedoed 20 miles off the New Jersey coast.

A GI sits guard over a shell hole in California soil. It was made by a 5-inch shell fired at the flat oil storage tank (at top, slightly left of center) just off the beach at Ellwood, 12 miles north of Santa Barbara, by a Japanese submarine that had surfaced at dusk and bombarded Ellwood's oil fields for 15 minutes.

John L. DeWitt, the general in charge of the Western Defense Command, decided early that Japanese-Americans were dangerous customers, still linked to their ancestors by "undiluted racial strains" and therefore potential saboteurs. "The very fact that no sabotage has taken place to date is a disturbing and confirming indication that such action will be taken," the general reasoned. No branch of the U.S. government chose to challenge DeWitt's conclusions, not the war department, the military, not Congress, the courts or the President himself. Consequently, on one man's recommendation 112,000 Japanese-Americans, two-thirds of whom were American citizens, lost their property and were confined in concentration camps for the duration.

The first contingent of Japanese-Americans removed by federal fiat from their homes on the Pacific Coast carry their luggage to rude dormitories in California's mountain-girt Owens Valley.

1942
What It Will Take to Win the War

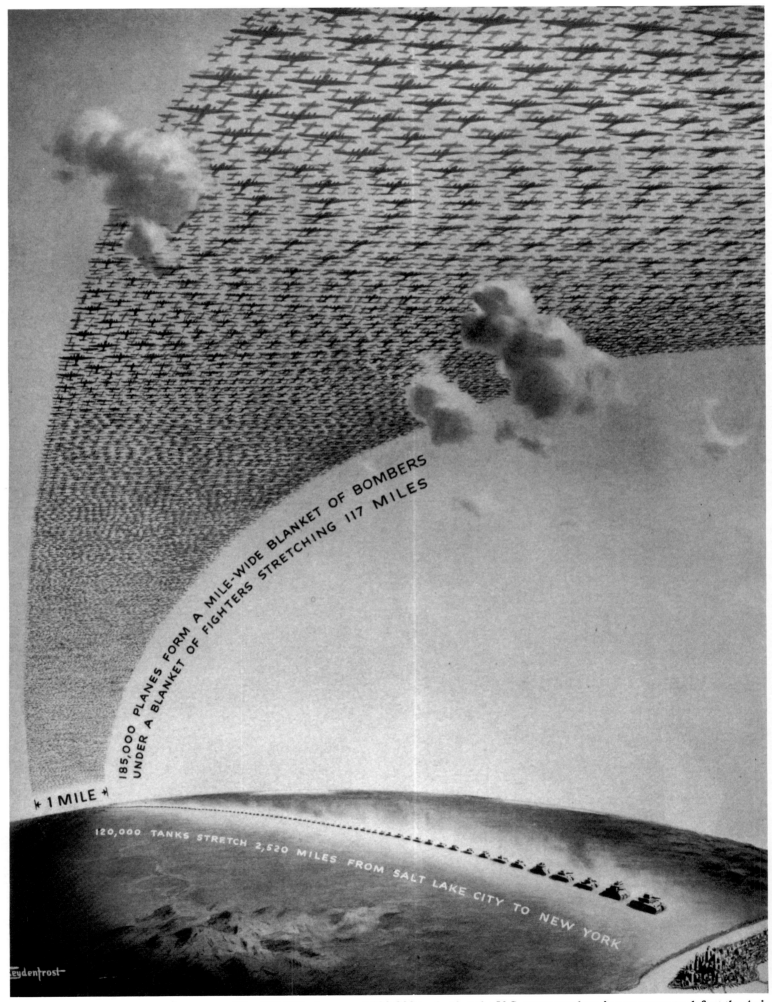

185,000 PLANES FORM A MILE-WIDE BLANKET OF BOMBERS
UNDER A BLANKET OF FIGHTERS STRETCHING 117 MILES

← 1 MILE →

120,000 TANKS STRETCH 2,520 MILES FROM SALT LAKE CITY TO NEW YORK

The 185,000 planes and 120,000 tanks that the U.S. must produce in two years to defeat the Axis powers are visualized in a LIFE drawing. A solid blanket of fighters flying above a second one of bombers makes a mighty two-layer cloud one mile wide and 117 miles long. The tanks, in single file, stretch more than 2,500 miles, a column that would reach from Salt Lake City to New York.

Symbolically pointing toward the Axis capitals, scale models of 4,500 Army and Navy planes hang from the ceiling of Chicago's Union Station. The plywood aircraft fleet, with wingspreads ranging from 1 foot (fighters) to 4 feet (bombers), was inspired by the LIFE drawing.

Desert Fighting

North Africa was a lung-choking, sandy horror that Britain—and, for that matter, Germany—got into reluctantly, and only because it meant control of the Mediterranean. In 1940 Mussolini had 450,000 troops in his African empire, plus a Mediterranean fleet of six battleships, 19 cruisers and more than 100 submarines. Britain, with only 82,775 soldiers, spread from Egypt to Palestine, and a fleet consisting of four battleships and seven cruisers, had thin prospects of holding the Mediterranean. When despite the odds General Archibald Wavell captured 130,000 of Marshal Rodolfo Graziani's Italians, never using more than two divisions, Hitler sent General Erwin Rommel to be his "hero in the sun." The Desert Fox captured the Libyan supply port of Benghazi and pushed the British east to Tobruk, almost at the Egyptian border. Britain upped its Western Desert force to an Eighth Army of two corps and pushed him back almost 200 miles beyond Benghazi. At the outset of 1942, Rommel regained Benghazi, recovering 350 desert miles in 17 days.

In May he really poured it on. Although he was outnumbered in men, tanks and planes, he drove Wavell's forces past Tobruk into Egypt. His Afrika Korps exhausted, he was forced to stop at El Alamein, 65 miles short of Alexandria. Then, after the German navy lost control of the Mediterranean, a new Eighth Army commander, General Bernard Law Montgomery, came at him with vastly superior forces, in men, tanks and aviation, and chased him half the breadth of North Africa to Mareth, in Tunisia.

British desert infantrymen with bayonets rush in to capture an Afrika Korps tank man.

Fighting the desert war, RAF fighters take off abreast in clouds of sand.

British tanks pursue Rommel's panzers, following lanes cleared through German mine fields.

British infantrymen, tanks looming behind them in the dust, move across the desert in support of advance troops.

Far from Britain's green fields the night before an attack, a violin-playing chaplain leads tank men singing hymns and old airs.

Operation Torch: The U.S. and Britain Strike All Along Africa's Coast

U.S. infantrymen keep low in a landing craft as they prepare to hit the beach at Oran. Shock troops wear netted helmets for camouflage.

The mission of the operation code-named Torch, the huge Allied offensive that initiated the U.S. into desert warfare, was to trap Rommel's desert army between the invaders, to his west, and General Montgomery's forces to the east, at the same time clearing the Mediterranean for an eventual assault on Hitler's *Festung Europa*. Rear Admiral Henry K. Hewitt commanded the U.S. landings and British Admiral Andrew Browne Cunningham the British. The Germans were caught napping; the worst they expected from the concentration of ships was an Allied attempt to relieve Malta. History's greatest armada thus far went miraculously unharmed. The main U.S. objective, Casablanca, was defended by French colonial troops loyal to Vichy. Major General George Patton's forces took their first two towns in 10 hours and the Allies overran Morocco and Algeria in four days. East of the Tunisian border was another matter.

The U.S. component of the invasion armada steams across the Atlantic headed for Morocco's ocean coast. Map (left) shows how the Allies split up the operation.

Monty and the Desert Fox

General Rommel, wearing a
plaid scarf and captured
British sun goggles against
the desert sun and sand,
leads the panzers of his
Afrika Korps across the
top of Africa.

This extraordinary
picture shows a
parachutist from the
Italian Folgoro division
throwing himself
under a British tank to
blow it up with a mine.

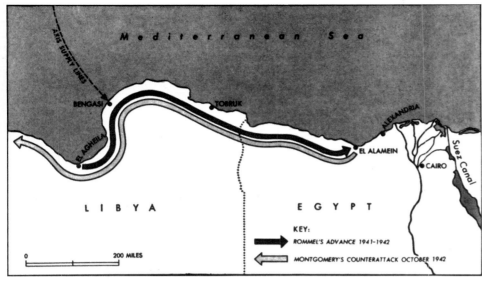

Montgomery pursued Rommel's army over four months, from El Alamein clear across Egypt and Libya into Tunisia.

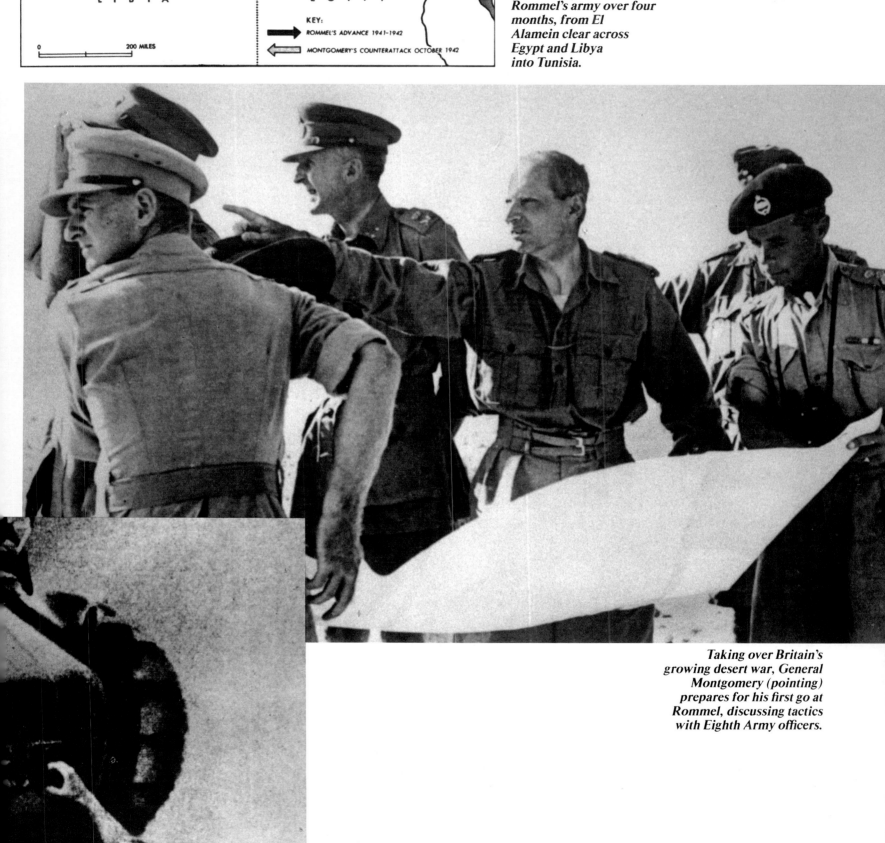

Taking over Britain's growing desert war, General Montgomery (pointing) prepares for his first go at Rommel, discussing tactics with Eighth Army officers.

1942

A Fox Hunt Along the Coast of Egypt

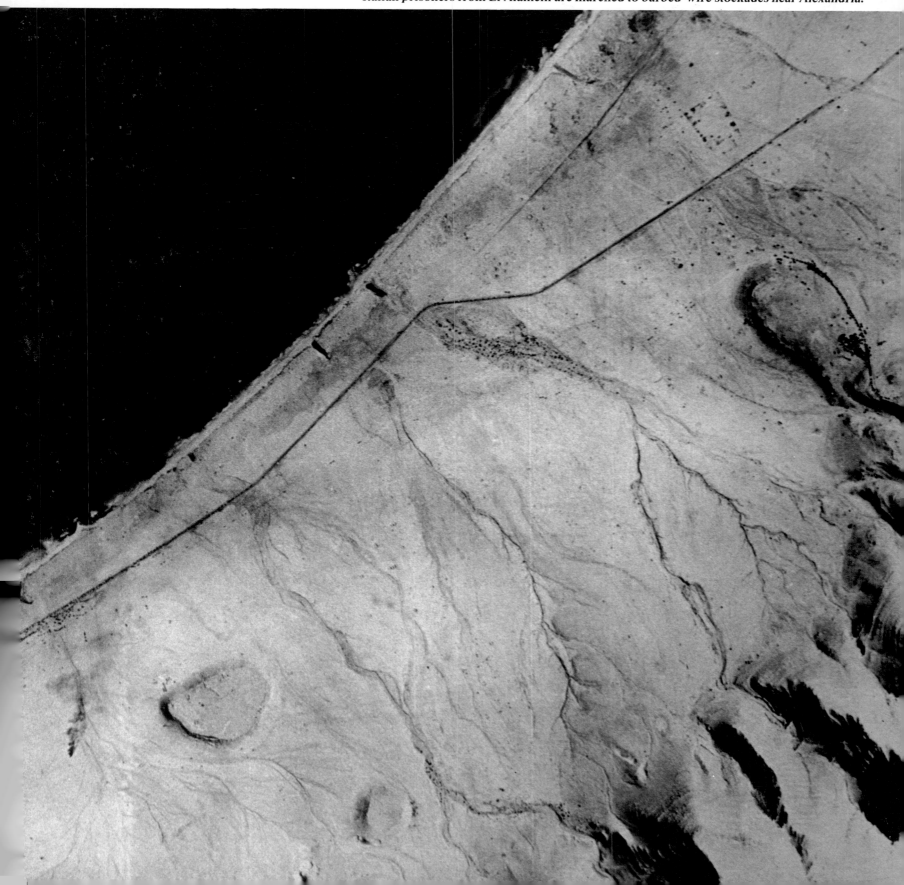

"Bumper-to-bumper" traffic strings out along Egypt's coastline as Rommel's army, pictured from a British reconnaissance plane at 20,000 feet, tools westward in retreat. More than 1,000 vehicles of every kind, from tanks to motorcycles, form this five-mile arc from Halfaya Pass, at extreme right, to El Salum's Observatory Point, at extreme left. Inset: German and Italian prisoners from El Alamein are marched to barbed-wire stockades near Alexandria.

BATTLEFRONTS: *The War Beneath the Sea*

U.S. Coast Guardsmen on the cutter Spencer watch one of their depth charges blow a submarine, the U-175, to the surface (above). Blasted to the surface (right), the sub lies open to the cutter's gunfire. Opposite page: One of the U-175's submariners pleads for rescue from the icy April waters.

As losses on the Atlantic mounted (5,579 U.S. merchant seamen were killed during the war and 487 taken prisoner), military and civilian America worked frantically on antisubmarine devices and techniques. Citizens in small spotting planes patrolled offshore waters. The Navy called on the Army Air Forces to help its Atlantic patrol fleet. What paid off, over the long run, was high-grade weapons, experience and ever more land- and carrier-based aircraft. These last were equipped with radar, which could find the U-boats when they surfaced. (German technology did come up—just too late—with snorkel subs, which did not have to expose themselves to radar.)

Inside one of the German navy's star undersea raiders, the U-96, her commander, Heinrich Lehmann-Willenbrock, and his crew are shaken by the explosion of a depth charge.

In the Pacific, a U.S. Torpedo Takes Its Toll

A Japanese destroyer goes down, photographed through the periscope of the U.S. sub that sank her. Two crewmen in white scramble up the fire-control tower as she goes under. The shoe was on the other foot in the Pacific, where in U.S. eyes as often as not the submariner was the hero.

Into the valley of death rode the six hundred. This time the paean was Italian. The Red Army had stiffened as the Axis juggernaut reached the Don River before Stalingrad. At the river town of Serafimovich it launched a fierce counterattack, against a sector held by Italian troops. Outmanned and outgunned, the Italians, giving new luster to their image, tarnished in Greece and Africa, not only held but even regained the offensive. With cries of "Avanti, Savoia!" a 600-man regiment of the Savoia Cavalry thundered down on some 2,000 Russians. They wiped out two battalions, captured their machine guns and artillery and took 500 prisoners.

Chomping his cigar, Prime Minister Churchill takes the controls of the flying boat that flew him back to England after a visit to the U.S. to inspect the "Arsenal."

Chiang Kai-shek, Free China's Generalissimo, and Mahatma Gandhi, the voice of Britain's subject India, meet in Calcutta. Between them they led one-third of the world's people.

Commander in Chief of the Pacific Fleet Chester W. Nimitz dances with a USO girl in Hawaii.

Architects of war: the top U.S. brass. Army Chief of Staff General George C. Marshall (second from left) confers with other Joint Chiefs (left to right) Admiral Ernest J. King, Admiral William D. Leahy and Lieut. Gen. Henry H. Arnold.

King George inspects the royal piggery at his farm at Windsor.

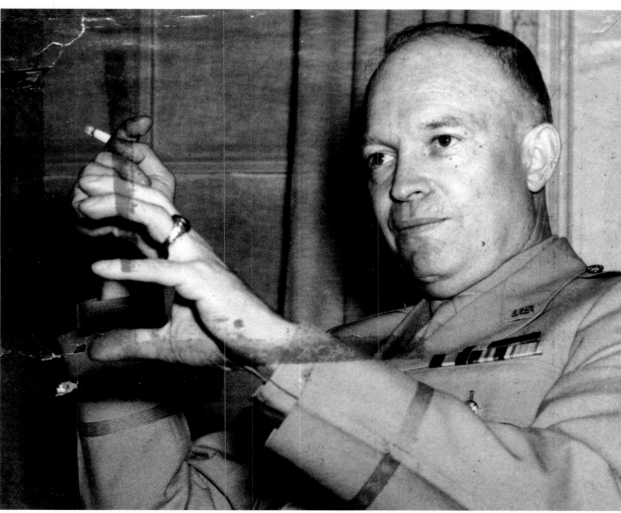

Lt. Gen. Dwight D. Eisenhower, commander of all U.S. forces in Europe, reflects on his options in a two-ocean war.

1942
Keeping the Troops Content

A dancer from home performs in an "encouragement show" for Japanese troops at Rabaul.

Saturday night was the loneliest night of the week, especially for servicemen far from home. The Japanese, at the zenith of their expansion, had forces farther from home than anybody else, except perhaps the Aussies. They missed the Saturday dance as much as the enemy did. Tokyo sent performers to all the fighting fronts to stage "encouragement shows," much as did America's United Service Organization. The American Theater Wing, a Broadway theater group, opened the Stage Door Canteen, where almost any talent in show business, from chorus girls to Helen Hayes, was likely to show up to

Actress Dorothy McGuire jitterbugs with Private Ed Maron at the Stage Door Canteen.

entertain servicemen who found themselves off duty in the Big Apple. Irving Berlin immortalized it by adding a new standard, "I Left My Heart at the Stage Door Canteen," to his World War I classic, "Oh How I Hate to Get Up in the Morning." But it was the USO troopers who got to the GIs where they were loneliest, in unfamiliar places far from home. The USO sent stars, mostly females who'd be so nice to come home to, all around the world, to deserts and jungles, mountains and islands, to rouse them to clapping their hands and stomping instead of dreaming of a white Christmas (that Irving Berlin again).

Hollywood Does Its Bit

A touring war hero, Air Pilot Dick Riddell from Scotland, writes autographs for stars at the Hollywood Canteen. From left: Patricia Morison, Ann Sothern and Donna Reed. At rear: Virginia O'Brien, Joan Bennett, Eleanor Powell, Marcia Hunt, Mrs. L. B. Mayer, Loretta Young and Jean Rogers.

In rehearsal for a jitterbug number in He Kissed the Bride, one of Joan Crawford's legs indicates 12 o'clock high. Both she and her partner, Allen Jenkins, were former dancers. The star donated her salary for the movie, $112,500, to charities; the government waived tax on it.

Counterclockwise around Navy flier Donald Mason (author of the famed war report: "Sighted sub, sank same") are Claudette Colbert, Carole Landis, Betty Grable, Ruth Hussey and Army fighter pilot George Welch, who shot down four attackers at Pearl Harbor.

Rita Hayworth, chosen by GIs at Camp Callan,
California, as their away-from-home mother, sews
a fine seam on the trousers of Private Luther Eklund.

Show Business Spreads the Word

Carol Landis, her much publicized legs demurely skirted, peeks as producer Cecil B. De Mille gives blood at a Hollywood Red Cross blood center. The actress had registered to do the same.

Jane Russell, standing in a hole in the side of the freighter Absaroka through which a seaman had been blown into the sea off the California coast, holds up a slightly edited Navy poster.

A Marine prepares to throw a hand grenade in the Battle of Guadalcanal.

A Norman Bel Geddes topographical model of Guadalcanal in LIFE, in a view looking south, shows two of the island's strategically vital features, the harbor of Tulagi (at left, on the Guadalcanal side of Florida Island) and, facing it on the big island, Henderson Field.

In one of the great coincidences of history, the fate of the civilized world hung in the balance as two sets of combatants, on opposite sides of the world, closed in on two dots on the globe and made them the most precious pieces of real estate on earth. Guadalcanal, discovered in the 16th century by a Spaniard who named it for his home town, was the key to the South Pacific. It contained both the finest harbor in the Solomons, at Tulagi, and strategically placed Henderson Field, from which the Japanese attacked U.S. warships attempting to reinforce embattled jungle fighters. The island's fall initiated the island-by-island reversal of all of Japan's conquests. At Stalingrad, the industrial city on the Volga that bore the name of Hitler's most hated enemy, the Red Army surprised the world by turning around the German juggernaut and starting a two-year rollback to the heart of its homeland.

Strung out on the Volga's west shore, Stalingrad shows the battering of months of siege. The Wehrmacht had fought its way to the concentration of tractor and metallurgical plants at right. The Russians continued to repair tanks there until German infantrymen came in through the windows.

'Guadal' Starts a Great U.S. Counterattack

LIFE correspondent John Hersey, whose novel A Bell for Adano *won a Pulitzer Prize in 1945, here reports on the Marines of Guadalcanal. As Hersey shows, the American fighting man's feelings toward the enemy became inflamed under the terrifying pressures of jungle combat.*

Marines are human. If you look at a typical private after he has been out on a Guadalcanal patrol for three days and nights—his chin covered with stubble, his eyes tired and fierce, his battle uniform torn and maybe bloody—you are apt to mistake him for a thug. But when he has shaved and bathed in the Lunga, when he has had a few hours' rest, you find that you would be willing to meet him on a dark night after all—if you were on his side . . .

As a fighter, he is a cross between Geronimo the Indian chief, Buck Rogers, Sergeant York and a clumsy heartsick boy. He knows how to use a knife—or a screwdriver if he has to. He knows how to lie as silent as an adder. He knows about close-in work, and he is a crack shot. But he is human: when mortar fire lands within 20 feet of him, he may turn and flee. So might a Jap, and so might a German . . . A legend has grown up that this young man is a killer; he takes no prisoners, and gives no quarter. This is partly true, but the reason is not brutality, not just vindictive remembrance of Pearl Harbor. He kills because in the jungle he must, or be killed. This enemy stalks him, and he stalks the enemy, as if each were a hunter tracking a bear cat. Quite frequently you can hear Marines say: "I wish we were fighting against Germans. They are human beings, like us. Fighting against them must be like an athletic performance—matching your skill against someone you know is good. Germans are misled, but at least they react like men. But the Japs are like animals. Against them you have to learn a whole new set of physical reactions. You have to get used to their animal stubbornness and tenacity. They take to the jungle as if they had been bred there, and like some beasts you never see them until they are dead . . ."

GIs hack their way through Guadalcanal's steaming jungle. The tangle of vegetation is 100 feet high; near the ground are thousands of kinds of insects.

After a bloody battle for a 1,500-foot peak euphemistically called Grassy Knoll, battle-stained infantrymen clean their weapons.

Celebrating Christmas on Guadal, a GI Santa hands out presents to wounded at a field hospital.

In a good-size stream, the troops tak laundry break to wash the island from their clothes and bod

A Japanese warrior's burnt skull, all that remained of his corpse after fire gutted his tank, is propped up on the machine's exterior.

The Inch-by-Inch Struggle in Stalingrad

*Defenders of Stalingrad move through trenches built to enable them to move
from house to house. Every building had been turned into a fortress.*

Red Guardsmen dash across open ground, one of them falling,
hit. A German shell blast mushrooms just beyond them.

Red riflemen pour fire on attackers from an apartment fortress. The
defenders couldn't be smoked out because there was nothing left to burn.

1942
The Frightful Cost of Allied Victories

Two young Stalingrad women carry their possessions from their home in a cellar without a house.

Japanese soldiers who tried to overrun U.S. Marine positions on Guadalcanal's coast lie half-buried on an Ilu river sandbar.

1943 THE TIDE

In what proved in hindsight to be the conflict's year of turnaround, a classic concept and at least one instrument of war came of age. So decisive was the former, the long-debated theory of strategic bombing, that 1943 became a year of high-level conferences, as Allied political leaders became emboldened enough to differ over grand strategies for both hemispheres. As the U.S. and Britain, in their different ways, punished Germany's home territory and smashed its war-making facilities by long-range, high-altitude bombing, it was no longer possible to deny the efficacy of strategic air power, as distinct from tactical aviation, which supported surface forces at the battlefronts. While British, American and Free French troops were teaming up to drive Rommel's Afrika Korps into POW pens in Tunisia, the Aussies and Yanks "down under" were establishing a collaboration that would power General MacArthur's vision of an island-by-island rollback of the Japanese all the way to the Philippines and thence to Japan's home islands. Meanwhile, Churchill joined President Roosevelt in the White House's great map room to pore, through a thicket of braid and brass, over the network of war fronts that circled the globe. The pair had met with De Gaulle at Casablanca and before the year was out would sit down with Chiang Kai-shek and with Stalin, each of whom had his own idea of appropriate Allied grand strategy.

For reasons of geography, strategic bombing came first to the European theater. The Continent was within the range of U.S. B-17 Flying Fortresses based on the "unsinkable carrier," Britain. The RAF's Lancasters and Halifaxes had been blasting the industrial cities of the Ruhr since 1940. Losses had forced the big bombers to break off daylight attacks on specific targets and

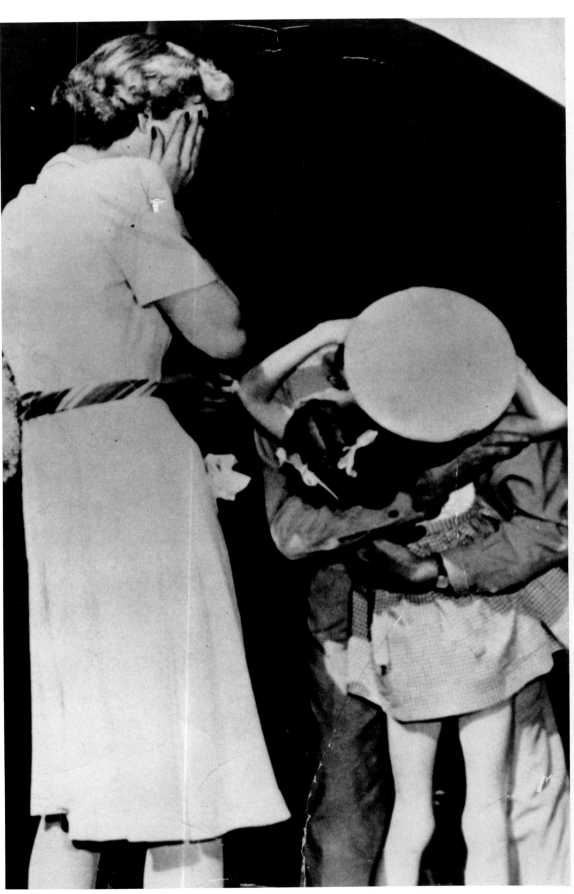

Some came home. The wife and small daughter of Bob Moore, the corner druggist of Villisca, Iowa, are overwhelmed as he returns from the African desert a hero with a Silver Star.

Others didn't. Three GIs who died on the gory beach at Bu
New Guinea, shocked America when the end of the ban on picture
U.S. casualties permitted them to be shown in all their anonym

FINALLY TURNS

A New Word in the Epic Struggle: Rollback

The arrows of war start, at long last, to stab across the shrinking peripheries of the Axis empires all over the globe.

turn to nighttime area bombing. The Americans, who possessed a closely guarded "secret weapon," the superior Norden bombsight, opted for daylight raids of what the Eighth Air Force called precision bombing and "pinpoint bombing"—a locution greeted with derisive laughs by infantrymen who found themselves in the neighborhood of the occasional not-so-near miss—but that did succeed in taking out huge amounts of German production.

The strategic bombing of Japan, protected by thousands of miles of ocean and "unsinkable carriers" of its own in armed islands, awaited longer-range bombers than the B-17s and B-24 Liberators. In the meantime, the strategic air fleet was limited to destroying raw-materials sources and supply routes such as those in New Guinea, Burma and Southeast Asia. An intra-U.S. difference of grand strategies pitted General MacArthur's plan, a systematic advance from New Guinea to the Philippines and beyond, against a naval-centered campaign of attack westward from Pearl Harbor. An Allied conference in Quebec decided to go both ways.

The land-locked rollback of the Wehrmacht in Mother Russia, which started in January with its disaster at Stalingrad and the Red Army's almost simultaneous lifting of the 17-month siege of Leningrad, was punctuated in July by a monumental clash of armies 200 miles east of Kiev. Despite their immense losses, the Germans still held some 400,000 square miles of scorched earth and had 4 million troops on their side of the 1,750-mile Eastern Front, facing 5 million resurgent Russians. The Soviets pushed a salient into the midsection of the front north of Kharkov, setting the stage for history's greatest tank battle. The Wehrmacht closed an armored pincers on the bulge, hurling 1,000 tanks, including Porsches and Panthers, the biggest ever built, against an equal number of smaller but more maneuverable Red ironclads. The Russians matched the Nazis' firepower, and the combination of smoke and the close range of the fighting kept tactical aircraft at bay. The Red infantry, moreover, found the armored behemoths were vulnerable to flamethrowers directed at their ventilation shafts. Hitler, his panzers done in, ordered the cease-fire himself.

Such victories did not end Stalin's calls on the Allies for a Second Front. In the middle of the night of July 9-10, U.S. parachute and glider troops, followed by other Allied units, landed on the island of Sicily, just across the narrow Strait of Messina from the toe of the Italian boot, in the war's first campaign against the enemy on his own soil. German troops defended airstrips fiercely but, reinforced after dawn by foot soldiers off new infantry landing craft, the invaders took the island's southern tip. The Italian defenders put up much less of a battle, and the civilian populace seemed welcoming. General Patton's Americans on the west coast and British forces under General Montgomery on the more rugged east coast raced northward and reached Messina in almost a dead heat, Patton having taken Palermo along the way. They found that the Germans had ferried 109,000 troops and their matériel to the mainland to fight again.

On the night of December 14, a fleet of odd-looking topless vessels crept across the Coral Sea toward the jungled southern coast of New Britain. This was the first invasion of Operation Cartwheel, a pincerlike series of island-to-island leaps aimed at the great Japanese naval base of Rabaul, on the island's eastern tip, and each unit of the curious fleet was a vessel that was to become indispensable to amphibious warfare (and to future crossword puzzlers): the LST, for Landing Ship, Tank. Heavily defended Rabaul was the apex of a wide, squat triangle, its base reaching from New Guinea in the west to Guadalcanal in the east, that aimed toward Japan. The main New Guinea landing force, commanded by General MacArthur, slashed through the jungle up the triangle's left leg. From Guadalcanal, amphibious forces under Admiral William F. Halsey pushed their way up the eastern leg by way of New Georgia and Bougainville. The whole Operation Cartwheel was coordinated with a series of leaps up the Gilbert and the Marshall islands in battles whose headlined names became synonyms for carnage: Tarawa, Eniwetok, Kwajalein.

The second full year of two-hemisphere war ended with the Allies on the offensive in every theater. Readers in the U.S. and Britain, at long last, could open their newspapers (and followers of the BBC everywhere could tune in) without gloomy trepidation.

History unfolded like a cinematic montage. Taking Tarawa cost the U.S. Marines more dearly (1,026 dead, 2,296 wounded, out of 5,000 who landed) than Guadalcanal or the Battle of Chateau-Thierry in World War I. The U.S. and Britain dropped millions of leaflets the length and breadth of Italy warning the nation to end Fascism. Mussolini was placed under house arrest and the king ordered Marshal Pietro Badoglio to form a government. Italy declared war on Nazi Germany soon after the Allies invaded its mainland, the Canadians and British at Reggio di Calabria, on the toe of the boot, the U.S. at Salerno, on its shin. U.S. bombers from Africa blasted oil fields at Ploesti, in Rumania, cutting Germany's supply by a third. The Allies ousted the Germans from Naples. The Nazis occupied Rome, which was declared an open city.

The Allies, misguidedly heading for Rome through the mountains to its south, were halted at the Rapido River before the abbey of Monte Cassino, which reared atop a mountainside fortified by the Wehrmacht as part of its Gustav Line. The RAF bombed a secret Baltic base where engines were made that propelled aircraft and "flying bombs" by passing air through them. The Red Army drove the Wehrmacht out of the Caucasus and liberated Smolensk and Kiev. Roosevelt, Churchill and Stalin, at Tehran, agreed on coordinated drives on Germany from south, west and east. Then, on Christmas Eve, F.D.R. announced his choice to lead the invasion of Europe: General Dwight D. Eisenhower.

In an image filled with dire symbolism for Japan, 12,395-foot Fujiyama, Nippon's sacred volcano, only 70 miles from Tokyo, is photographed through the periscope of a U.S. submarine.

CHRONOLOGY 1943

January	February	March	April	May	June
1 *● New law limits U.S. salaries to $25,000, later revoked*	**2** ● Last Germans surrender at Stalingrad	**2-4** ● Battle of Bismarck Sea, heavy losses for Japanese	**7** ● Mussolini and Hitler meet near Salzburg	**2** ● Darwin, Australia, bombed by Japan	**1** ● Monsoons stop operations in India, Burma
2 ● Allies take Buna Mission, New Guinea ● Germans begin withdrawing from Caucasus	**7** ● Final Japanese evacuation from Guadalcanal	**5** ● In Ruhr Valley, heavy Allied bombing begins	**13** ● Mass grave of 4,000 Polish officers uncovered in Katyn Forest	**3** ● Final Allied offensive begins in Tunisia	**11** *● F.D.R. asks Italians to overthrow Duce* ● Pantellaria Island occupied by U.S.
5 ● Japanese start quitting Guadalcanal	**8** ● Kursk reoccupied by Soviets	**10** ● Rommel called home	**17** ● Hitler orders all Hungarian Jews jailed	**7** ● Allies take Bizerte and Tunis	**12** ● Lampedusa Island surrenders
8 ● Madagascar turned over to Free French	**14** ● Rostov recaptured by Soviets	**13** ● Nazis close Warsaw ghetto ● Attempt to kill Hitler fails	**18** ● Admiral Yamamoto shot down and killed	**11-27** *● Washington conference*	**13** ● African campaign concluded with German defeat
10 ● Reds close ring around Germans at Stalingrad	**16** ● Kharkov reoccupied by Soviets	**14** ● Germans recapture Kharkov	**19** ● Battle of Warsaw ghetto begins	**11-31** ● Battle of Attu	**16** ● Tojo tells Diet war has reached critical stage
12-18 ● Soviets launch Leningrad offensive	**18** *● Madame Chiang Kai-shek addresses U.S. Congress*	**16-19** ● Battle off Newfoundland between subs and convoy escorts	**28-30** ● Last German armored attack in North Africa	**12-13** ● With 238,243 prisoners taken, North African campaign almost over	**17** ● Goebbels proclaims Berlin free of Jews
14-23 ● Casablanca conference	**22** ● Rommel withdraws through Kasserine Pass in Tunisia	**20** ● Battle of Mareth, Tunisia ● Second March attempt on Hitler's life by his own men	**28-May 6** ● Heavy losses inflicted on U-boats	**14** ● Japanese sub torpedoes Australian hospital ship	**20** ● RAF "shuttle-bombing" of Germany starts
18 ● 900-day siege of Leningrad lifted	**25** ● RAF starts round-the-clock bombing	**21** ● Deep mud on Russian front slows action	**30** ● Stalin told Murmansk convoys are being suspended	**16** ● Of final 60,000 Warsaw Jews, 56,065 are dead	**22** ● U-boats withdrawn from North Atlantic
20 ● Jews of Warsaw ghetto rise up	**26** ● U.S. bombs German U-boat pens	*This month Allies lose 120 ships in Atlantic*		**18** *● United Nations food conference opens*	**30** ● U.S. operations in northern Solomons begin
23 ● British enter Tripoli, Libya	**28** ● German forces contained in Tunisia			**20** ● Yamamoto's death announced in Tokyo	
26-27 ● First U.S. air raids on Germany				**21** ● Japanese offensive begins along Yangtze River	
28 ● Nazis mobilize women for military service				**25** ● May 1, 1944, picked for invasion	
30 ● RAF raids Berlin				**30** ● Attu secured	
				This was "Black May" for German navy: Battle of the Atlantic virtually ended	

■ **War in Europe**   ■ **War in Asia**   ▨ **U.S.A.**

July	August	September	October	November	December
1 • *MacArthur opens Allied Pacific offensive*	**1** • *U.S. air raid on Ploesti oil fields*	**3** • *British and Canadians land in southern Italy* • *Italy sues for peace*	**1** • *Allies take Naples* • *Germans begin withdrawal from Kuban Peninsula*	**1** • *U.S. lands on Bougainville*	**1** • *Stalemate along Gustav Line*
2 • *U.S. lands on New Georgia*	**2** • *J.F.K.'s PT-109 sunk*	**4** • *U.S. and Australians land near Lae*	**5-6** • *U.S. hits Wake Island*	**2** • *Naval Battle of Empress Augusta Bay*	**4-7** • *Second Cairo conference, Big Three resume in new setting*
5 • *Germans launch offensive at Kursk*	**5** • *Russians recapture Orel and Belgorod*	**8** • *Italy surrenders*	**6** • *U.S. lands on Kolombangara*	**3** • *Russians launch drive to recapture Kiev* • *Nazis kill 17,000 Jews in Maidanek camp*	**5** • *Japanese raid Calcutta in daylight first time*
6 • *U.S. shells Kiska in Aleutians*	**6** • *Battle of Vella Gulf in Solomons, Japanese defeated*	**9** • *German troops occupy Rome* • *Allies land at Salerno*	**12** • *U.S. drive on Rome* • *Greatest Allied air fleet hits Rabaul*	**5** • *Allies bomb Vatican* • *Massive U.S. attack on Rabaul*	**9** • *Japanese victors in Changteh*
10 • *Invasion of Sicily*	**13** • *Rome declared open city*	**12** • *90 Germans in gliders rescue Mussolini*	**13** • *Italy declares war on Germany*	**6** • *Reds reconquer Kiev*	**12** • *Hitler appoints Rommel as man to stop invasion*
11 • *Red offensive against Orel*	**15** • *Allies land unopposed on Kiska*	**21-22** • *British midget subs attack Tirpitz in Norway*	**15** • *From India, Chinese advance into Burma*	**15** • *Germans withdraw to Gustav Line south of Rome*	**15** • *Arawe landing ends U.S. Solomons offense*
12 • *Largest tank battle in history for Kursk*	**17** • *Allies take Messina; conquest of Sicily complete*	**22** • *First Soviet bridgehead across Dnieper*	**19-30** • *Moscow conference of Big Three foreign ministers*	**20-24** • *U.S. landings on Makin and Tarawa*	**17** • *U.S. invades New Britain Island in New Guinea*
13 • *Naval Battle of Kolombangara*	**17-24** • *First Quebec conference*	**24** • *Mark Clark's Fifth Army moves north from Salerno* • *Reds liberate Smolensk, Germans in retreat*	**30** • *Reds drive Germans out of Caucasus*	**22-26** • *First Cairo conference—F.D.R., Churchill and Chiang Kai-shek*	**24** • *F.D.R. names Eisenhower to lead invasion of Europe*
14 • *Messina hit by Allies*	**22** • *Russians take Kharkov by storm*	**30** • *Germans driven from Naples*	**31** • *Heading for Rome, Allies halted at Monte Cassino* • *By now, half of German cities have been bombed*	**23** • *Makin secured*	**26** • *U.S. lands at Cape Gloucester, in Solomons*
17 • *Soviets take Taganrog* • *Hitler orders more men to Balkans*	**23** • *Japanese bomb Chungking, the first time in two years*	*A million dead this month as famine sweeps Bengal*		**28-Dec. 1** • *Tehran conference—F.D.R., Churchill, Stalin on invasion*	**30** • *Allies end assault on Gustav Line*
19 • *Allies bomb Rome*	**27** • *U.S. lands on Arundel Island in Solomons*			**29** • *Tito is leader of Yugoslavia*	**31** • *Soviets retake Zhitomir, west of Kiev* • *More than 2,000 planes set Berlin afire*
21 • *Pope deplores Rome bombing*	**29** • *Danes revolt, King seized by Germans* • *U.S. has "trustworthy information" on Nazi atrocities*				
22 • *Palermo taken*					
25 • *Mussolini overthrown, is arrested* • *Hitler sends Rommel to Greece*					
28 • *Japanese secretly leave Kiska* • *B-17s raze Hamburg*					

Hitler's 'Final Solution'

News of Adolf Hitler's "Final Solution" to his long-festering problem with Jews—kill them all—did not circle the earth with the speed of a war dispatch about a battle with a death toll of 6 million. The word genocide did not exist, and few, in either the Allied or the Axis world, seemed sufficiently moved by the enormity of the policy to coin it. Holocaust it literally was, although the word would not become a proper noun until long after the fact. The horror of the numbers of its victims and of the Nazis' endlessly inventive methods of accomplishing their annihilation seemed too great for the civilized mind to comprehend. Every method of execution was employed by SS specialists in cities and towns and in the field—shooting, hanging, stabbing, poisoning, burning, suffocation by live burial and of course the highly efficient mass gassing of the death camps. But some Nazis were in positions to exercise more ingenuity, particularly Nazi doctors. Heinrich Himmler was said to abjure sadism, but he had a keen interest in scientific research. Doctors demonstrated, with decompression experiments on prisoners provided by Himmler, how altitude kills (it first bursts the eardrums), what degree of cold humans could endure before they froze to death (these tests were spoiled by the subjects' loss of consciousness before they congealed), what happened in children's bodies before they died of starvation, and precisely how viruses kill. The Final Solution was no secret to its potential victims, however; awareness that genocide was official Nazi policy was the final blow that set off the epochal uprising of the 60,000 Jews still alive in the Warsaw ghetto. With pathetically few smuggled weapons they resisted furiously a "special action" started April 19 by 2,000 troops to eliminate them in three days. It was not until May 16 that all but a handful (the official count was 56,065) were killed or sent off to the death-camp ovens for "cleansing" by the same methods that had expunged their 100,000 Warsaw predecessors and 240,000 more European Jews up to that time.

Somewhere in the vastness of the Eastern front an SS trooper performs his specialty, taking careful aim at a Jewish mother and child for whom terrified peasants prepare a grave. Left, Jews of the Warsaw ghetto, ending their rebellion, surrender under the stony gaze of the guard they called Frankenstein. A one-man atrocity team, he helped trigger the uprising by randomly beating and murdering ghetto residents and raping their women.

Women from the ghetto of Riga, Latvia, are herded toward an excavation that is to be their grave. Nazi soldiers shot them, the impact of the bullets hurling them into the pit.

A Polish Jew kneels at the edge of a mass grave to receive his SS executioner's shot.

1943
Who to Die, Who to Live

In a rare photograph, Joseph Mengele, at the foot of the railroad ramp at Birkenau, hand-picks victims for the death camp's ovens.

The Final Solution produced a new rank for the SS: Angel of Death. That was the name given to the most famous of the officers who assumed the role of God at each of the six major death camps by deciding which prisoners should die and which live, at least long enough to perform slave labor. This was Joseph Mengele, a medical doctor who wielded his finger of death so efficiently that he became a legendary figure at the most infamous of the camps, Auschwitz. (The other death factories were Belzec, Chelmno, Maidanek, Sobibor and Treblinka.) Not only did he survive the war and escape the United Nations' war crimes tribunals but he even managed to live to almost the biblical span. Until 1949, he played the harmless physician, with his wife and son, not far from his family home in the Danube town of Günzberg. Then, feeling the hot breath of Allied and Israeli Nazi hunters, he fled through a Nazi network via Italy to Spain, where he was provided with false papers that got him into Argentina and then Paraguay. His subsequent existence, shuttling as a respectable citizen between cities in Paraguay, visiting South American resorts and traveling to Spain, Italy, Greece and Egypt, always just ahead of Israeli intelligence, turned the legend of the Angel of Death almost into myth. As the numbers of death-camp survivors diminished, more and more of the unconcerned wondered whether he had ever existed. Occasionally people tipped off the Israelis to his whereabouts—and shortly thereafter turned up dead. In 1985 the corpse of a 67-year-old victim of a swimming accident was dug up outside São Paulo, Brazil, and after exhaustive forensic examination investigators from West Germany, the U.S. and Brazil, with the concurrence of the Israeli Nazi-hunter Menachem Russek, decided that it was the remains of the Angel of Death.

Hungarian Jews arriving at Auschwitz pass a camp officer who decides whether they live or die.

1943
Torture, Humiliation and Back-Breaking Slave Labor

A sentry stands guard over a sea of naked prisoners in Mauthausen's main courtyard. Inmates, especially newcomers, were often made to stand thus for a day and a night.

Like the slaves who built Egypt's great pyramids, prisoners struggle under enormous chunks of granite up the steep steps of a quarry near Mauthausen. Finished with their crushing chore, they would be flogged into torturous runs.

Unspeakable Genetic Experiments, 'Shower Baths of Death'

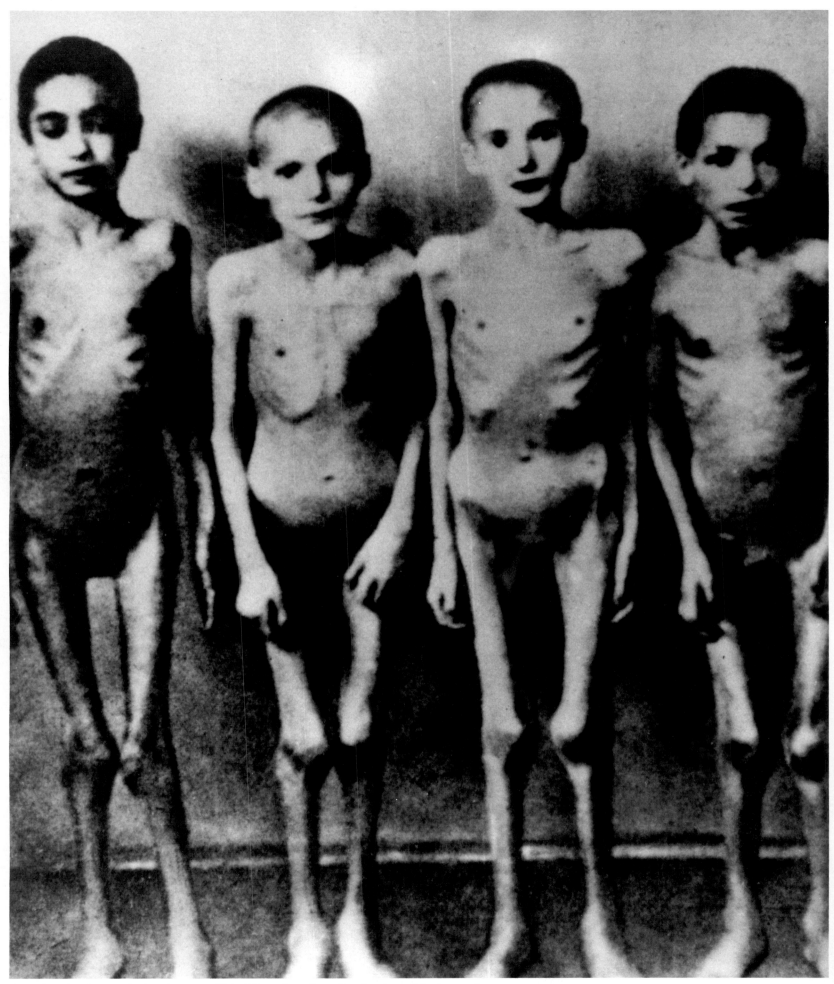

Emaciated twins await the pleasure of Dr. Mengele, whose fascination with the products of multiple births well suited the purposes of his mentor, Himmler. Mengele experimented on 200 sets of twins, of Auschwitz's "inferior racial stock," in order to discover genetic secrets that would enable German mothers to produce a "superior race" faster through multiple births.

A large gas chamber at the Maidanek camp in Poland stands mercifully empty after the Nazis' downfall. Some 1.3 million prisoners met their deaths at Maidanek. New arrivals were ordered to strip and shower. When "shower baths" like this one were packed tightly with naked men, women and children, the metal doors clanged shut and lethal gas was released through the ventilating system. Afterward, bodies were removed by hooked poles and ice tongs to conveyor belts that took them to the ovens and graves awaiting them.

A ghastly hand protrudes from an oven door in an unidentified death camp. It is not known whether the photo was made by an Allied soldier after the camp's liberation or by an SS officer before.

1943
Squeezing the Axis out of Africa

The landings of Operation Torch by no means chased Rommel out of North Africa. Widespread and deadly desert warfare, rolling back and forth across the top of the continent, would have to be waged before the Fox was whipped. For one thing, the Allies did not have clear-cut air superiority across the theater. The RAF's experienced Desert Air Force did chase the Afrika Korps along the Mediterranean. But in the west the U.S. 12th Air Force had to cope with short supplies, overcast skies and inexperience. At first Major General Jimmy Doolittle reported that only 200 of his 600 planes, based too far off in Algeria, were operating effectively. When forward airfields started up they were so muddy that steel mats sank into them. The Luftwaffe flew from weather-proof Tunis airport. Ground battles were bloody, particularly for the green U.S. troops. In their first important combat, they let the 10th and 21st panzer divisions break through their line at Kasserine Pass, in the mountainous waist of Tunisia. When they saw their buddies falling dead and wounded, more than 2,400 Yanks surrendered. Although Goebbels made the most of their embarrassment

The map of the area encompassed in the photograph at right shows Tunisia's twin cities of Tunis and Bizerte, including the former's all-weather airport, which the Luftwaffe used punishingly and which was the target of Allied bombing raids from distant fields in Algeria. In the photo, looking northeast across Tunisia's coastal plane to Bizerte and the Mediterranean, B-17 Flying Fortresses head for home as smoke columns rise from bombed planes and ammunition dumps on the Tunis airfield.

Searchlight beams (thick, diffused lines) and tracers from antiaircraft guns (thin, sharp lines that disappear into clouds) slash the night sky above Gibraltar. The vital naval stronghold at the entrance to the Mediterranean was a constant nightmare to Allied generals fighting in North Africa at the end of supply lines that depended on it.

and General Harold Alexander, Eisenhower's operational deputy, sent British officers to train them for combat, the blooded Americans had learned a lesson. Rommel's victory was short-lived. His men captured several airfields, but the panzers were overextended and the Germans were forced back through Kasserine. With the Axis pinned against the Mediterranean, fierce battles raged for weeks before Bizerte. (Unlike most of the strange names that combat brought briefly into the headlines, this one stuck in the minds of geography-shy Americans because it brought forth a hit tune, "Dirty Gertie From Bizerte.") Especially bitter was the struggle for Hill 609, a flat-topped natural fortress at Mateur, the mountainous gateway to Bizerte. Major General Omar Bradley's U.S. II Corps, led by the 34th Division finally took it; Bizerte and Tunis fell and Kasserine Pass was avenged. Rommel left his cornered forces in Tunis and returned to Germany to appeal to Hitler to abandon North Africa and thereby save his troops from being wiped out. Hitler, incredibly, called him a coward, turned down his plea, relieved him of his command and lost the battle, the troops and the continent.

Britain's Field Marshal Bernard L. Montgomery and U.S. General Dwight D. Eisenhower, in the field, discuss their combined operations. They were the figurative pincers, "Ike" moving his fresh forces east and "Monty" leading his desert veterans west, that closed on Rommel and squeezed the Axis out of Africa, setting up the war's next phase, their joint invasion of Europe via Sicily and Italy.

The End of the North African Campaign

German and Italian troops who surrendered to end the war in Africa pour into a prison
compound near Mateur, west of Tunis. Next stop: POW camps in Canada, Britain or the U.S.

Sicily, a stepping-stone to Italy, was the first objective. Here men and matériel of Montgomery's Eighth Army move onto a beach on the big island's east coast. Patton's Seventh Army landed on the south at the same time.

The Capture of Sicily Knocks Italy out of the War

A U.S. ammunition ship explodes after being hit off Gela by German bombers attacking the Seventh Army invasion convoy.

The amphibious part of the British and U.S. landings on Sicily went off smoothly, but its airborne accompaniment had difficulties. High winds blew gliders into the sea and chutists off their targets. U.S. airborne reinforcements two nights after the landings arrived right in the thick of a Luftwaffe bombing. Still Patton's and Montgomery's converging forces met and entered Messina five weeks after their Sicilian D Day.

The immediate consequence of their victory was the surrender of war-weary Italy. With his forces fighting listlessly or giving themselves up to the Allies, King Victor Emmanuel III abruptly imprisoned Mussolini and appointed the old war hero Marshal Pietro Badoglio premier. Badoglio immediately started negotiating for peace. Hitler, smarting for his humiliated ally, arranged to have a parachute rescue team snatch the Duce from prison. He headed north, to the foothills of the Alps—Hitler's *Festung Europa*, or Fortress Europe, to lick his wounds. On September 8, Eisenhower announced Italy's surrender.

A Seventh Army medical corpsman gets a Palermo shoeshine, while another GI waits to get one too, the better to impress his new Sicilian amica.

Hitler walks with Mussolini after Il Duce's rescue from prison. The dictator without a country holed up in his estate on Lake Garda and set about doing what the Führer encouraged him to do: establishing a "republic" in northern Italy.

'The Four Days of Naples'

For four days, from September 28, when the Germans started to evacuate the city, until October 1, when the Allied armies entered it, Neapolitans were a people between conquerors. The Nazis had a particular hatred for these swarthy, street-singing, unbuttoned Italians. Among the atrocities that U.S. officials enumerated for F.D.R. were the deliberate destruction of the water supply and the sewage disposal, electrical, telephone and transportation systems; the university and its library; the planting of time bombs against civilians; the release of dangerous criminals from 13 prisons and the looting of hospitals. As the Wehrmacht grip weakened, anti-Fascist Italians

The American landing force digs in on the beach at Salerno, Italy, harassed by constant bombing and frequent Wehrmacht counterattacks from the north.

Three young snipers of Naples who fought the Wehrmacht for four days until the U.S. Fifth Army reached the city hold their fire. The smoker was nine years old.

One of 20 Naples youngsters, ages 14 to 20, who died fighting the Germans is borne from a schoolhouse used as a mortuary. As with several other young defenders, the body was too large for the children's coffins the Neopolitans had collected.

came into the open. In what came to be known as the Four Days of Naples, they poured their fury on the departing occupiers with whatever arms they could scrape up. Organized with help from a leftist group called the Party for Italian Liberation, youths of school age, ranging from nine to 20, using to great effect their knowledge of city neighborhoods, sniped from windows and leaped from housetops and walls that lined steep, narrow streets. A group in Vomero was led by a professor, Antonino Tarsia. Armed with rifles they had seized from Fort St. Elmo, they surrounded the Germans in the Fascist Youth headquarters; 20 boys from one school were among those killed in the bloody skirmishing.

Mothers of Naples lament their children who died defending them in guerrilla fighting that raged from the heights of Vomero to the Bay of Naples.

BATTLEFRONTS: RUMANIA   Record-Breaking Air Attack in the Balkans

As early as a month after Pearl Harbor, the U.S. Army Air Forces started planning to bomb Europe's prime strategic target, the Rumanian oil fields of Ploesti. The great center, 35 miles north of Bucharest, was the site of 10 major refineries, which produced 60 percent of Germany's crude oil. First planned as a small, high-altitude attack, Operation Soapsuds evolved into a more dangerous but much more destructive low-level mass raid. Early on August 1, 177 four-engine B-24 Liberators, in five groups, took off from Benghazi, Libya, and flew, southeast of Italy's heel and across Greece, Albania and Yugoslavia, to Rumania. They drove in boldly on the refineries, at treetop height, through forests of balloon cables, intense flak and Messerschmitt fighters. With a loss of 54 planes and 532 fliers, the raid temporarily destroyed 42 percent of Ploesti's refining capacity.

B-24 Liberators of the Ninth Air Force leave the Ploesti oil fields in billows of oily smoke after their mighty blow at the Axis war machine.

A B-24 maintains its low-level flight, virtually at treetop height, across the Astra Romana factory.

The smoke and fumes of many fires of petroleum in various stages of refinement mix in a vast overca

Half-starved, half-frozen German soldiers taken prisoner by the Stalingrad defenders stand in a compound, dazed by months of bitter struggle and ultimate defeat. More than 90,000 of them died of cold and starvation; 100,000 were killed in battle in just the last three weeks. It was almost impossible to see in Stalingrad's Wehrmacht remnants the polished military machine that had knifed into Mother Russia, much less the ideologically dedicated Hitler Youth (above) whence many of them had sprung.

Surrounded by the gutted buildings of Stalingrad, victorious Red Army soldiers indulge in their other field specialty, singing and dancing. The music was even sweeter accompanied by an accordion "liberated" from the invaders.

Leningrad's Epic Seventeen-Month Siege

German artillerymen race to hurl another shell at Leningrad from one of their big siege guns.

For 515 days, the huge siege guns pounded Leningrad, and all the other elements of Field Marshal Wilhelm von Leeb's armies hurled steel at Peter the Great's beloved "window to the sea." The besiegers comprised two German armies and four panzer divisions, plus 12 Finnish divisions under Field Marshal Mannerheim, who thirsted to get back what Stalin had plucked from him in 1940. The refusal of the Leningraders to surrender astounded the world. Day after day for those 17 months shells crashed incessantly into their streets and buildings till virtually nothing was left intact. Women and elderly men daily attacked the rubble and piled it into little mountains. Corpses lined the streets, and sometimes the only traffic visible was handcarts or trucks carrying coffins. With reservoirs ruined, residents drew water from street snow

Corpses lie on the Nevsky Prospekt as artillery shellbursts further punish Leningrad's principal avenue.

and the Neva River. Despite the murderous gunfire, the great dispenser of death was hunger. Although the Red Army, holding the attackers at bay, managed to push some food across frozen Lake Ladoga, it was a mere trickle. One half of the citizenry died during the winter. Among those who did not was the composer Dmitri Shostakovich. As Tchaikovsky had immortalized Napoleon's retreat from Moscow in his *1812 Overture,* Shostakovich composed a paean to his city, his *Seventh Symphony.* Deep in the siege's second winter, Russians commanded by Marshals Zhukov and Voroshilov pierced the ring of German iron around the city south of Lake Ladoga, and took other strategic Wehrmacht positions. Leningrad, miraculously, lived, although the great counterattack to drive the invaders completely out did not take place for another year.

Cold and Hunger Are Siege's Greatest Weapons

Leningraders collect precious water from streets turned to glaciers. The unpleasant process was made even more frustrating by Leningrad's winter temperatures, which inhibited melting even on days when it didn't snow.

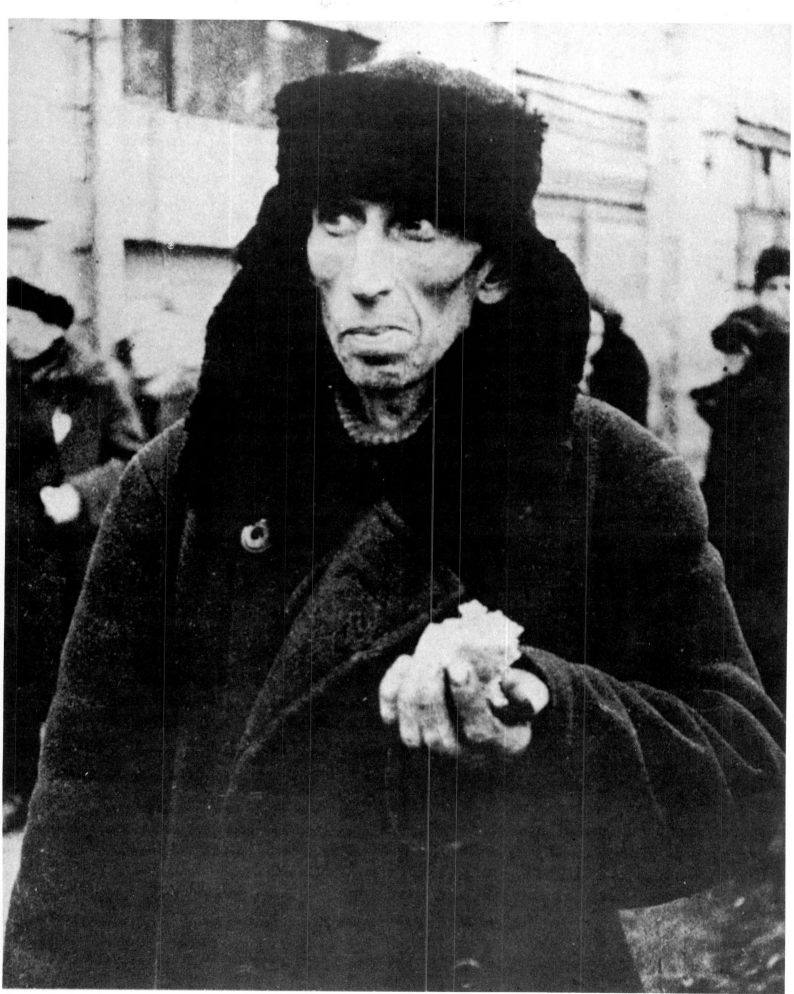

A gaunt Leningrader holds his daily ration of bread. Even this staple was usually an
odd-tasting concoction of whatever ingredients could be scraped up—sometimes literally.

Partisans Take Aim at the Hated Invaders

A Partisan "zeros in" his rifle, the standard Red Army infantryman's weapon, adjusting its sights as a comrade-in-arms looks on. The cruelty of much of the fighting and the utter devastation of the scorched-earth policy, of both the invader and the invaded, made most of the able-bodied civilian population thirst for Nazi blood. The Partisans' knowledge of local terrains made them particularly effective guerrillas.

A group of Yugoslav Partisans flock through a forest near Miljevina after escaping encirclement in a German-led anti-Partisan campaign that was a testament to the effectiveness of Tito's guerrillas. More than 6,000 of them died in the month-long battle.

Russian farm women wielding pitchforks (right, above) lunge at a collaborator being marched out of the village to be executed by a firing squad (right).

At the Tehran conference, F.D.R. turns to grasp the hand of Sarah Churchill Oliver, Winston's actress daughter, as Foreign Minister Molotov, Averell Harriman and Major General Edwin M. Watson look on.

En route to Tehran to meet with Churchill and Stalin *(above)*, F.D.R. and his top military men (including generals Marshall and Arnold and admirals Leahy and King) almost met with disaster. Aboard the U.S. battleship *Iowa* 350 miles east of Bermuda the President and his brass came close to being blown up by a torpedo from one of their own warship escorts. At the time the U.S. destroyer *William D. Porter* was engaged in a running combat drill with the *Iowa* as the target for realism's sake. Suddenly the ship mistakenly let go a forgotten live torpedo from one of its firing tubes. Fortunately it missed, exploding in the *Iowa*'s wake. The President's log commented: "Had that torpedo hit the *Iowa* in the right spot with her passenger list of distinguished statesmen, military, naval and aerial strategists and planners, it could have had an untold effect on the outcome of the war and the destiny of the country."

At a Washington meeting on military strategy, Churchill and Roosevelt sit before (from left) Lieut. General Hastings Ismay, deputy secretary (military) to Britain's war cabinet; Air Chief Marshal Charles Portal; General Alan Brooke, Chief of the Imperial General Staff; Admiral of the Fleet Dudley Pound, First Sea Lord; Admiral William D. Leahy, F.D.R.'s Chief of Staff, and General George C. Marshall, U.S. Army Chief of Staff.

Molotov signs the four-power Moscow Pact that resulted from a conference in the Soviet capital. Looking on are U.S. Secretary of State Cordell Hull (left) and Britain's Foreign Secretary Anthony Eden. Chinese Ambassador Foo Ping-sheung was the fourth signer.

Stalin kisses the British-forged "Sword of Stalingrad" at the Tehran conference.

1943
Churchill's Inner Sanctums

A war map indicating England's defense sites in case of invasion dominates the concrete-and-steel shelter 70 feet below London that was the P.M.'s office-bedroom throughout the Blitz. It was protected by 16 feet of concrete, gasproof doors and a steel net designed to catch bombs.

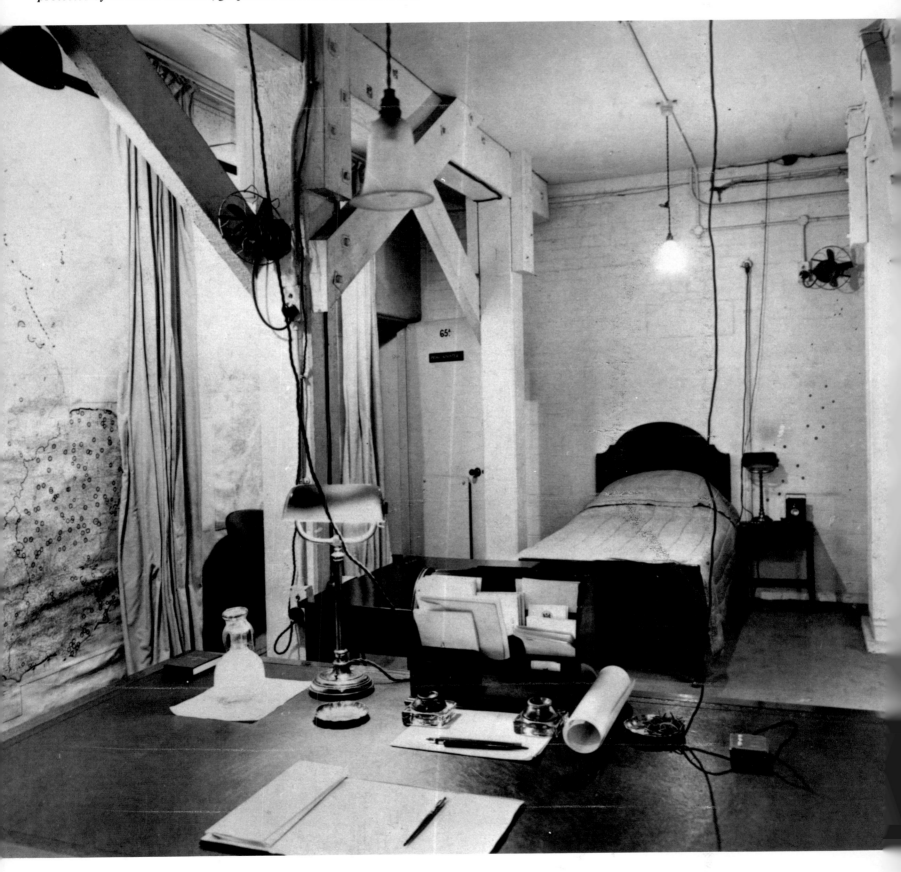

Churchill's personal pressure chamber, created to pressurize the P.M. (to the equivalent of 5,000 feet) on high-altitude flights, is demonstrated by its designer. It was so comfortable and convenient, with its built-in ashtrays and telephone, that Churchill liked to lie in it with his stogie even when the pressure—the chamber's pressure, that is—was off.

Members of the Bristol, Connecticut, ration board mass behind their barricade of ration cards and government directives. From left: Valmore Pilon, a war plant assistant superintendent; Mrs. Claire Hotkoski, housewife and ordnance inspector; Milton C. Richardson, metal forger; board chairman Joseph M. Donovan, lawyer; Christen Wyrtzen, factory superintendent; Mrs. Florence Sanborn, hospital superintendent and diet expert; and office manager John C. Donovan.

Pigs stand on their Seattle packing-plant pen, smashed when a prototype of the B-29, on a test flight from the nearby Boeing airfield, crashed into it, killing the pilot and 10 others on the superbomber's development team.

Lieutenant John Hancock Spear kisses his brand-new bride, Ester, goodbye in New York's Penn Station before returning to Camp Blanding, Florida.

War workers in Detroit's Woodworth plant sit under the dryers in the beauty shop that the company installed to combat absenteeism.

A Curtiss-Wright engineering cadet, Mary Lou Hansen, 19, sketches an engine mount at Rensselaer Polytechnic Institute, hoping to go on to a job with the aircraft manufacturer.

A Mexican-American youth in L Angeles wears a "zoot suit," style popular with some urban civilia but not at all with GIs. Wh servicemen and police in L.A. met in rie with racial overtones, the city ma wearing such garb a misdemean

Meat cuts, marked with Office of Price Administration ceiling prices and ration point values, are displayed on a butcher shop counter.

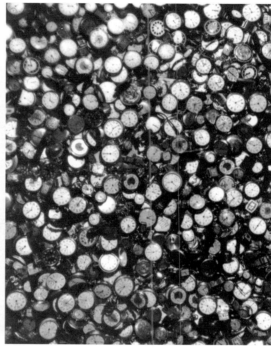

Watches donated to a "Watches for Russia" campaign in Seattle await checking of their condition before being shipped to America's ally.

U.S. Navy Waves, in uniform for the duration, gaze at a model in a nightie at a fashion show in New York City's Ritz-Carlton.

The Army's first all-black combat division, the 93rd, parades at Fort Huachuca, Arizona, after a 25-mile hike in sweltering heat.

The current craze called the Lindy Hop (which had been created by Harlem blacks after Lindbergh's 1927 Atlantic flight) is demonstrated by Stanley Catron and Kaye Popp, young dancers from the Broadway musical Something for the Boys.

The new kid on the block of crooners, Frank Sinatra, sings for 1,600 Waves at their naval training station in New York. A first for young Blue Eyes: there was not a scream or squeal, just the sound of gloved hands clapping. Waves had discipline.

1943

Victory Gardens, Victory Girls

The grounds of Jane Addams High School in Portland, Oregon, get a working over by girl students. Eight thousand square feet of lawn having been turned into a Victory Garden, increasing U.S. agricultural production and providing an object lesson in Home Economics at the same time.

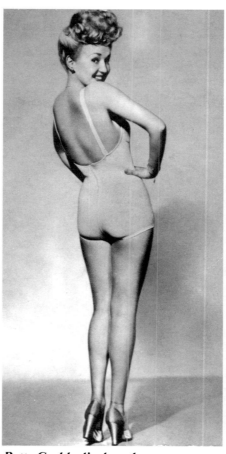

Starlet Chili Williams, appearing in a small picture in LIFE to promote polka dots, not oars, was brought back, full page, by reader demand, to become the magazine's all-time pinup champ.

Betty Grable displays the legs that made her by most counts the No. 1 pinup among U.S servicemen around the world.

In this picture, made at the request of the War Production Board, Veronica Lake's fans got to see both her eyes at the same time. The honey blond movie star, whose trademark hairdo always obscured the right side of her face, was showing war plant workers that long hair and drill bits don't mix, or mix most uncomfortably.

A woman welder at a Gary, Indiana, plant of the U.S. Steel Corp. cuts through a sheet of steel. At Gary alone, women were also employed as grinders, oilers, coil tapers, foundry helpers, loaders, painters, engine and furnace operators, packers, shippers and draw bench operators and held down dozens of other kinds of jobs. Before the war the only women workers in the Gary area were tin-mill sorters.

261

The tremendous importance of the capture of Guadalcanal is apparent from the reconnaissance photograph at left and the map below. Possessing the island's Henderson Airfield made possible the bombing of Rabaul, the keystone of Japan's defense of both the South and the Southwest Pacific, and hence to the Allied island-by-island rollback of its empire. Ever since the Japanese had occupied the immense, volcano-girded natural harbor at the eastern tip of New Britain, they had used its land and sea facilities, along with Truk to the north, as a major base from which to supply their operations on New Guinea, Guadalcanal, Munda and Australia's approaches. The picture at left is the first look that the U.S. had of the huge Japanese base, taken on a long-distance reconnaissance flight in the spring. At the moment the photograph below it was taken, six months later, Flying Fortresses were blasting some 80 ships they had surprised in Simpson Harbor, off the town of Rabaul (see map), and a dozen more in Blanche Bay, between Simpson and Greet Harbor, to the right.

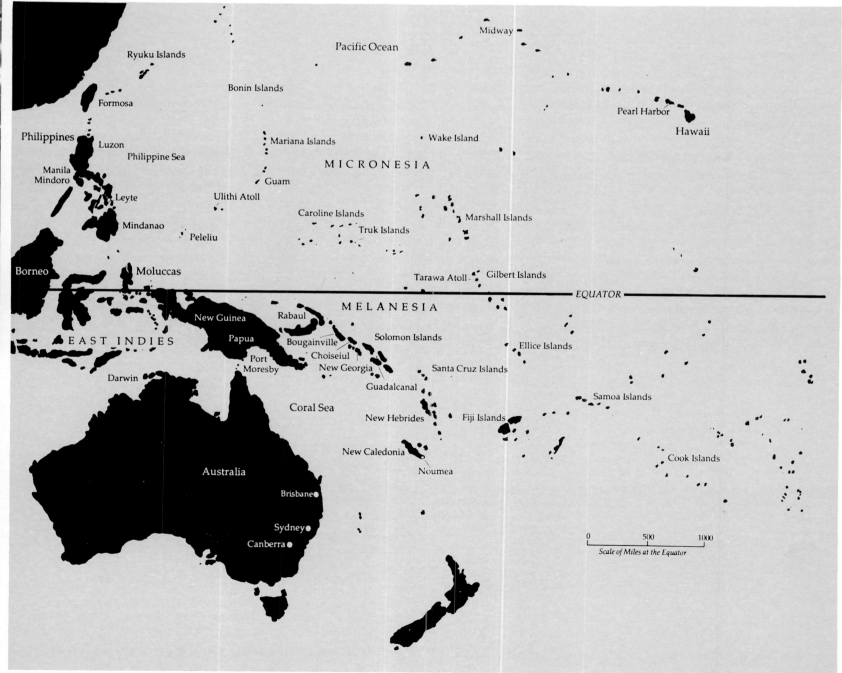

A Hazardous Rescue in Burma

One of the fictionlike stories to come out of the Pacific hostilities—which pointed up the gripe of troops in the China-Burma-India theater that theirs was "the forgotten war"—was the activities of a merry and devastating little band of British marauders assembled by 39-year-old Brigadier Orde Charles Wingate. A Scottish Plato devotee with the strange idea that trained Englishmen, and others from the Raj, could match the Japanese at their highly touted specialty of jungle fighting, he took a second-line Lancashire regiment, added Gurkhas, Kachins, Shans and Burmese, and trained several thousand of them in the Indian jungle. He led them across the Chindwin River into North Burma. "Wingate's Gang," a.k.a. Chindwins, looking like something out of a Warner Bros. spoof of Robin Hood, spread havoc throughout Japanese forces 200 miles inside their lines. Supplied by planes from Assam in India, they destroyed bridges and railways, delaying a Japanese Chindwin offensive and relieving a cut-off Burmese force. An entire division was concerned with destroying this ghost army. It never did.

The crew of a U.S.-made C-47, flying supplies for "Wingate's mob" over Japanese territory, mans machine guns against enemy Zeros. The big transport made a hazardous landing 170 miles inside Burma and brought out 17 sick and wounded Chindits, Wingate raiders named after the ferocious stone lions that guard Burmese temples. Without this successful rescue mission they would almost surely have died at the hands of the Japanese.

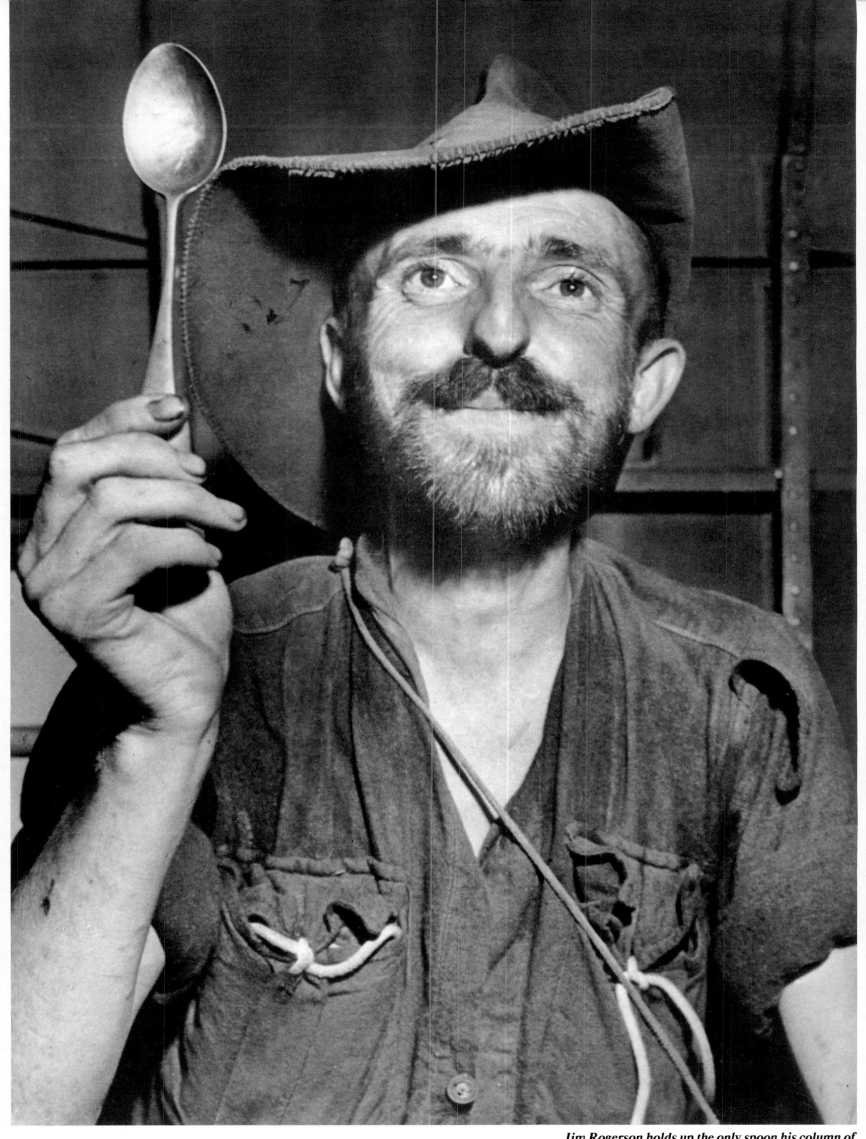

Jim Rogerson holds up the only spoon his column of Chindits had left after its hazardous mission.

1943
The Real Bridge over the River Kwai

Deceptively primitive-looking bamboo scaffolding sheathes the huge bridge of concrete and steel being built by POW laborers across the main Khwae Noi, or River Kwai, bridge in

Thailand. The span, which actually crossed the
Mae Klong River just above its juncture with
the Kwai, was the prototype of the one in Pierre
Boule's novel and the subsequent Columbia movie.

An early lesson on the road back is learned by green U.S. troops, hip-deep in the surf of Butaritari Island in Makin Atoll as they wade toward enemy oil dumps hit by naval gunfire. Although they had 20-to-1 superiority and were supported by tanks, they took four days to capture the island and suffered 218 casualties.

U.S. Marines in camouflage fatigues blast a Japanese blockhouse in their painfully slow, yard-by-yard advance across Tarawa's Betio Island.

With Tarawa Finally Won, the Gilberts Are the Allies'

In the bloody eastern phase of Operation Cartwheel, the seizure of the Gilbert Islands (map, far right), Admiral Nimitz brought up the Second Marine Division from New Zealand and elements of the Army's 27th Division, just completing training on Oahu. The green troops drew the landing on lightly held Makin Atoll, the Marines Tarawa. Tarawa's one-square-mile main island, Betio, proved to be the most dearly won battlefield in the Corps' history. Before the November 20 landing, 3,000 tons of bombs and naval gunfire were poured on the little island. But its 4,836 Japanese defenders, dug in be-hind coconut-log pillboxes and concrete blockhouses, poured murderous fire on the invaders. The first wave of Marines swept through the water in new amphibian tractors, but later groups found the water over the reef too shallow and had to wade half a mile of surf through a deadly storm of mortar and machine-gun fire. Nevertheless they piled over the seawall with rifle, bayonet and flamethrower. Over 76 hours the Marines lost 990 killed and 2,296 wounded, but they won the island and put to rest an old Japanese taunt that Americans couldn't fight because they were afraid to die.

A Marine throws a grenade into the smoke of battle. His buddy at right, exhausted, takes a drink although he is open to Japanese snipers from three sides.

Still exposed to enemy fire from several directions, Marines swarm over a blockhouse. This was the only way such redoubts could be taken: by climbing them and firing down on their occupants.

986 MILES
TO SAIPAN

TAONGI

BIKINI   RONGERIK

ENIWETOK

MARSHALL

UJELANG

UJAE   KWAJALEIN   WOTJE

MALOELAP

MAJURO

ISLANDS   ARNO

KUSAIE   JALUIT   MILI

Ocean

Pacific   MAKIN

TARAWA   GILBERT

EQUATOR   ABEMAMA

OCEAN   ISLANDS

0   300
NAUTICAL MILES

Marines march off one of the few
prisoners they took at Tarawa. He had
been stripped to prevent suicide.

Amid the Killing, Astonishing Pictures of Kindness

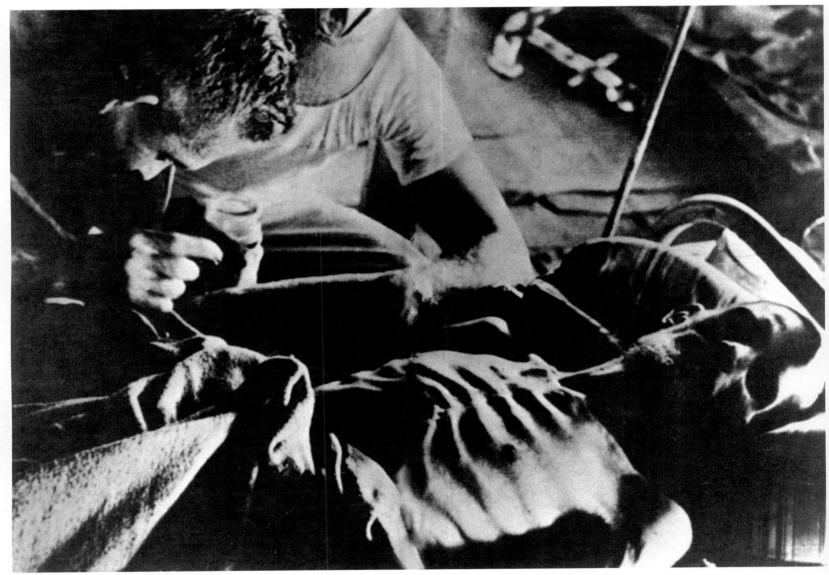

A captured American medic in the Philippines POW camp at Cabanatuan tries to treat an emaciated fellow prisoner. The picture was taken with a homemade camera using X-ray film.

An Aussie infantryman blinded by a shellburst is led from
the New Guinea battlefront near Buna by a Papuan native.

1944 *THE BEGI*

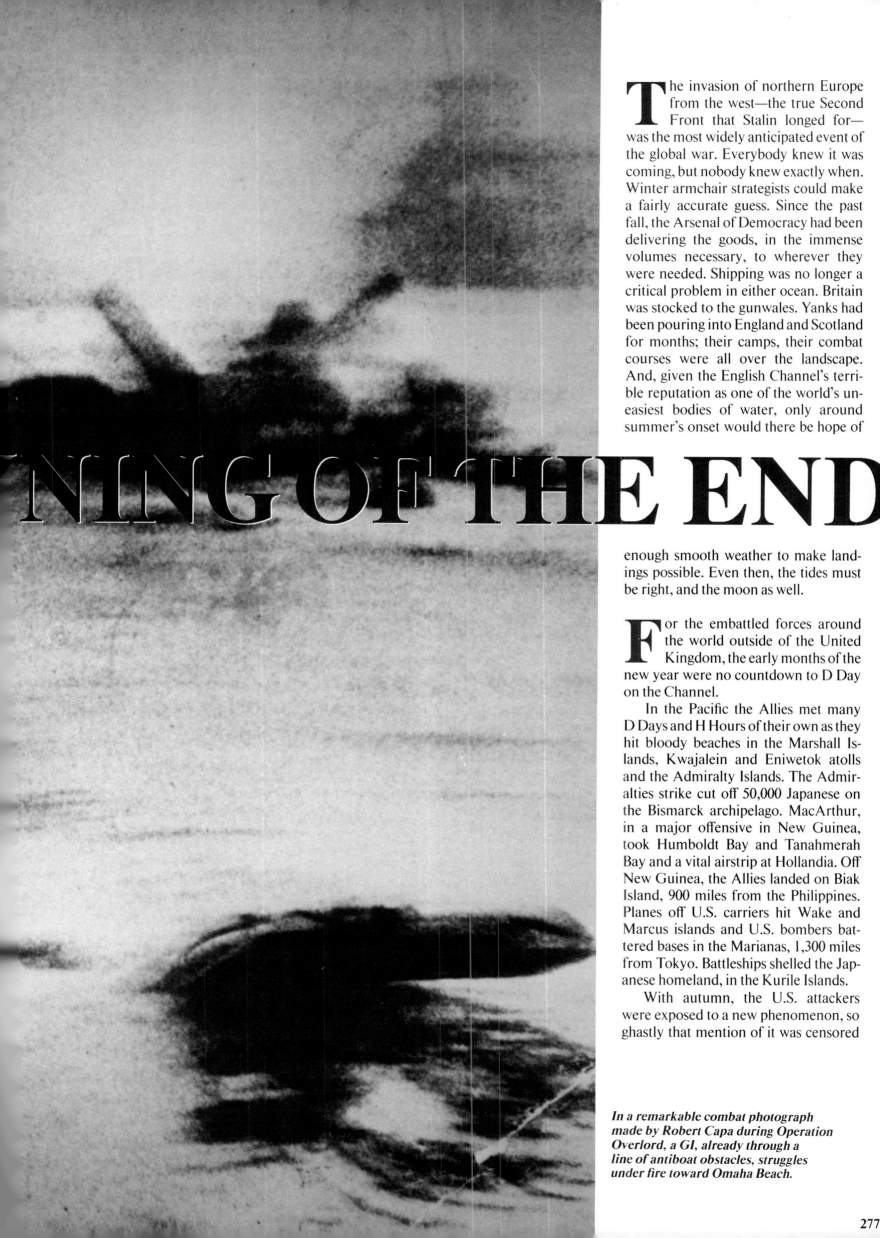

The invasion of northern Europe from the west—the true Second Front that Stalin longed for—was the most widely anticipated event of the global war. Everybody knew it was coming, but nobody knew exactly when. Winter armchair strategists could make a fairly accurate guess. Since the past fall, the Arsenal of Democracy had been delivering the goods, in the immense volumes necessary, to wherever they were needed. Shipping was no longer a critical problem in either ocean. Britain was stocked to the gunwales. Yanks had been pouring into England and Scotland for months; their camps, their combat courses were all over the landscape. And, given the English Channel's terrible reputation as one of the world's uneasiest bodies of water, only around summer's onset would there be hope of enough smooth weather to make landings possible. Even then, the tides must be right, and the moon as well.

For the embattled forces around the world outside of the United Kingdom, the early months of the new year were no countdown to D Day on the Channel.

In the Pacific the Allies met many D Days and H Hours of their own as they hit bloody beaches in the Marshall Islands, Kwajalein and Eniwetok atolls and the Admiralty Islands. The Admiralties strike cut off 50,000 Japanese on the Bismarck archipelago. MacArthur, in a major offensive in New Guinea, took Humboldt Bay and Tanahmerah Bay and a vital airstrip at Hollandia. Off New Guinea, the Allies landed on Biak Island, 900 miles from the Philippines. Planes off U.S. carriers hit Wake and Marcus islands and U.S. bombers battered bases in the Marianas, 1,300 miles from Tokyo. Battleships shelled the Japanese homeland, in the Kurile Islands.

With autumn, the U.S. attackers were exposed to a new phenomenon, so ghastly that mention of it was censored

In a remarkable combat photograph made by Robert Capa during Operation Overlord, a GI, already through a line of antiboat obstacles, struggles under fire toward Omaha Beach.

277

D Days in Mountains, Islands, Jungles and One of the World's Uneasiest C

This map, drawn from the perspective of an eye looking southeast, from Wales across the Cornwall peninsula toward Normandy and the invasion beaches of Overlord, shows the routes of the British, Canadian and U.S. forces from their various staging areas.

for six months: noble death for emperor and homeland. On October 19, at a Japanese staff meeting on Luzon, the desperate new tactic was hatched. Called Kamikaze, or Divine Wind, after the typhoon that did away with Mongol invaders seven centuries before, specially picked pilots were now asked to ride their bomb-laden Zeros right down into their targets, on the principle of one life for many—in the case of carrier attackers sometimes one life for hundreds. On Saipan, the first invaded island with a Japanese populace, U.S. Marines had already encountered a less official, civilian version of the noble-death philosophy: many Japanese trapped on its northern point deliberately committed suicide by walking into the sea.

On the other side of the world, the Red Army, with no thought for D Day, cracked Wehrmacht lines in a mighty winter offensive. It hacked its way back through the Ukraine, liberated Odessa and cut off 100,000 Germans in the Crimea on its way to recapturing the great naval base Sevastopol, after a 24-day siege. It fought all the way to Hunga-

ry as its armies in the north, chasing the Nazis out of Russia, crossed the old Polish border.

In the Mediterranean theater, the Allies struggling north toward Rome found that the strategists' picture of Italy as "the soft underbelly of *Festung Europa*" was a misconception. Their every move toward the open city was controversial. They had bitten off a chunk of topography far beyond their powers of mastication. The land was nothing but mountains. Field Marshal Albert Kesselring could choose just which peaks and valleys he wanted to defend—and he defended them with troops trained in mountain warfare. General Harold Alexander's forces—the U.S. Fifth Army on the left flank, the British Eighth on the right—were flatland troops right to their combat boots. In two months of battle before the Winter Line along the rugged valley of the Rapido River, General Mark Clark's Fifth had ground out just eight miles—measured horizontally—at a cost of 15,930 casualties. With Eisenhower,

Omar Bradley, Montgomery and Arthur Tedder having left Italy before the new year to plan the Normandy invasion, GIs, using the same language as their brethren in Burma, called their campaign "the forgotten war." Said General John P. Lucas, Clark's boss: "I hope I never see a mountain again as long as I live."

The Allied commanders halted at Cassino, a small town on the Rapido before the 1,700-foot abbey-crowned fastness of Monte Cassino, decided that the 6th century Benedictine monastery was being used as a German observation post and must be destroyed. On February 15, 255 Allied bombers hit the sanctuary and thousands of rounds of heavy artillery helped blast its upper structure to powder. The Germans who moved into the rubble-strewn remains of the 10-foot-thick lower walls easily turned back the New Zealand and Indian infantrymen who scrabbled up the mountainside below them. A month later, 564 bombers dumped 1,110 tons and artillery fired 195,969 rounds of high explosives to similar avail. The planes that failed to dislodge the mountain defenders finally severed Kesselring's supply lines and, as tough Polish troops made it up to the fortress ruin, he withdrew from the rubble pile that was Cassino. Allied troops who in another controversial bit of tactics had stormed ashore at Anzio to outflank the Cassino Germans and then had been pinned down within a 135-mile perimeter for 123 days broke out in time to join forces with the Cassino victors. The conquerors entered the Eternal City to the cheers of many Romans.

Long before H Hour, 6:30 a.m. on Tuesday, June 6, perilously close on the heels of a violent storm that had postponed it for two nail-biting nights, Eisenhower's Operation Overlord had thousands of men afloat and in the sky. The first paratroops hit the silk over Normandy shortly after midnight. The assault troops, who had been in their assorted landing craft all night, leaped into the boiling surf at their appointed time. The plan was to land, under cover of intensive air and naval bombardment, on the beaches of the Seine estuary, storm the bluffs and cut off the port of Cherbourg on the Cotentin Peninsula, where a stream of men and matériel could flow in to roll back the Wehrmacht. Even aside from the fact that troops untried in combat were pitted against the world's most experienced fighting force, the logistics of the operation were forbidding. The planners tried to anticipate every contingency. To assure a usable port, complete floating harbors fabricated in Britain were put into place even as infantrymen splashed up the five beaches (from west to east,

Utah and Omaha were American; Gold, British; Juno, Canadian; and Sword, British). Concrete caissons and metal pontoons towed across the Channel were sunk to form breakwaters that protected supply points. Prefabricated fuel pipelines were dropped on the bottom. The green troops were equal to their task. By 7:30, despite breakers, shallow-water military obstructions and German gunfire, two regiments and some tanks were ashore at Utah. (At Omaha, and even more at Gold, Juno and Sword, farther east, the remains of the storm swamped tanks and made unloading difficult.) By the weekend all the beachheads were consolidated and the Allies were moving inland.

The invasion's essential strategy had been laid out at the conferences in 1943 (Stalin carried out his Tehran promise by launching an offensive in Karelia even as the Omaha and Utah Beach Americans were joining forces), but even without air superiority the Wehrmacht made the going tough and slow south of the Cotentin Peninsula. Cherbourg—after a week's siege—and St.-Lô were the U.S. First Army's and the British had what was left of Caen, but moving through Normandy was a hedgerow-to-hedgerow firefight. After the Allies had liberated Paris, the Americans closed on Bordeaux, the last German pocket in France, and the Wehrmacht headed east.

The Allies raced eastward too, liberating northern France and the Low Countries—up to the Holland sites of the Führer's new V (for Vengeance) rocket weapons and the German border. Americans, buoyed by news of MacAr-

thur's return to the Philippines, started thinking that the war was almost over.

In October "Bull" Halsey and his fleet did battle with the Japanese imperial navy in history's greatest naval engagement. Even though errors abounded on either side, when the smoke cleared, the battle for Leyte Gulf had crippled the Japanese navy to such an extent that it would never be a factor during the nine months of fighting left. More island triumphs followed and offensive strikes at the Japanese homeland should have proved to the enemy that the war was lost. But the Japanese people were not told of their ever more hopeless position and those who ran the war would rather die than give up. The war was still anything but over.

It still had time to run in Europe, too. The Germans, on their own soil, were a different kind of enemy. The First Army fought through the Ardennes, then battled for 10 weeks through the fir-shrouded Huertgen Forest into the Saar Basin. As winter loomed, gains were being measured in yards. When the First, along with the U.S. Ninth and the British Second, were bearing down on Cologne and the Ruhr Valley, the Wehrmacht opened a huge counteroffensive in the Ardennes. With three armies in the north and two in the south of the 450-mile front, the Germans pushed a 50-mile salient into the hard-won Allied territory. At year's end, with wintry skies limiting the Army Air Force's operations, Patton's Fourth Armored Division was fighting to relieve the all-but-encircled forces, in the Battle of the Bulge.

With bandages covering wounds he received during the invasion of Leyte, a U.S. officer lies on a cot while Mass is sung in a Leyte church converted into a hospital.

CHRONOLOGY 1944

January

2
• U.S. lands at Saidor, New Guinea

5-15
• Battle of the Rapido

6
• Allies attack Monte Cassino
• San Vittore falls to U.S.

8
• Reds capture Kirovograd

9-15
• Chinese take Kantan in North Burma

13
• 1,400 U.S. bombers destroy three German aircraft factories

16
• Ike becomes supreme commander of Allies in Europe

21
• U.S. repulsed at Rapido River

22
• Allies land at Anzio

24
• Hitler orders troops to hold Gustav Line at all cost

25
• Allied raid on Rabaul destroys 83 Japanese planes

27
• Blockade of Leningrad lifted

28
• Germans contain Anzio beachhead

29
• USS Missouri, world's greatest battleship, launched

31
• U.S. landing on Kwajalein in Marshall Islands

February

1
• Gestapo chief in Poland assassinated

3
• Reds surround 66,000 Germans in Ukraine

7
• Heavy Russian bombing of Helsinki

8
• Reds take Nikopol
• Kwajalein secured

12
• Allies halted at Cassino

15
• Cassino leveled

16-19
• Heavy fighting at Anzio

17-21
• U.S. invades Eniwetok in Marshall Islands

18
• U.S. demolishes Japanese installations at Truk
• Reds take Staraya Russa

20-25
• Intensive USAAF raids throughout Germany

21
• Tojo takes direct command of Japanese army

22
• Large U.S. carrier force attacks Saipan and Tinian

23
• U.S. bombers hit Mariana bases 1,300 miles from Tokyo

25
• Merrill's Marauders fight Japanese in North Burma

29
• U.S. cuts off 50,000 on Bismarck archipelago

30
• U.S. battleships shell Kuriles

March

2
• Chindit force crosses Chindwin River

4
• U.S. bombs Berlin for first time

6-29
• Japanese counterattack on Bougainville repulsed

6
• Japanese drive on Imphal in India invasion

15
• Japan invades India

15-23
• Germans repulse Allies at Anzio

17
• U.S. bombs Vienna

19
• Germans buckle under Red push in Ukraine
• Germans invade Hungary

22
• Tojo tells Diet that situation is "truly grave"

23
• Red breakthrough near Tarnopol

24
• Bloody Gestapo reprisal in Rome
• Japanese routed at Bougainville
• General Wingate killed in Burma crash

30
• U.S. fleet attacks Palan
• Hitler relieves von Manstein and von Kleist

31
• Japanese surround Merrill force in North Burma

April

1
• SS kills 86 French civilians in reprisal for train sabotage

2
• Russians enter Rumania
• Imphal isolated

8
• Reds launch Crimean offensive

9
• Admiralty Islands secured

10
• Reds recapture Odessa in Ukraine

13
• Reds cut off 100,000 Germans in Crimea

15
• Reds take Tarnopol in Ukraine

16
• Reds take Yalta

19
• Japanese begin offensive in Honan region of China

22
• MacArthur in major New Guinea offensive

27
• Hollandia area of New Guinea secured

29
• U.S. attacks Truk

30
• Tito wants Allies to recognize him as Yugoslav chief

May

1
• Conference of Commonwealth P.M.s opens in London

4
• Aitape section of New Guinea secured

8-9
• Reds recapture Sevastopol

11
• Allies drive for Rome against Gustav Line

13
• Hitler okays withdrawal from Russia

17-20
• U.S. takes Wake Island

18
• Allies capture Cassino

23
• Allies break out at Anzio

27
• Allies land on Biak Island in New Guinea

Strategic bombing interrupted most of month for coming invasion

June

4
• Allies take Rome

5-6
• Allied glider landings behind Normandy lines

6
• D Day
• U.S. planners set Oct. 1, 1945, as date for Japan invasion

9
• Soviets attack Finland

10
• Nazis kill all 642 in French village of Oradour-sur-Glane in reprisal for capture of SS officer

11
• U.S. carrier planes attack Japanese bases on Saipan, Tinian, Guam, Palau

12
• Mao Tse-tung says he will support Chiang Kai-shek

13
• First V-1 hits London

15
• First Superfortress raid on Japan hits Tokyo
• U.S. lands on Saipan

18
• Reds pierce Mannerheim Line

19-20
• Battle of Philippine Sea, Japanese defeated

21
• 1,000 Allied bombers, 1,200 fighters over Berlin

23
• Reds break through German lines in central Russia

27
• U.S. forces take Cherbourg

28
• Republican Convention in Chicago nominates Dewey

■ **War in Europe**   ■ **War in Asia**   ▨ **U.S.A.**

280

July	August	September	October	November	December
2-6 • *U.S. takes Noemfoor Island in New Guinea* **3** • *Allies take Siena* • *Recapture of Minsk* **8** • *British take Caen, France* **13** • *Saipan secured* **16** • *U.S. attack on St.-Lô opens* **18** • *Yanks take St.-Lô* **19** • *Tojo Cabinet resigns* **20** • *German officers' attempt to kill Hitler fails* • *Battle for Florence begins* **21** • *Marines land on Guam* **24** • *Marines land on Tinian* **25** • *Allies begin breakout of Normandy* **26** • *Strategy conference in Hawaii* **27** • *Reds take Lvov*	**1** • *Patton breaks out of Normandy beachhead into Brittany* • *Polish Resistance army rises up against Germans in Warsaw* **6-10** • *Germans counter at Avranches* **8** • *Japanese take Hengyang in China* **10** • *Guam completely recaptured* • *Fierce resistance in Warsaw* • *U.S. planes bomb Nagasaki* **11** • *Allies take Florence* **14** • *Invasion of southern France begins* **16** • *With monsoon assistance Japanese driven out of India* **18** • *Reds reach German border* **21** • *60,000 Germans trapped in Argentan-Falaise pocket* **23** • *Rumania surrenders to Soviets* **25** • *Allies liberate Paris* • *Rumanian army surrenders to Reds* **28** • *Allies take Marseilles*	**1** • *Soviets take Bucharest; Dieppe liberated* **2** • *Allies take Pisa* **3** • *Allies take Lyon* **4** • *Finland makes peace with Russia* • *Antwerp liberated* **5** • *Allies take Brussels* • *Soviets declare war on Bulgaria* **8** • *First V-2 hits England* • *Reds and Bulgaria make peace; Bulgaria declares war on Germany* **10** • *Allies take Luxembourg* **10-16** • *Second Quebec conference* **15** • *RAF damages Tirpitz off Norway* • *U.S. forces land on Peleliu in Palau Islands* **16** • *F.D.R. agrees to redirect war effort to Pacific* **17-26** • *Disastrous U.S. landings in Holland* **21** • *U.S. carrier planes hit Manila area* **25** • *In Germany, teenagers and old men are drafted* **27** • *After two weeks hard fighting, Allies give up Arnhem pocket*	**2** • *Germans put down last of Warsaw uprising* **5** • *British land on Greek mainland* **9-10** • *Third Moscow conference* **12** • *Peleliu secured* **12-16** • *Battle off Formosa* **14** • *Liberation of Athens* **15** • *On orders from Hitler, Rommel kills himself* **20** • *Battle of Leyte starts invasion of Philippines* **21** • *U.S. takes Aachen* **23-26** • *Japanese thoroughly beaten in Battle for Leyte Gulf* **25** • *MacArthur wades ashore at Leyte*	**5** • *B-29s pound Singapore* **7** • *F.D.R. elected President for fourth term* **12** • *Japanese convoy destroyed off Leyte* • *Tirpitz sunk* **18** • *Allies break into Saar Basin* **22** • *U.S. captures Metz* **23** • *U.S. captures Strasbourg* **24** • *From Saipan, B-19s hit Tokyo by daylight* **30** • *Soviet breakthrough in southern Hungary*	**3** • *Civil war begins in Greece* **8** • *Biggest U.S. air raid on Iwo Jima* **10** • *In Philippines, U.S. takes Limon and Ormoc* • *Japanese offensive in China ends* **15** • *In Philippines, U.S. lands on Mindaro* **16** • *Germans counterattack in Ardennes as Battle of Bulge starts* **24** • *Soviets surround Budapest* **25** • *In Philippines, Leyte secured* **28** • *Ledo-Burma road linking China and Burma completed* **31** • *Battle of the Bulge rages*

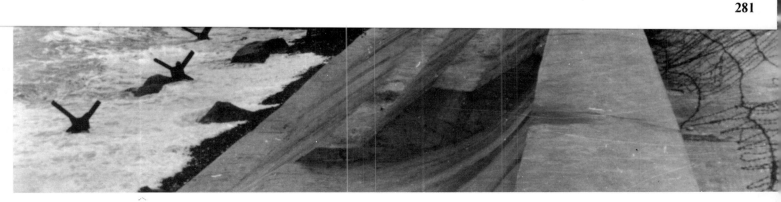

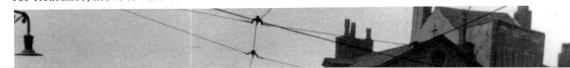

Traffic is heavy in Liverpool as U.S. P-51 fighters, wingtips removed for clearance, move toward an air base to be readied for Overlord.

More than two years before the invasion, its planners had re-

1944

Three Million Troops Stand Ready

THE ENEMY

"YOU ARE ABOUT TO EMBARK UPON A GREAT CRUSADE"

—EISENHOWER TO THE ALLIED FORCES, JUNE 6

What is this crusade?

It is a crusade against a man, a gang, a nation and an idea which have threatened and still threaten the life and hopes of our Western civilization. These ideas, this gang, this man, with their grip on that nation, cannot live in the same world with us. It is we or they.

In this crisis let us remind ourselves that our Western civilization depends for its life on three great beliefs. We believe that every human soul is sacred, whether small or great, and that the birthright of every man is freedom. The Nazis deny it. We believe that men can best govern themselves through laws and live peaceably together by obeying these laws or lawfully changing them. The Nazis deny it. We believe that man was given the power to reason, and therefore owes his fellow man the duty to be reasonable all around the borders of his faith. The Nazis deny it and have moreover buried all civilized faith beneath a mass of tribal superstition. This tribal superstition gives them a sanction in their own mad, ambitious minds to commit any wickedness, from the torture of defenseless flesh to the planned conquest and enslavement of the world. Our crusade is that of Western civilization which is fighting for its life.

Why is America involved in this crusade? Because we are a part of Western civilization and because our nation, too, is in danger.

THE MAD GERMAN DREAM

It is not a joke nor an exaggeration that the Germans wished and wish to rule the world. Some of them have wished it and planned for it since 1890, the year of the founding of the worldwide Pan-German League. Pan-Germans believed with Fichte that Germans are "the people who are entitled to rule the earth."

Schemes like this were in the mind of Wilhelm II. They are in the minds of the Prussian militarists who have been the ruling class of Germany for over 50 years. Schemes like this are in the mind of Hitler.

Hitler, in fact, took these old schemes and made them the daydreams of the whole nation. He rose to power by dinning in the German ear the notion that all Germans are chained supermen, victims of a "plutodemocratic" plot. He made daydreaming a national habit. Were Europe alone left under Hitler's heel, it would be a base for the same fantastic German imperialism at some future opportunity. The American nation, without allies, is not safe against a tyrant who commands all Europe. That is one reason—a rea-

son of power politics and self-defense—why we Americans are fighting Germans.

The Nazi system must expand or die. Its expansion threatens not only our American security, but the American democratic political system. "There is no such thing as security for any nation—or any individual—in a world ruled by the principles of gangsterism," said President Roosevelt. "Gangsterism" is a precise description of the Nazi political methods and beliefs, which are not beliefs but their opposite: nihilism. America has known gangsters, but never one who operated on a world stage.

For this stage, Hitler transmuted the simple gangster's lust of money and power into a mystical nationalism. He asks his Germans to fight for no more rational purpose than national self-assertion. Comprehensible things like loot, women and slaves are offered as mere by-products of conquest. The motive, the inspiration is a fanatical zeal which finds as much pleasure in war as in peace, as much fulfillment in dying as in life.

We believe in reason and in life, not in unreason and death. That is another reason why we fight Germans.

A TRIBE IS AMOK

For 5,000 years great prophets and thinkers of all lands have tried to mitigate the curse of Earth: man's injustice to his fellow man. For nearly 2,000 years we of western Christendom have made slow, painful but steady headway toward that end. All our religious doctrine and most of our rational reflection have taught us that all men are brothers, equal in the sight of God and entitled to an equal chance to prove themselves in life. Said Hitler, "We are not out against the hundred and one different sects of Christianity, but against Christianity itself." And he has proved it! The Nazi state can and does sterilize whomever it sees fit to sterilize. In addition to the Nuremberg anti-Semitic laws, it can forbid any marriage which its minions think may contaminate the purity of the so-called Aryan *Volk*. This master race, when purified, is to be a race of Nietzschean heroes, to which all other races are inferior. A permanent caste system in continental Europe is a professed part of Hitler's New Order, as it would eventually be a part of his plan for the world. Frenchmen, Poles, Norwegians, Belgians, imported by the millions to work in the Reich, already know what this slavery means.

Where most Americans would fit in this international caste system has never been made quite clear. It will never be made clear.

Our American blood is generously mixed, and to avoid the ignominy of having to unmix it is another reason why we fight.

Rational and humane people throughout the world are arrayed against Hitler and his nation. Since this is so, it is often supposed that the Germans will suddenly realize the hopelessness of their cause, awake from their dream, collapse. They have not collapsed and will not until they are beaten. The world's enmity does not scare them; it adds to the ferocity with which they fight. For the Germans have scuttled their rational and humane impulses and replaced them with the superstitions of a tribe. No instinct other than primitive tribalism can explain or sustain so much nonsense, defiance and cruelty as the Germans have shown.

They have defied all law and the very concept of law, human, international, and divine. They have taught their youth false anthropology, false economics, false geography, false history, false religion. They have corrupted science itself by forcing it to serve other ends than truth. Without warning they attacked Austria, Czechoslovakia, Poland, Norway, the Lowlands, Yugoslavia, Greece, Russia. To win and to rule they have revived barbaric cruelties and invented refinements of them. Throughout their fear-ruled empire they have killed hostages, uprooted civil populations, looted, raped and burned.

In Lidice near Prague the 1,200 inhabitants were suspected of sheltering the killers of Reinhard Heydrich. In June 1942 the Nazis shot every man in Lidice, sent every woman to a concentration camp and razed every building in Lidice to the ground. They have given the same treatment to seven other Polish cities, in cold blood.

When the Nazis entered Warsaw in September 1939, they gave each German soldier 24 hours for looting. At a hospital in Starotitarovskaya in Russia they bled 40 children to death to supply their own blood bank. They dive-bombed Rotterdam after it had surrendered. They have systematically starved Greece. They have sent trainload after trainload of Jews to the Belzec Crematory near Lwow, where they are electrocuted en masse, then burned. It is not mere passion; it is according to plan. Wrote Herr Werner Best, a Nazi theoretician, "Historical experience has shown that the destruction and elimination of a foreign nationality is not in the least against the laws of life, provided that destruction and elimination are completed."

There will be neither peace, nor freedom, nor good feeling in the world until these people are at our mercy. There can be no room for mercy until then.

Yanks preparing for the cross-Channel adventure march briskly along an English country road. Above is the editorial LIFE published at the time of the invasion.

Finishing Touches by the Commander in Chief

Ike watches units in last-minute maneuvers.

The Commander in Chief chats with paratroopers of the 101st Airborne Division, their faces already in their night invasion camouflage, before they depart from their base near Newbury to attack heavily fortified emplacements in Normandy.

The Supreme Commander, having made his decision on the delicate timing of the invasion, had no qualms about it, even though the weather made it necessary to postpone it to almost the last possible minute. But realizing how many men would die in it, he was deeply concerned about his troops. His goal, as the countdown to H Hour proceeded, was to speak to every unit in the invasion. He moved among them listening intently to the stories and jokes with which they covered up their apprehensions. It bucked up their morale, and morale, he told his aides, "is supreme on the battlefield." At the jump-off, as the transports and landing craft plowed across the Channel behind 200 protective minesweepers, radios blared forth his order of the day: "You are about to embark upon a great crusade . . . Good luck! And let us all beseech the blessing of almighty God upon this great and noble undertaking."

A motorized artillery unit moves up the ramps of cavernous landing vessels.

1944
Hitting Omaha Beach

GIs jump into the surf from an LCT and start wading toward the tank obstacles and barbed wire of the section of Omaha Beach called Easy Red. The area was relatively lightly defended, but by day's end, when Omaha's beaches had been cleared, the attackers, the First Division, veterans of Africa and Sicily, and the 29th National Guard Division had suffered 3,000 casualties. Left: a landing craft bearing Canadian infantrymen plows toward a horizon virtually obscured by columns of the invasion fleet.

D Day

Robert Capa photographed the invasion for LIFE. *His description of D Day appeared in his book* Images of War. *In 1954 Capa was killed in Indochina on another* LIFE *assignment.*

At 4 a.m. we were assembled on the open deck of the USS *Chase.* The invasion barges were swinging on the cranes, ready to be lowered. Waiting for the first ray of light, the two thousand men stood in perfect silence; whatever they were thinking, it was some kind of prayer . . . I too stood very quietly. I was thinking a little bit of everything; of green fields, pink clouds, grazing sheep, all the good times, and very much of getting the best pictures of the day . . . The first-wavers stumbled into their barges, and—as if on slow-moving elevators—we descended into the sea. The sea was rough and we were wet before our barge pushed away from the mother ship . . . In no time the men started to puke . . . The coast of Normandy was still miles away when the first unmistakable popping reached our listening ears. We ducked down in the puky water in the bottom of the barge and ceased to watch the approaching coast line . . . It was now light enough to start taking pictures, and I brought my first Contax camera out of its waterproof oilskin. The flat bottom of our barge hit the earth of France. The boatswain lowered the steel-covered barge front, and there, between the grotesque designs of steel obstacles sticking out of the water, was a thin line of sand covered with smoke—our Europe, the "Easy Red" beach . . . My beautiful France looked sordid and uninviting, and a German machine gun, spitting bullets around the barge, fully spoiled my return. The men from my barge waded in the water. Waist deep, with rifles ready to shoot, with the invasion obstacles and the smoking beach in the background—this was good enough for the photographer. I paused for a moment on the gangplank to take my first real picture of the invasion. The boatswain who was in an understandable hurry to get the hell out of there, mistook my picture-taking attitude for explicable hesitation, and helped me make up my mind with a well-aimed kick in the rear. The water was cold and the beach still more than a hundred yards away. The bullets tore in the water around me, and I made for the nearest steel obstacle . . . It was still very early and very gray for good pictures, but the gray water and the gray sky made the little men, dodging under the surrealistic designs of Hitler's anti-invasion brain trust, very effective . . . Seven days later, I learned that the pictures I had taken on "Easy Red" were the best of the invasion. But the excited darkroom assistant, while drying the negatives, had turned on too much heat and the emulsions had melted and run down before the eyes of the London office. Out of one hundred and six pictures in all, only eight were salvaged.

Slogging ashore at Omaha with the First Infantry Division's 16th Regiment, Capa, shooting before any of his companions start firing, captures on film a GI's fall.

Second-wave riflemen pinned down by German gunfire at H Hour plus 1 huddle in heavy surf behind beach obstacles.

First-wave attackers exchange fire with the Wehrmacht from behind a thicket of long logs implanted in the sand bottom to halt invasion craft.

A disabled U.S. amphibious tank and the Germans' own beach obstacles provide GIs with cover from murderous enemy fire.

1944
Why It Was the Longest Day

Commandos of the British Fourth Brigade take cover and concealment from German mortar fire on a smoke-hazed road at St. Aubin.

Wehrmacht troops surrender to GIs battling toward Cherbourg on D Day plus 3.

Normandy fishermen gaze at American dead, assembled amid the ruins of battle on Omaha Beach to be transported to England.

An LCT, having put ashore its load of tanks, shuttles back to the attack transports with a cargo of U.S. wounded.

The first dead of the invasion are placed in white bags and laid in neat rows on a U.S. hospital ship that will take them to England for burial.

'These Dummkopfs, Thank God They Have Finally Made a Landing'

One thing that worked to the Allies' advantage was the division in the German general staff about where the landings would come. Gerd von Rundstedt, Hitler's commander in chief in the west, believed they would be in the Somme-Calais area; Rommel, now the commander in France under Rundstedt, felt, as did Hitler, that Normandy would be the target. The old Fox started months before the invasion to build up Normandy's coastal defenses, making the "Atlantic Wall" for the first time more than a myth. Von Rundstedt planned to trap the invaders ashore, then blow them away with a massive counterattack. Rommel insisted they be stopped in the water.

They worked out a compromise: infantry was moved forward, armor back. Rommel's men, firing big guns from cliffs up to 200 feet high, wreaked havoc on the beach and sea approaches of Omaha, making that sector a scene of terror and frustration—and heroism—for the invaders.

To play down the inadequacy of the general staff's strategic intelligence, Hitler, when he was being briefed on D Day, before staff and Axis visitors, about the actual sites of the landings, said, "These Dummkopfs, thank God they have finally made a landing."

On July 20, a group of German army officers tried to kill the Führer in his bunker at his field headquarters. Although Operation Valkyrie was well organized, it failed through a mischance at the last minute: an officer kicked over the briefcase containing the bomb at Hitler's side. Four men died, but the Führer lived. He ordered an investigation throughout the Wehrmacht. Himmler's SS executed nearly 5,000 soldiers and civilians. For the top eight conspirators, Hitler ordered especially painful deaths. "I want them hung up like carcasses of meat," he said. His order was carried out precisely by the SS. The executioners looped nooses of thin cord around the culprits' necks and hoisted them so that they slowly strangled. Hitler never trusted the army again: he more than ever relied on the SS.

On D Day morning, in a castle near his Berchtesgaden HQ, Hitler and air chief Göring are briefed on the Normandy landings by General Alfred Jodl. Center: the Führer visits an aide wounded in the assassination attempt a few weeks later. Far right: the death chamber at Plötzensee prison. On the meathooks at rear the strangling plotters who tried to kill Hitler were impaled.

A week after D Day, Omaha Beach still bustles with newly landed troops and machines being staged to move to the battlefronts. Barrage balloons cannot yet be dispensed with.

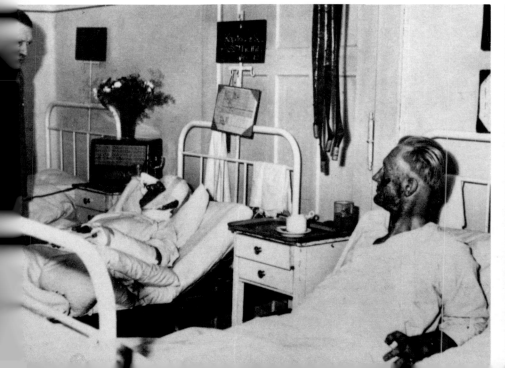

BATTLEFRONTS: ITALY   *Cassino Resembles the Ruins of an Earthquak*

The battle for Cassino, the town, began January 16. The U.S. Fifth and the British Eighth armies, having inched their way north from Naples for months, had reached the Rapido. In their first attack they crossed the river but were driven back. In the second they crossed again and tried to capture a steep-sided hill surmounted by a monastery but never got to the top. The third try started with an artillery and bomber barrage that reduced the town to rubble. The artillery occupied three-quarters of the ruins but Kesselring's *Alpenjaeger* clung to strong points in the higher sections and artillery positions on the mountainside from which they could blast all the Allied positions. It was a textbook example of mountain warfare, and the Allies had neither the textbook nor the mountaineering skills needed for the job. "The simple fact is that the Germans stopped us," Secretary of War Henry Stimson said, summing up the fiasco. Combined with the inability of the Allies to expand their Anzio beachhead, it disillusioned many back in the States about the whole Italian campaign.

From a knoll in the Liri Valley, three infantrymen of a U.S.-Canadian task force cover a patrol of their buddies.

Allied bombers and artillery combine their destructive power to pulverize Cassino in their third massive attack. This view looks across the Rapido River toward the local landmark, Castle Hill, and other foothills of 1,700-foot Monte Cassino. The destruction of the town was of no help in driving the mountain-trained Germans out of the abbey, on the summit far above this scene.

1944
Surrender in Rome, Retreat from Florence

As the Allies close on the open city of Rome, armed Germans with fear-filled faces surrender to an American sergeant. Berlin propaganda had told them that when Americans did take captives they treated them brutally.

American Martin B-26 bombers hit military targets in German-occupied Florence. Despite the fliers' care in "pinpoint" bombing raids, many art treasures near such targets were destroyed.

The shattered remains of the Ponte di Santa Trinità across the Arno, Michelangelo's gift to his native city, often called the world's most graceful bridge, are shrouded with smoke from explosive charges laid by the retiring Germans. Though they pledged to respect the city's artistic riches, the Wehrmacht blasted Florence's trove of beautiful bridges, all but the Ponte Vecchio. They blew up the approaches at both ends of the old structure.

BATTLEFRONTS: RUSSIA *Victory After Victory Lights Up the Moscow*

When the Red Army won a victory at the front, Moscow saluted it with rockets and guns. Right from the year's outset, as the early course of the war was reversed to a westward chase, combat scenes like those at left, of Soviet troops driving in on the faltering Wehrmacht at Leningrad and (bottom) chasing the Nazis back across the Ukraine toward the Hungarian border, touched off Muscovite pyrotechnics. Opposite page: how Moscow celebrated the captures of a few cities.

Odessa, April 10, wins a Moscow salute of 24 salvos of red, white and green flares and 324 massed guns. This is Red Square, with the Kremlin at right.

Sevastopol, May 9, gets the same salute as Odessa. At the far end of Red Square is the 16th century Cathedral of St. Basil.

Vitebsk, June 26, a victory in which 31,500 Germans died, is hailed in Pushkin Square, near the International Book House.

Minsk, July 3, warrants a celebration of 24 salvos by 324 guns, seen here in the night sky across the Moscow river. The Kremlin lies beyond.

Polotsk, July 4, the gateway to the Baltic states, is celebrated with flares bursting over the Hotel Moscow. The University of Moscow is at left.

Molodechno, July 5, opening the way to East Prussia, calls forth a skyful of flares that halts a jam of cars on the Moskvoretsky Bridge.

These three pictures are representative of hundreds that were taken during WWII showing the barbarism of the Nazis toward the Polish people. Here a group of citizens are marched down a Warsaw street on their way to concentration camps or execution.

Nazi firing squads like this one mowed down thousands of Poles in villages across the country.

Uprising

A transport filled with Poles, blindfolded and condemned to death, is unloaded by the Germans in the forests of Palmirsk near Warsaw, a favorite killing ground of the Nazis.

As the Red Army rolled westward across Poland and Soviet bombs started falling on Warsaw, Polish partisans attacked the Germans behind their lines. When the Russians reached Lublin, they promoted the creation of a Committee for National Liberation to rival the Polish government in exile based in London. Throughout Poland there was exultation that the Wehrmacht was on the run. This was tempered, however, by the suspicion among many, recalling their history, that Red occupying forces might be no great improvement over the Germans and that the Lublin Committee were Soviet stooges. Among them was General Bor-Komorowski, commander of the Polish resistance, organized by the government in exile. On August 1, when the Red Army was within sight of Warsaw on the other side of the Vistula River, the general called his 40,000-strong Home Army into the streets of the capital to wrest it from the German occupiers. The fight was desperate, casualties mounted, food ran short. On October 3, after 200,000 had died, the fighting ceased. The Red Army had stayed on its side of the river throughout. Reportedly, Stalin was outraged that even some Communists had joined the Home Army and refused to order his soldiers to help the uprising. The Home Army, and with it the leverage of the government in exile, had been eliminated.

Members of the Polish underground army fire from a rubble barricade on a Warsaw street.

BATTLEFRONTS: ENGLAND   *Rocket Bombs and Rocket Guns*

A V-1, in the pregnant silence of the last, motorless seconds of its flight, hurtles toward the English earth.

The V in the designations of the V-1 and V-2 flying bombs that the Germans hurled at England in one more futile attempt to break civilian morale was, in true Hitlerian style, not for Victory but for Vengeance. The first of the *Vergeltungswaffen*, or vengeance weapons, the V-1, was a jet-powered missile that made a lot of noise in achieving its top speed, 400 mph. The terror of the "buzz-bomb," as the Londoners, its first and principal victims, dubbed it, was enhanced by the few seconds of eerie silence between the cutoff of its engines and the blast of the bomb. RAF fighter pilots, although even their latest Spitfires could not match the V-1's speed, developed a technique of diving on them, momentarily exceeding their speed, and exploding them with gunfire or tipping them over so that they crashed. The V-1 killed more than 6,000 and wounded 17,000 before it was replaced with the progenitor of the ballistic missile, the rocket-fired, supersonic V-2, a 12-ton, 46-foot missile with speed up to 4,000 mph. The V-2 caused about twice as many casualties as a V-1, and 1,817 of them were fired at England before their launch sites were captured by the Allies.

An RAF Spitfire pilot edges in on a V-1 and (below) gingerly slides his wingtip under the bomb's wing to tip it into a crash.

A London rescue squad bears a woman through the dust of the V-1 blast that destroyed the bus she was riding in.

A battery of rocket Z-guns lets go at flying bombs attacking London. Rocket artillery was not new, as singers of "The Star-Spangled Banner" are aware, but these were state of the art. They were fairly effective against V-1s, hardly at all against V-2s.

Liberté Returns to France

Kneeling before the ramp of an LST on a tidal flat in France, a soldier of General Jacques Leclerc's French Second Armored Division, dressed in U.S. government issue, scoops up a handful of lovely French silt.

A GI meets a local jeune fille on the hood of a half-track in Chartres. The Americans moved through France with choruses of their fathers' World War I drinking song "Mad'moiselle from Armentières" in their mind's ear, but, racing through the countryside along with the French in a wave of liberation, they seldom had time for more than a hello-goodbye kiss.

1944
The Resistance Clears the Way for De Gaulle

A Resistance fighter fires at snipers on a rooftop near Notre-Dame as a soldier of Leclerc's army dashes to a firing position.

Parisians give an exuberant greeting to the French Second Armored Division rolling into the capital.

Charles de Gaulle's march along the Champs-Elysées at the head of Leclerc's army was the supreme moment for the leader who eight days after the Normandy landing had returned to French soil for the first time since 1940 to start setting up his new government. He and these Free Frenchmen had waited a long time and gone through much for this moment. During the previous year a contingent of them had walked 1,200 miles across the Libyan desert to join the Allies in Tunisia. The drama of their arrival was heightened for the long-waiting citizenry by outbursts of battle in the streets (top left), which continued sporadically for days as veteran guerrillas of the Resistance and civilian Parisians engaged diehard Nazis and collaborationists.

1944
Place de la Concorde, Paris

Parisians cram the history-laden Place de la Concorde, site of the guillotine of the French Reign of Terror just 150 years before and where Germans had camped after the Siege of Paris in 1871. After General de Gaulle ended his victory march here, he sped off by car to the Hôtel de Ville, Paris's city hall, where he was received as head of the provisional government by the Paris Committee of Liberation.

1944
Swift Retribution for Collaborationists

On a platform in a town outside of Paris, a woman, shaved bald for having fraternized with the Nazis, grimaces as she tries to avoid looking at herself in a mirror held by her ceremonial accuser, a French GI.

Four French patriots on a Rennes street gang up on a collaborationist who kneels and begs for mercy. Such physical punishment was meted out for even having entertained Wehrmacht soldiers or solicited their trade.

A shorn collaborator is paraded through the streets carrying her German-fathered child to the taunts of her neighbors. Such offenders were sometimes stripped and made to carry signs reading, "I whored with the Boches."

Villagers in St.-Mihiel, 140 miles east of Paris, jeer at a captured German soldier as he is marched through their gauntlet by a member of the Resistance.

Hitler's Last Gamble: The Battle of the Bulge

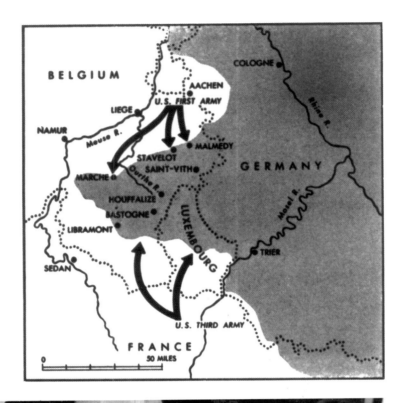

A U.S. sergeant on leave in Spa, Belgium's eponymous hot-springs health resort, wallows in its famed warm mud, a far cry from the cold stuff he wallowed in in combat.

Just when the Allies, careering across Belgium toward the Rhine, had become heady with victory, Hitler, in a desperate, bold move, hurled most of his remaining armored reserves at them through the fog-shrouded Ardennes. His gamble was to capture enough gasoline to regain Liège and Antwerp. He ordered the Seventh and the Fifth and Sixth Panzer armies—14 infantry and 10 tank divisions—to attack on December 16 over a 75-mile front held by five U.S. divisions.

The strike took the Allies by surprise. The sector was supposed to be a good place to be just before Christmas, after the bitter fighting through the snows of Huertgen Forest. GIs relaxed with Luxembourg beer or got leave to visit spas. With Allied aviation out of action because of the thick overcast, the Wehrmacht tore two great gaps in the Allied lines. The Second Infantry slowed them in heavy fighting and the Seventh Armored hung on grimly at St.-Vith to split their advance. The First Army turned south to block the way to Liège and Montgomery sent troops to prevent a Meuse crossing, while Patton smashed at the southern flank. At Bastogne, Brigadier General Anthony C. McAuliffe and his 101st Airborne were cut off and surrounded by the forces of General Hasso von Manteuffel. When Wehrmacht emissaries demanded their surrender, McAuliffe made a laconic reply that has become legendary: "Nuts!" The Germans then commenced a siege that threatened to starve the paratroopers.

On December 23 the weather cleared and the Air Forces began demolishing the panzers, as Patton's Fourth Armored smashed its way northward to relieve the forces trapped in the Bulge. Von Rundstedt withdrew right after New Year's Day. His armies had lost more than 600 tanks and suffered some 90,000 casualties, but they had upset the Allied timetable, diverting four Allied armies from their drives on the Ruhr and Saar valleys.

GIs inspect a German tank turned turtle in a counterattack on the Bulge front. The tank toppled into the crater made by a bomb dropped right in front of it by an Allied plane. Everyone in its crew was killed by the blast.

Inside the Bulge, a Variety of Miserable Weather and Terrain

A panzer officer orders his men, advancing with the infantry, up a rise past a wrecked U.S. half-track.

Advancing from tree to tree through wet snow cascading off the Ardennes spruces, uncamouflaged GIs offer brief targets to the enemy. Their vulnerability was increased every once in a while when unpredictable breaks in the fog sharply silhouetted their olive-drab outlines against the snow.

Moving up to relieve Bastogne, U.S. infantrymen walk across an open field to get past a pocket of German resistance. As automatic fire erupts from the left, they hit the frozen ground (right), there to remain until tanks can clean out the machine-gun nest. As the Germans fell back, they often left behind a single machine gun to slow the Allies' advance.

Allied Airmen Turn Germany to Rubble

Congregants of a Cologne church, surrounded by debris, worship under the open sky. Many other churches, and buildings of all kinds, had even less left standing as Allied bombers flattened German cities.

Hamburg's medieval quarter, seen from the bell tower of St. Nicholas Church, is a charred skeleton. Sixteen other churches, six theaters and countless structures throughout the city fared no better.

A Berlin mother, in her gas mask after an air raid, wheels her baby p bombed-out theater. Its billing reads JOURNEY INTO THE PAST. *In the three y after the Allies adopted the policy of bombing cities, more than a million of bombs leveled 11 million dwellings and took some half a million civ lives. The Germans tried to confuse the Allied navigators by covering a w lake with gauze and building five fake Berlins close to the capital as w several "dummy" Hamburgs to try to divert some of the devasta*

The looks of Winston Churchill, without his trademark cigar, and Franklin Roosevelt, without his cigarette holder and already showing signs of the illness that was to take his life, belied their improved military situation, at their second Quebec meeting.

Josip Broz, Yugoslavia's Marshal Tito, the Croat Communist Partisan commander who turned his following into a guerrilla army that routed the Nazis, communicates with his field officers on the telephone in his mountain cave headquarters.

Supreme Commander Dwight D. Eisenhower is flanked by his Anglo-American staff at a planning meeting for Operation Overlord. From left: Lieut. General Omar Bradley, Admiral Bertram Ramsay, Air Chief Marshal Arthur Tedder, Ike, General Bernard Montgomery, Air Chief Marshal Trafford Leigh-Mallory and Lieut. General Walter Bedell Smith.

At a field conference with Generals Bradley (cen and Montgomery, General George S. Patton wears famous pair of pearl-handled revolv

Four-star chiefs of the Army and the Air Forces, Generals George C. Marshall (left) and Henry "Hap" Arnold (behind the man with the water can) wash up on a visit to the field in Normandy.

General Douglas A. MacArthur wears his newest decoration, the Most Honorable Order of the Bath, awarded to him by King George and presented by Australia's Governor General Gowrie at Canberra.

Back Stateside, the Big Apple Has Its Biggest War Boom

One look at Broadway and it was clear to the most inexperienced eye that "Brother, Can You Spare a Dime?" had segued into "We're in the Money."

Nobody had held a watch on it, but all of a sudden the Great Depression seemed long ago and far away. All those jobs in war production, all that weekend overtime meant lots of money. The national income for 1944 was running around $158 billion, the highest of all time, and New York City was enjoying its greatest boom ever.

People were buying $15,000 bracelets, $3,500 mink coats and $29.75 lace panties and paying $1 a throw for drinks. Civilians were snapping up theater tickets (*Oklahoma!* was the big one) from scalpers for as much as $29. Consumer spending was figured to hit $95.5 billion, as much as the total national income of 1941. Unless you had lost a dear one in the war, it was easy, stateside, to accentuate the positive.

Chorus girls Diane Van Alst, Mara Williams and Mary Mullen get off their feet in the dressing room of the Copacabana nightclub.

The American Kaleidoscope

A Hitler authentic enough to shoot gets a haircut in Hollywood. Paramount was making what was not yet called a docudrama, a movie called The Hitler Gang. Looking on, and looking almost as convincing, are (from left) Göring, Goebbels, Himmler and Hess, all in quotation marks.

Starlet Elyse Knox hits the silk, trying on the parachute of Lieutenant Tommy Harmon of the Army Air Forces, her fiancé, for a wedding dress. The gridder from Michigan, twice All-American and twice survivor of air crashes, used the chute when he was shot down over China.

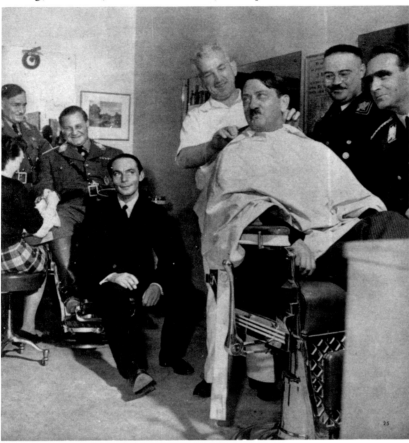

By permission of the U.S. Supreme Court, a black dentist of Houston, Lonnie Smith, sets a precedent voting in the Texas primary. The court had ruled that "Negroes," as proper parlance of the time had it, could not legally be barred from voting in the Lone Star State's primary.

Charles de Gaulle, 6 feet 4 inches, responded to New Yorkers' cheers with his greatly elevated V for Victoire on the steps of City Hall during his flying visit to the U.S. to win recognition for his Committee of Liberation as the de facto provisional government of metropolitan France. (He got it.)

A "pressure boy," as young relocated Japanese-Americans were called, exercises his right to sing the blues in the stockade of Tule Lake Segregation Center, in Newell, California.

A Phoenix, Arizona, war worker, Natalie Nickerson, writes a "Thank you, I think" letter to her Navy boyfriend for the Japanese skull he sent her.

Chicago boss Ed Kelly lifts the arm of Missouri Senator Harry Truman, victorious in the race for the vice presidential nomination at the Democratic Convention.

Lists of U.S. war casualties—close-typed, sadly—stand in silent eloquence in the Library of Congress.

To the American fighting men, most of whom had been brought up to feel that life was precious and every individual mattered, the Japa- nese attitudes on human existence seemed barbaric. The way their troops fought to the death and often preferred suicide to surrender frightened the Westerners and made the enemy emi- nently easy to hate.

In these two pictures the gulf be- tween cultures is demonstrated to the

A Marine at the bloody end of the drawn-out Battle of Saipan tenderly lifts the only living thing the victors found among hundreds of corpses in a cave, a badly hurt, fly-covered baby.

extreme—a GI saving the life of an otherwise doomed child and a Japanese extinguishing the life of a prisoner. LIFE's reportage said that the Japanese were both sentimental and moral about this form of killing, finding it "in accordance with the compassionate mercy of Bushido."

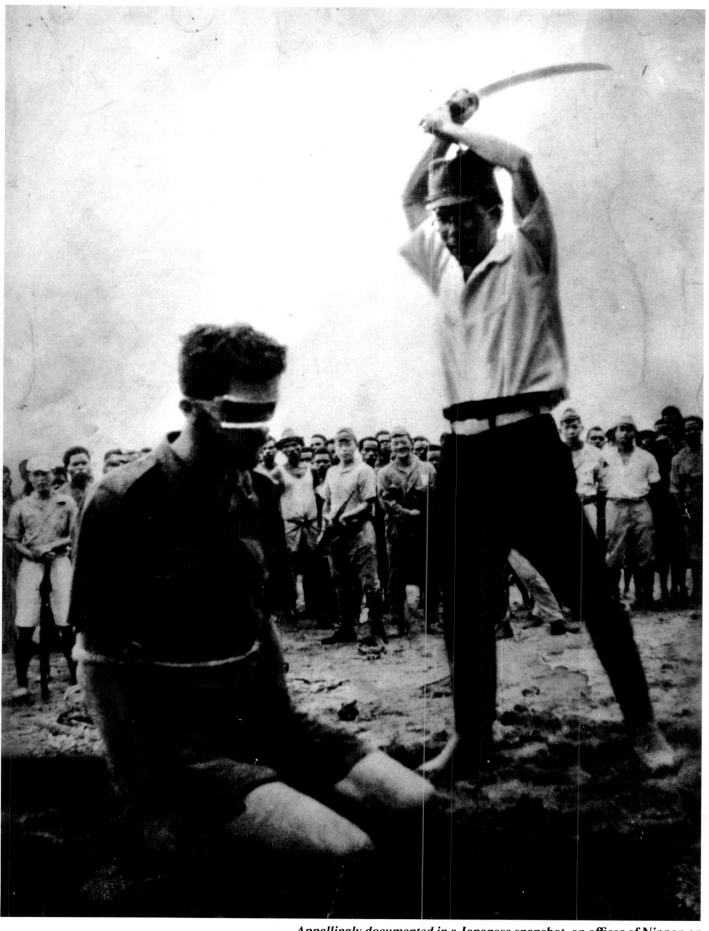

Appallingly documented in a Japanese snapshot, an officer of Nippon on New Guinea prepares to behead an Allied flier with his samurai sword.

As the Japanese carrier Zuikaku *lists sharply before it slides into the Pacific
off the Philippines, crewmen raise their arms and voices in a banzai cheer of farewell.*

Suicide Is Turned into a Weapon

The idea of "noble death"—that it is a fine thing to die for others, for one's family, for one's nation, for king or emperor—was not invented by the Japanese. Religions had been founded on it. Revolutions had battened on it. Nathan Hale had allegedly regretted that he had but one life to give for his country. But in Western nations even the noblest death was not an occasion of joy, a consummation devoutly to be wished. In modern Japan it had become just that. Furthermore, death by one's own hand had been ritualized in *seppuku*, what Westerners called hara-kiri. The ritual, a particularly painful way to go to eternity, consisted in disemboweling oneself with an antiseptically wrapped short sword. It had been romanticized in a classic drama of the 1700s, *Chushingura* (The Tale of the Loyal Retainers), based on an actual event. Its hero is forced to commit the act because of a transgression: drawing his sword in a Shinto shrine (even though in defense of his wife). The powerful scene moved generations of Japanese to believe that suicide is ennobling; from it flowed the tactic of the self-immolating infantryman and the airman riding the Divine Wind of Kamikaze.

A Japanese sergeant major who led an ill-fated breakout attempt at an Australian POW camp hangs from a noose he rigged in a camp kitchen.

Instead of execution, hara-kiri (or seppuku) was the privilege of the gentry in Old Japan. In the woodcut below, the doomed man is about to take up the ritual sword and disembowel himself while his second, standing behind him, will strike off his head at a signal from the dying man.

A Kamikaze pilot and his fellow fliers are regaled with sake and special rations at a farewell party on an airfield.

After their final, suicidal attack on the Americans seeking to recapture Attu, Japanese, dead mostly at their own hands, carpet the tundra. The man in the foreground is one of many who turned themselves into human bombs, clutching his grenade to his chest as he hurled himself on the attackers.

Japanese pilots salute their commander before taking off for a session in the air that their enemies might consider eerie: training for a Kamikaze flight.

1944

A Kamikaze Attack off Leyte

A Kamikaze fighter pilot dives toward double destruction: that of his target, the U.S. carrier Essex, *and of himself . . .*

. . . Hit by an antiaircraft shell seconds before the crash, the plane continues on course leaving a trail of white smoke. The Essex *suffered only minor damage.*

1944

The Divine Wind Blows a Ship in Half

Hit amidships by a Kamikaze west of the Philippines, the escort carrier St.-Lo explodes in a fiery cloud. It sank in half an hour.

Crewmen of an American aircraft carrier wash off the results of a
Kamikaze pilot's failure to take them to eternity along with himself.

ISLAND FIGHTING: The Battle for Eniwetok Atoll

Lay a long enough ruler across Kwajalein and Eniwetok in the Marshall Islands and its north-westerly end will cut squarely across the heart of Japan. The leaping frog that was the amphibious U.S. war machine was right on course when, having taken Kwajalein Island in a textbook invasion so smooth that it demoralized the Japanese, it repeated the offense at Eniwetok.

U.S. planes attacked Truk Island, the heart of Japan's Pacific defense, as a diversion. Then Army, Navy and Marine forces, under the command of Rear Admiral Richard Kelly Turner, attacked Eniwetok. Carrier planes and battleships' 16-inch guns blasted the island's excellent air facilities and large military barracks and then covered the troops as they stormed ashore. Engebi Island, with an airstrip and a radio station, Japan's main position in the atoll, was the first to fall.

A Marine drags a dead comrade out of the surf on the coral beach of Eniwetok's Engebi Island under fire from a Japanese pillbox, off to the left.

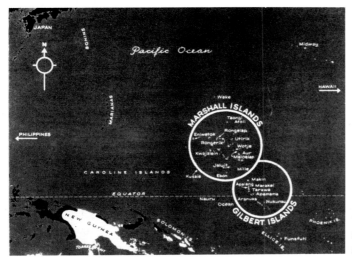

The Gilberts and the Marshalls are seen in relation to the rest of the Pacific, thrusting northwestward toward Japan's home islands.

A Japanese soldier burns from a burst of fire from a Marine flamethrower after trying to throw a grenade from ambush.

1944

Horrifying Fighting on Saipan

In the summer of '44 the U.S. set out to take the Mariana islands of Saipan, Tinian and Guam, only 1,300 miles southeast of Tokyo. To accomplish this the greatest armada the world had ever known was assembled to back up the invasion forces. Saipan came first and with it came some of the most bizarre and bloody Pacific fighting, including a massive charge of beaten men—the most horrifying banzai assault of the war—when cooks and typists and hospital patients on crutches joined troops in a club-wielding, grenade-throwing attack on U.S. positions. It was a human landslide of drunken, crazed warriors bent on going to their deaths with blood on their hands and honor in their hearts. Even after the fighting had calmed, the suicides continued as hundreds of Japanese civilians joined soldiers in leaping off high cliffs into the sea and blowing themselves up with grenades obtained from their own soldiers. Robert Sherrod, LIFE's great war correspondent, was an eyewitness: "What the Americans found at the battle's end staggered their imagination, strained their credulity. To understand, they had to throw away all their Occidental con-

The first wave of Marines, keeping low, moves up the Saipan beach past an Amtrac amphibious tank.

As a jeep bears a wounded American to the rear, a bulldozer scoops out a mass grave for Japanese

Saipan Victory Ends in Mass Suicide

cepts of the human thinking process. There, on the northernmost point of Saipan, a large segment of the Japanese civilian population was calmly, deliberately committing suicide. Hundreds of human beings, perhaps thousands, had chosen to die as what the Japanese so fondly call 'shields for the emperor' . . . The volcanic rocks on Marpi Point between the 200-foot cliff and the water's edge cached hundreds of bodies of civilians who had snuggled into the jagged earth with grenades against their bellies . . . More strange and unbelievable was the sight of civilians stoically drowning themselves. Sometimes groups would join hands and wade into the water. There was no diving. The Japs simply walked to the edge of the slippery rocks, slid into the waves and went under. 'Yesterday,' a Marine told me, 'I saw a father throw his three children off, then jump down himself. Sometimes the parents cut their children's throats before they threw them off the cliff.' "

"On the edge of the slippery, tidewashed rocks," Sherrod continued, "I watched a Japanese boy of perhaps 15, attired in knee-length black trousers, walking back and forth. He would pause in meditation, then he would walk on, swinging his arms. He sat on the edge of the rocks, then he got up. He sat down again, waiting . . . When a high wave washed the rock, the boy let it sweep him into the sea. At first he lay face down, inert on the surface of the water. Then his arms flailed frantically, as if an instinct stronger than his willpower bade him live. Then he was quiet. He was dead."

Undecided now in the face of shouted pleas by Marines and others not to kill themselves, a small group of civilians run back and forth. Below: After some 45 minutes, the decision is made for them. From a cave a Japanese sniper fires at his countrymen. One falls; his wounded mother drags herself after him.

Carnage at Peleliu

On September 15 LIFE artist Tom Lea was with the U.S. First Marine Division as it hit the beaches of
Peleliu. Ranking by war's end with Tarawa, Saipan and Iwo Jima among the four bloodiest battles
in the 169 years of the Marines, Peleliu presented ghastly scenes like these for Lea's sketch pad.
The last step before death of this mortally wounded Marine was also described in words: "Mangled
shreds of what was once an arm hung down as he bent over in his stumbling, shock-crazy walk. Half his
face was bashed pulp. The other half bore a horrifying expression of abject patience." On his
first combat assignment, this Marine "never saw a Jap, never fired a shot."

Now it was the Palau Islands; the carnage on Peleliu defied description. But artist Tom Lea tried his hand at it in paint for LIFE, and company commander Captain George P. Hunt, one of the true Marine heroes of the Pacific who was destined to become managing editor of LIFE two decades later, tried it in words. "The human wreckage I saw was a grim and tragic sight. Wounded and dying littered the edge of the coconut grove from where we had landed to the point. As I ran up the beach I saw them lying nearly shoulder to shoulder. I saw a ghastly mixture of bandages, bloody and mutilated skin; men gritting their teeth, resigned to their wounds; men groaning and writhing in their agonies; men outstretched or twisted or grotesquely transfixed in the attitudes of death; men with their entrails exposed or whole chunks of body ripped out of them. There was Graham, snuffed out a hero, lying with four dead Japs around him; and Windsor, flat on his face, with his head riddled by bullets and his arms pointed toward a pillbox where five Japs slumped over a machine gun."

Battle fatigue is mirrored in the stark, staring eyes of this Marine painted against the backdrop of "Bloody Nose Ridge," a mile-long jagged cliff that was the strongest Japanese redoubt on Peleliu. Lea's notes add to the man's story. "He left the States 31 months ago. He was wounded in his first campaign. He has had tropical diseases . . . He half-sleeps at night and gouges Japs out of holes all day. Two thirds of his company has been killed or wounded . . . he will return to attack this morning. How much can a human being endure?"

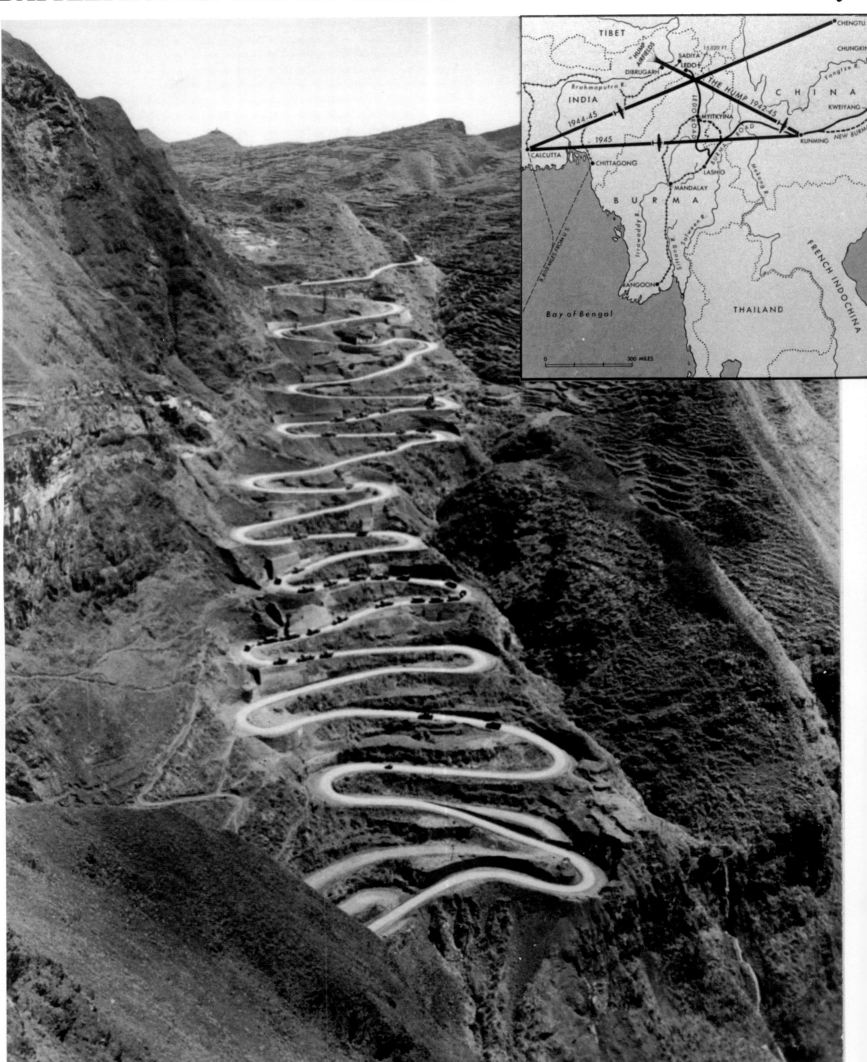

A U.S. convoy headed for Chungking moves tortuously up the Hump's notorious "21 curves."
The map shows the relation of the old rail supply lines to the new Burma and Ledo roads and the
Hump airlift that kept China in the war in the long months when they were building.

No war theater produced more recrimination than China-Burma-India (CBI). The President wanted Chiang Kai-shek's China to contribute more to the war. Churchill directed Britain's effort toward returning Singapore, Hong Kong and Rangoon, not to mention Mandalay, to the empire. The CBI was split in two, the C versus the BI. The Americans were split among themselves. General Joseph (Vinegar Joe) Stilwell wanted to fight overland, despite the rugged terrain; Major General Claire Chennault, who shared with Vinegar Joe a mutual low regard, had a faith in combat aviation that approached the religious; he had promised Roosevelt a year earlier that if he was given 147 planes he would "accomplish the downfall of Japan."

Stilwell disdained Chiang, although he was his chief of staff; Chennault liked Chiang but loathed his own Air Forces superiors. For seven months B-29s had attempted to bomb Japan from China bases but the distance was too great. No wonder the GIs and other ranks in the theater insisted that CBI stood for Constant Bickering Inside.

Chinese refugees from East China cities threatened by the Japanese cram a westbound train in Kwangsi Province. When Chennault's 14th Air Force started bombing Japanese shipping and rail lines from these cities, the Japanese launched a retaliatory sweep, panicking Hankow and other cities. Left: a refugee "rides the rods" under a freight car, lashed in by ropes.

1944
Decisive Clash of Two Mighty Fleets

Indicative of the might of the Japanese fleet that clashed with the U.S. Navy in the first Battle of the Philippine Sea, waged while the struggle for Saipan was in full fury to the west, battleships of the Rising Sun, in attack formation, fill the entire horizon.

Just one part of the U.S. task force, pictured before the two fleets clashed, tells much about the dimensions of the strategic engagement and the history of the war. Of the six battleships, nine carriers, countless cruisers, destroyers and cargo ships, nearly all had been built since Pearl Harbor.

Under attack by carrier planes of Task Force 58, a portion of the fleeing Japanese fleet writhes and twists to avoid bombs. The carrier at right is taking many hits.

A deck officer on the Enterprise leaps to extricate a Hellcat pilot who has come in on fire.

With no enemy on the horizon, the immense 275-yard flight deck of the Big E is put to happier uses. Here, during a "field day," a dive-bomber pilot wins the 220-yard dash.

1945 THE

The hands of a watch pinpoint the instant its wearer died in the searing blast.

INAL FIRE

Miserable though the Ardennes winter was for embattled GIs fighting snow and a wraith-like enemy in the fog-shrouded conifer fastness, it was worse for Adolf Hitler, who had returned to the Reich Chancellery in Berlin. It was a long time since anyone had called the Führer a military genius.

On the Eastern front the Red Army, having crushed 25 German divisions in its rush through Poland—the worst defeat in Wehrmacht history—and driven the Nazis out of Hungary, was inside the Reich and headed for Berlin. No German soldier stood anywhere on Russian soil. The Western Allies had overrun northern France and the Low Countries in their rush toward his industrial heartland, the Ruhr valley, and had destroyed two of his armies in the process.

The Battle of the Bulge, which was shaping up as the war's biggest in Western Europe, was the result of the Führer's attempt to regain the luster of his glory days of the Blitzkrieg. His grand plan for halting the Allies' march to the Ruhr—implemented over the objections of his generals—was suitably grandiose. If it had worked it would have been brilliant. His idea, to launch a two-pronged counterattack aimed all the way to the port of Antwerp, was that the overextended Allies would have to rest and await resupply and reinforcement while he could reorganize his forces behind his Switzerland-to-Holland West Wall. The stroke, by the Fifth and Sixth Panzer armies with the Seventh and 15th armies protecting their flanks, did catch the overconfident British and

Moments after the epochal Hiroshima blast, members of the "walking dead," people who survived the shock wave to die later of radiation burns, move about dazedly, snapped almost reflexively by one of their number.

F.D.R. Did Not Live to See Hitler's Defeat

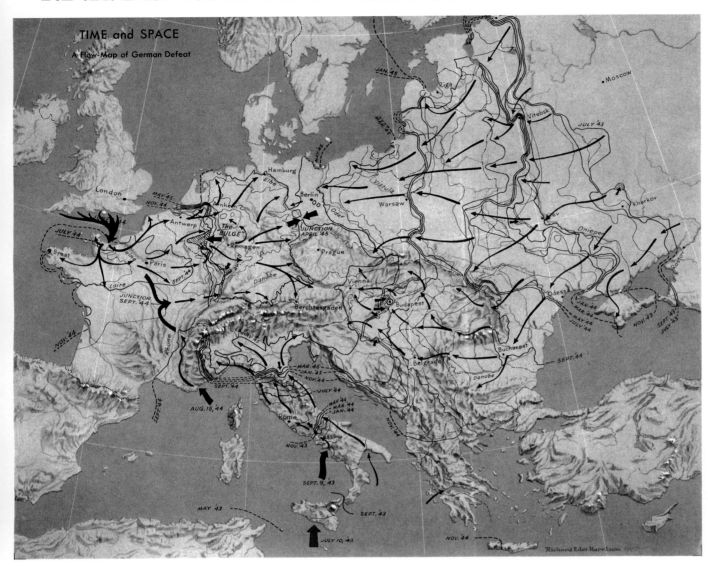

TIME and SPACE
A Flow-Map of German Defeat

The undoing of Hitler, the master strategist, is evident on this map of the Allied advances on the Wehrmacht, from three directions, in Fortress Europe and the increasingly desperate homeland.

Americans by surprise, and the dent in the American line, across a 75-mile front, was the result. But the Second Infantry Division and the Seventh Armored, at the point of the salient, fought savagely, the tanks holding on to split the panzers at St. Vith. General Courtney H. Hodges's First Army turned south to block the way to Liége, Montgomery prevented a Meuse crossing and Patton hit the southern flank hard. The Army Air Forces zeroed in on German tanks and trucks and by January 28 the Battle of the Bulge was over.

Hitler's defeat, like his plan, was outsized. Gerd von Rundstedt lost 600 tanks and 90,000 casualties. Worse, the battle had shown that the Luftwaffe was a waning threat even close to home. After the Bulge, as one of his generals put it, the Führer started a "corporal's war." There were no more grandiose plans, just a succession of piecemeal fights.

The Allies, their timetable set back by the battle, slashed through the Siegfried Line and headed for the Rhine, one of Europe's greatest natural barriers, which no invader had crossed since Na-

poleon in 1805. The Allies did it at many places by quick, low-level parachute drops on its east bank. The Wehrmacht blew up the bridges, but the Allies speedily used their crossing equipment: 2,500 boats, 6,000 pontoon floats, 100,000 tons of bridging material, 315,000 feet of wire rope and 8,000 feet of chain. The U.S. Navy provided assorted landing vessels, some 1,000 sailors and a complement of Seabees (members of Construction Battalions).

But the first surface crossing was by the Ninth Armored Division, which raced other First Army units to the one remaining Rhine span, the 1,200-foot Ludendorff Bridge at Remagen, and got there before the bewildered German engineers managed to demolish it. Once across, the Allies' columns laced the German landscape in a series of branching patterns as they rolled almost unhindered to the east.

In their march across Poland, the Russians had come upon something new in the horrors of war. At the Nazis' Auschwitz concentration camp, where many thousands of civilians, men, women and children, had been put to death in gas chambers, the soldiers found

5,000 living corpses, most of them Jews, who had not yet been gassed when the ovens were turned off before the Red Army's arrival. Sixty thousand others had been lined up and started on a forced march toward Germany. Laggards were beaten or killed. The Americans, sweeping later across Germany, found similar horrors at Buchenwald (which had been founded in 1933 to handle German Jews but, which, 50,000 deaths later, contained more than a dozen nationalities), Dachau and others. The Allies liberated a total of 23 such major installations and more than a hundred lesser ones.

The Western Allies made up for lost time and met the Red Army at the town of Torgau, on the Elbe some 90 miles southwest of Berlin. The zones the individual Allies were to occupy had been worked out at a Big Three conference at Yalta in February, but the Western generals chafed at being restrained from sweeping into Berlin along with or ahead of the Russians, who already had entered the capital. Eisenhower, however, considered Berlin strategically out of it, and wanted to main-

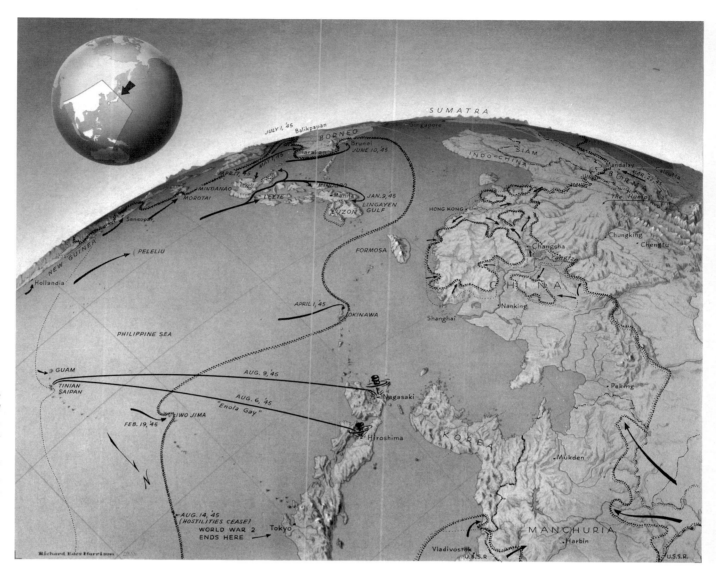

This map of the Pacific, an unusual polyconic projection southward from a point over northern Asia, charts the Allies' inexorable waterborne advance upon Japan's home islands.

tain pressure in northern Italy, where Allied forces, led by the U.S. 10th Mountain Division, were driving Kesselring's Alpenjaeger from the Apennines to the Alpine underbelly of Hitler's *Festung Europa*, Fortress Europe.

One of Hitler's last orders was to "drown the Russians in a sea of blood and hold Berlin at all costs." Berlin fell, to the Russians, on May 2, forty-eight hours after Hitler's suicide in his bunker beneath the Reich Chancellery, 12 days after 2 million soldiers of the armies of Marshals Georgi Zhukov and Ivan Konev had started their final attack, 42 months after the Wehrmacht had been beaten back from the gates of Moscow, and 988 years short of fulfilling the Führer's prediction of a "thousand-year Reich." Five days later Germany surrendered, unconditionally.

President Roosevelt did not live to see that consummation he had so devoutly wished. Having been ailing for months (he was noticeably drawn at Yalta), he died on April 12. His death shocked the world, and particularly the U.S. forces at home and abroad. (It postponed for two days the final offensive of the Allied armies poised in

the Apennines for the breakthrough to the Po valley and the Alps). It was President Harry Truman who warned the cheering Americans that the war was only half won.

The other half moved violently but ineluctably toward its end. While MacArthur's troops mopped up the Philippines, the island-hopping amphibian forces embarked on their last two, brutally costly steps to Japan. The Marines' month-long battle for Iwo Jima (tougher, said Marine commander Lieut. General Holland Smith, than Tarawa, Kwajalein or Saipan) gave B-29s a base with fighter cover, and the 83-day bloodbath by the U.S. forces on Okinawa provided a foretaste of the invasion of Japan.

As the distance to Japan shrank, Kamikazes struck with more and more abandon. Trying to emulate the great, calm samurai warriors out of their history, these proud young men were treated like gods before their fatal assignments. They dove to their deaths with poetry on their tongues and reverence in their hearts, and the sight of one coming in on a ship filled the Americans on board with so much awe

and horror, and sometimes even pity, that there were instances when gunners froze and forgot for a moment to fire. During the three months in the spring of the year that it took to overwhelm and secure Okinawa—only 380 miles from Japan itself—279 ships were hit in 1,900 Kamikaze tries.

Nightly, the Superforts incinerated great areas in Japanese cities, including half the built-up part of Tokyo. In July, while the new Big Three—Truman, Clement Attlee, who replaced Churchill when the P.M. called for a general election, and the perdurable Stalin—were debating the future in Potsdam, the first atomic explosion was achieved in New Mexico. The trio drafted an ultimatum calling on Japan for unconditional surrender. Tokyo's answer was unsatisfactory. The terrible cost of Iwo and Okinawa fresh in his mind, Truman authorized the dropping of two atomic bombs on Japanese cities. On August 6, a B-29 from Tinian loosed one, equivalent to 20,000 tons of TNT, on Hiroshima, killing 66,000, and three days later another hit Nagasaki. By August 15, World War II was over.

January	February	March	April	May	June
1 • Hitler speaks out for first time in five months **9** • Luzon landing starts large-scale U.S. invasion of Philippines **12** • Soviets launch massive offensive in Poland and East Prussia • U.S. sinks 25 Japanese ships off Indochina coast **16** • Germans in defeat as Battle of Bulge ends **17-19** • Soviets occupy Warsaw **19** • Germans now in full retreat on Eastern front **20** • F.D.R. inaugurated for fourth term • Allies sign truce with Hungary **22** • Reopening of land route to China **27** • Auschwitz liberated • Soviets complete occupation of Lithuania **29** • U.S. forces land on Bataan **30-Feb. 2** • Malta conference—Big Three discuss war aims **31** • U.S. landings south of Manila	**1** • 513 U.S. survivors of Death March rescued **3** • U.S. enters Manila • Allies drop 3,000 tons of bombs on Berlin **4-11** • Yalta conference—Big Three discuss war aims **7** • Japanese take Kanchow **8** • Allied offensive for Rhine begins **13** • Allied offensive on Germany's railroads starts • 50-day Soviet siege of Budapest ends—159,000 dead **13-15** • Dresden devastated by Allied bombing **15-21** • U.S. wins back Corregidor **16-21** • U.S. hits Tokyo **19** • U.S. Marines land on Iwo Jima **21** • Bataan secured **23** • Turkey declares war on Axis • U.S. opens Roer River offensive **26** • Marines take Mount Suribachi on Iwo Jima • Midnight curfew begins in U.S.	**2** • U.S. takes Trier, Germany **3** • Manila secured • Finland declares war on Germany **5** • U.S. enters Cologne **6** • Chinese take Lashio **7** • Allies take Remagen Bridge over Rhine **9** • U.S. captures Bonn **9-10** • Massive fire bombing of Tokyo—100,000 killed **15** • American flag hoisted over Iwo **16** • Nazis flee toward Rhine after Patton wins Saar battle **19** • Clothing prices frozen in U.S. • Hitler orders scorched-earth policy **21** • Allies take Mandalay, Burma **22-23** • Allies cross Rhine **24** • Chinese halt advance in North Burma **27** • Last German V-2 hits England **29** • Allies take Mannheim, Frankfurt **30** • Soviets take Danzig, enter Austria	**1** • U.S. encircles Ruhr pocket • U.S. landings on Okinawa **6** • Kamikaze raids on U.S. fleet off Okinawa start • Koise Cabinet falls in Tokyo **7** • Soviets enter Vienna **11** • Allies reach Elbe River **12** • President Roosevelt dies, Truman becomes U.S. President **14** • Allies open final offensive in Italy on Gothic Line **16** • Reds steam ahead toward Berlin **19** • 300,000 German prisoners taken as Ruhr is cleared **21** • Allies take Bologna **23** • Red army enters heart of Berlin **25** • San Francisco conference on United Nations opens • U.S. and Soviets meet up at Torgau, Germany **26** • U.N. charter adopted • Allies take Bremen, Verona **28** • Mussolini captured and executed by Italian Partisans **29** • Allies take Milan, Venice, Genoa • Germans in Italy give up **30** • Hitler commits suicide	**1** • Berlin surrenders • Nazi propaganda minister Joseph Goebbels commits suicide **3** • Rangoon freed **4** • Germans surrender in Netherlands, Denmark, northern Germany **4-5** • Japanese counteroffensive at Okinawa repulsed **7** • German high command officially surrenders at Reims **8** • V-E Day **10** • Soviets enter Prague **20** • Japanese begin withdrawing from southern China **23** • Churchill resigns and calls for elections • Himmler kills himself **26** • Imperial palace hit in devastating Tokyo air raid	**4** • U.S. fire-bombing of Kobe **5** • Allies carve up Germany into four occupation zones **10** • Australians invade Borneo **12** • U.S. begins final offensive at Okinawa **21** • Okinawa secured **24** • Tarakan secured **26** • Chinese take Liuchow • United Nations established **30** • Luzon liberated

■ **War in Europe** ■ **War in Asia** ■ **U.S.A.**

July	August	September
10-Aug. 15 • *U.S. and British carrier raids on Japan* **14** • *Italy declares war on Japan* **16** • *U.S. explodes first atomic bomb at Alamogordo, N.M.* **17-Aug. 2** • *Potsdam conference on peace in Europe, final push on Japan* **26** • *Japan given surrender ultimatum* • *Clement Atlee becomes Prime Minister of Britain*	**6** • *Atomic bomb dropped on Hiroshima* **8** • *Soviets declare war on Japan, invade Manchuria* **9** • *Second atomic bomb dropped on Nagasaki* **11** • *Japan offers surrender* **12** • *Soviet troops enter Korea* **13** • *U.S. keeps up heavy bombing of Japan* **14-15** • *Japan surrenders, end of hostilities* **28** • *Japanese surrender in Burma* • *U.S. occupation of Japan begins*	**2** • *Japanese government formally surrenders aboard battleship* Missouri *in Tokyo Bay*

Out of the woods in the Ardennes, the Western Allies, exploiting their command of the skies, rolled into the Rhineland and Germans, for a change, watched foreign armor and air power churn up their landscape and set fire to their homes. With the Rhine behind them, the unspoken war cry in the minds of the airborne and the infantry was "On to Berlin!" In the heat of battle, particularly with the Wehrmacht falling back on its own soil, there were excesses of the kind proscribed by the Geneva Convention of 1864. On the Western front these no longer consisted of the calculated cruelties of the SS but of the commoner concomitant of war, the murder of prisoners and wounded, and, in one notable case, bombing overkill for partially political purposes *(page 367)*.

The body of a dead GI is borne off a snowy field in the Bulge by German POWs. Allied casualties in the winter warfare, before clearing weather reinstated Allied air superiority and opened the way for the invasion of the Rhineland, totaled 77,000.

Tracks across fields less than three miles from the Rhine tell the story of Ninth Army tanks that broke their file formation on a road to engage German self-propelled guns, visible beyond farmhouses set afire by U.S. artillery and dive-bombers.

American paratroops hit the ground on farmland east of the Rhine. The planes that dropped them have passed out of the picture to the left.

Mortars Across the Rhine

Displaying the teamwork that characterizes their specialty, a Third Army mortar squad pounding defenders on the east bank of the Rhine prepares to feed in another round even as the roar of the preceding shell reverberates.

'For Them, the War Is Over'

That line appeared in the caption of virtually every photograph of dead released by the wartime Soviet picture agency. And indeed pictures of the fallen, on whatever front and of whatever nationality, have the same look of finality, as here, where a GI killed by mortar fire sprawls on a Roer River footbridge and (right) an American machine gunner felled by a sniper lies crumpled on a Leipzig balcony.

War's Frightful By-Products: Massacre and Overkill

An American medic, murdered at the command of a Nazi officer, lies under rotting snow near Malmédy.

On the second day of the German counteroffensive that produced the Bulge, Wehrmacht tanks overpowered a column of American trucks near Malmédy. A panzer officer ordered 150 Yanks into a snow-steeped field, where most were cut down with a machine pistol at close range. Those who did not die immediately were shot in the head. Fifteen who had fled into a wood survived the massacre, which came to light when the snows melted in January.

The following month, on February 13 and 14, British and American bombers, following an initiative of Winston Churchill, who thought blitzing cities in eastern Germany would show Stalin the muscle that the Western Allies were using on Russia's behalf, raided Dresden, 100 miles south of Berlin. The old center of art and culture, some of whose buildings dated back to the 13th century, had been spared major bombing till then. On the night of the 13th, 234 British Lancasters, loaded with about 75 percent incendiaries, bombed it for 17 minutes (its antiaircraft guns had been sent to the Russian front), and three hours later 538 more dropped their bombs on the spreading fringes of the fire storm, which was devouring the city's mostly wooden buildings. The next day 311 American Flying Fortresses blasted rail installations by daylight. Although the techniques and the tonnages were not exceptional, the timing, at this late date, of such massive bombing of a vulnerable, low-priority target did not sit well with the public back home, who identified Dresden with beautiful, fragile chinaware. The fire-bombing of Dresden became the most controversial action of the Western Allies.

A stone figure atop Dresden's town hall looks out over the city's old quarter, her serene gesture become ironic amid the scene of ruin in the wake of the Allies' fire-bombing.

1945

For Russia, the Hour of Revenge

If the Western Allies were impelled toward Berlin by the scent of victory, the Russians were driven by the lust for revenge. The Red Army poured across the Reich's eastern border and laid waste everything in its path. It was as though every unit sought to make up all by itself for the Wehrmacht's atrocities in Mother Russia. In many German villages males were forced to watch as entire squads raped their wives, daughters, mothers. Officers pulled rank to violate the prettiest. Men or boys who resisted were shot or castrated or both. Women who fought back were bayoneted and disemboweled. Some were nailed to barn doors. Babies had their heads bashed in. German militiamen were doused with gasoline and turned into human torches. Word of the horror flew even faster than the motorized invaders. The sight of smoke on the horizon sent the inhabitants of even the remotest farms running for their lives. Usually their flight was futile; the Russians chased them in machine-gun-equipped sleighs or light trucks and cut them down in the fields with a fury that was biblical. Hitler had troubled his own house; his people inherited the wind.

Residents of Breslau's outskirts panic as Red Army artillery sets their village ablaze. Some of their horses have already been killed.

Tensely awaiting the approach of Soviet armor, German infantrymen keep machine guns and Panzerfäuste, an antitank weapon similar to a bazooka, at the ready.

Five days after crossing Germany's eastern border Russians man 76.2-mm field guns trained on Berlin.

Red Army soldiers emplace the hammer and sickle atop the Reichstag, not yet cleared of its defenders.

Friends Found, Friends Lost

The Americans and the Soviets join forces in a long-awaited meeting, symbolized by the embrace of lieutenants William D.
Robertson of the U.S. First Army and Alexander Sylvashko of the First Ukrainian Army, near Torgau, on the Elbe River.

A Schweinfurt woman sorrowfully covers the bodies of her neighbors' children, shot
their mother after hearing that their soldier father had been killed fighting the Russians
the city's gates. The closing in of the Allies set off a country-wide wave of Selbstm
(self-murder). This characteristically German phenomenon (police in America cal
suicide "the Dutch act") differed innately from Axis partner Japan's seppuku (page 332)
clue is in the word's root, Mord, murder, rather than Todt, death. Selbstmord is
joyous "noble death" but a despairing way out of facing a fate worse than dea

BODIES BURNED HERE

EMERGENCY EXIT

DR. MORELL'S OFFICE

EMERGENCY TELEPHONES

HALL, SCENE OF HITLER'S FAREWELL

HITLER MARRIED HERE

HITLER'S BEDROOM

STOREROO

EVA BRAUN'S BEDROOM

HITLER DIED HERE

a. Seydenfrost

Adolf Hitler's last home and headquarters was a 19-room bunker under the Reich Chancellery garden close to the center of Berlin. For the final few weeks of his life Hitler seldom left the stuffy confines of his concrete tomb with its inadequate communications and cramped quarters. At least it kept him separate from his generals based 20 miles away at Zossen; he was sure that if he let down his guard another assassination attempt on him would be made. So there in his bunker he stayed, attended by a few guards, servants, aides and his doctors, one of whom, a specialist in venereal disease and a notorious

quack, had been injecting his shaking, deteriorating patient with secret formula drugs for the past nine years.

The staff meetings Hitler held daily had less and less to do with reality as he began moving imaginary battalions and calling for strikes that could never take place. Waving a road map of Germany in the air, he would shout orders as if in the heat of battle and then, laying the map out on a table, he would show anybody within his reach the complicated maneuvers that would take place in order for the tide to turn. More and more he turned to the stars for his future, studying horoscopes and seeking balm

in their messages. Goebbels read aloud to him from Carlyle's *History of Frederick the Great* and paused at the passage in which Frederick decides to take poison if his onrushing defeat is not reversed. "Brave King," he is addressed. "Wait yet a while, and the days of your suffering will be over. Already the sun of your good fortune stands behind the clouds, and soon will rise upon you." Hitler's eyes filled with tears when he heard Goebbels tell how Frederick had been saved from suicide at the last minute by the death of his enemy. When the Führer's own horoscope was brought forth, it told of disaster in the

In a LIFE article H. R. Trevor-Roper, a young British historian who researched Hitler's last days, called Eva Braun, the Führer's wife for two days, "pretty rather than beautiful." "Unobtrusive, anxious to please," he wrote, "she soon achieved an ascendancy over Hitler, supplying that idea of restfulness which was so lacking in his political life but for which his bourgeois soul so hankered." Other Trevor-Roper conclusions are included on these pages.

1947 LIFE published this cutaway illustration of the underground bunker in which Hitler lived out his last frightened, neurotic days and where, finally, on the eve of defeat, he died.

early months of 1945 suddenly followed by an overwhelming German victory in the latter part of April. Could it be that Friday, April 13, the day of Roosevelt's death, was the turning point for which both men waited? "It is written in the stars," Goebbels told his leader. For the time being, Hitler could put thoughts of poison aside and wait for the prophecy to come true.

Bringing Hitler back to reality was the combination of the muffled rumble of the Russian advance far above the bunker and the shocking news that Himmler was negotiating with the Allies. There was nothing unreal about the fury that surged through the Führer as he contemplated the treachery of one of his most devout and trusted followers. "He raged like a madman," one of those present in the bunker remembered. "His color rose to a heated red and his face was almost unrecognizable."

In the turmoil of Nazi defeat almost half a century ago, LIFE correspondent Percy Knauth interviewed Hitler's stenographer, 35-year-old Herr Gerhard Gesell, who told him, "At the afternoon briefing of April 20, with the Russians already in Berlin, it was decided to evacuate the Führer's supreme headquarters

to Berchtesgaden. I volunteered to remain because I wanted to see what would happen at the end ... The decisive briefing began at 3 o'clock on the afternoon of April 22 and lasted until nearly 8 o'clock that evening ... Hitler suddenly announced his intention of staying in Berlin. At first hesitantly, then with increasing firmness, he declared that he wanted to die in Berlin. He repeated this 10 or 12 times during the conference in various phrases. He would say 'I will fall here' or 'I will fall before the Chancellery' or 'I must die here in Berlin' ... He thought it would be the greatest service he could render to the honor of the German nation."

Less than a week later, with the Russians laying waste to Berlin, the time to end it all was arriving. Longing for respectability, Hitler's longtime mistress and most trusted friend, Eva Braun, had moved into the bunker. Hitler ordered her to leave but Eva had her heart set on marriage and in the end the Führer could not deny her. On April 29 the two filled out a marriage license, Hitler claiming on it to have sprung from pure Aryan blood. The bride wore a black taffeta dress and, as a witness described, shed "tears of radiant joy." With a minor city official called in to preside over the occasion and make it legal, Hitler and Eva proclaimed they were married. Champagne flowed in the tiny room with six-foot-thick reinforced concrete walls 50 feet beneath the ground. That duty done, Hitler retired with a private secretary to dictate his will and political testament. Hitler left his personal possessions to the Nazi Party, or, "if this no longer exists" to Germany. "If the state, too, is destroyed, there is no need for any further instructions on my part," he concluded. In his political statement he appointed successors of whom he demanded continued war efforts as well as undying hatred of all Jews. Joseph Goebbels witnessed both documents.

The following morning Hitler was told that Benito Mussolini was dead, killed along with his mistress by Italian partisans, their bodies strung up by the feet and hideously mutilated. Suicide and the burning of his body, along with Eva's, would save Hitler from such ignoble fate. The final decision had been made.

No One Dared Picture What Was Happening Behind the Closed Door

When the sun rose on April 30, Hitler had been asleep but an hour. Still he seemed refreshed for his last day alive. Fifty feet above him in the open air a scene of horror worthy of hell itself was unfolding. Berlin was afire. Tanks roared through the streets. Shelled buildings gave way and crumbled to the ground. Rockets whined. Hot, sulfurous mists coiled and swam and choked the air. Bodies lay everywhere. Blood turned the canals red. Zoo animals, their cages blown open, roamed the streets. The raped, the wounded, the dying joined in a mighty shrill choir as the Russians, at 10 a.m., began their final assault on the Reichstag, still defended by several thousand SS troops. In his hideaway below, Hitler spent a quiet morning with old friends. Goebbels, who was there, prepared himself for the shooting of his wife, Magda, and their six young children along with his own suicide. Hitler ate spaghetti and tossed salad with his two secretaries and his cook. It was about 3:30 in the afternoon when Adolf and Eva shook hands with everyone present and retired to the Führer's personal chambers. No one dared picture what was happening behind the closed door to the soundproof suite. When Hitler's valet finally pushed the door open, the smell of cyanide and gunpowder drifted out. Finally, Martin Bormann led the way in, followed by Goebbels and two aides. The Hitlers were on the sofa, she dead of poison, he of a bullet administered through the mouth and into the brain. The bodies were quickly carried up the emergency stairway and laid side by side in a shallow shell hole in the garden. Hitler's chauffeur told LIFE's Percy Knauth that Eva was still warm and soft when he carried her. Gasoline was poured over the bodies and lit. As evening came, more and more gasoline was added and the burning continued. At midnight three SS troopers buried in a deeper shell hole whatever they could scrape up.

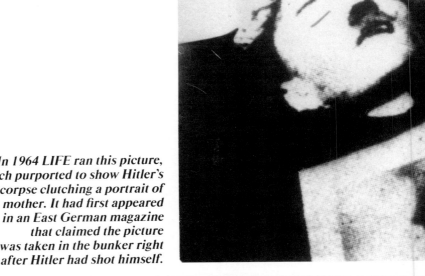

In 1964 LIFE ran this picture, which purported to show Hitler's corpse clutching a portrait of his mother. It had first appeared in an East German magazine that claimed the picture was taken in the bunker right after Hitler had shot himself.

LIFE photographer William Vandivert took this picture of a conference room in Hitler's bunker after SS troopers had tried to burn it up and the Russians had stripped it of evidence.

In the summer of 1945 LIFE correspondent Percy Knauth sifts through the dirt and debris in the trench where the bodies of Hitler and Eva Braun were thought to have been burned. Their suicides and cremation were carefully orchestrated and even rehearsed, at least in part to avoid an ignominious finale like the one Mussolini and his mistress underwent two days before (below).

*Exultant upon being liberated by the U.S. Third Army, prisoners of war
at Moosburg, Germany, climb fences and rooftops and jam a camp square.*

*On a road outside the Belsen death camp lined wit
those for whom release came in the form of death,
local youngster takes a walk. The Allies could ne
decide whether the German populace was indiffere
or inured to the death all around them*

Sights Too Ghastly for Liberators' Eyes to Grasp

Wiping away the Wehrmacht in the Western Allies' final sweep toward Berlin uncovered the unutterable atrocities of the concentration camps, particularly the extermination camps. As the Red Army had retched coming upon Maidanek, Treblinka and Auschwitz in Poland, the Americans and the British blanched at Buchenwald, Dachau and Belsen. Battle-hardened troops wept, and some broke down entirely, at sights their eyes could scarcely communicate to their brains: corpses, emaciated to stick figures, stacked like cordwood; huge mounds of spectacles, baby shoes and human hair, the only evidence that millions of other human beings had existed. For many of the stunned liberators, these remnants were verification of Army briefings they had refused to credit, believing (as Hitler in *Mein Kampf* had predicted Britishers and Americans would believe, recalling World War I atrocity stories about the Kaiser's *Reichswehr*) that reports of Nazi cruelties were just propaganda.

Assigned the chore of burying their victims, an SS officer and a female camp guard captured at Belsen stand knee-deep in corpses.

The head and forearm of a young political prisoner emerge from the crack under a door through which he tried to escape when the Nazis set fire to the building at Gardelegen, near Berlin.

The bodies of 3,000 of the Nazis' slave laborers are laid out on a street at Nordhausen before burial by Allied troops. They had been starved and beaten to death.

The living dead of Buchenwald stare blankly at the photographer accompanying their liberators. They were among those who could stand up and therefore survived.

1945
What Hath Hitler Wrought!

Buchenwald townspeople—who had for months, even years, seen corpses littering their landscape—stand shocked and weeping after being taken on a tour of the Buchenwald camp by the U.S. Army. Eisenhower, who had been sickened when he saw Ohrdruf, the first camp liberated, insisted that the carnage get the widest possible exposure. Ohrdruf's mayor and his wife committed Selbstmord after their tour.

After Germany's surrender, German war prisoners sit for a required screening of concentration camp scenes. Many said they could not believe the films were authentic.

At Long Last—Victory in Europe

In a London mad with joy over the fall of Hitler's Reich, East Enders, whose poor neighborhoods had suffered the most from the Luftwaffe's incendiaries, wave myriad flags and mill about—around, of all things, a fire they set themselves.

ed Army liberator, Marshal Ivan Konev, is greeted a roaring welcome by citizens of Prague. The Czech ital had endured six years under the Nazi heel.

Russian soldiers back from the front and civilians jamming a Moscow railroad station to meet them join in a noisy chorus celebrating the defeat of the Nazis.

A New Occupant for the Big Three's Middle Seat

Getting set for the official photograph of the Big Three's February meeting at Yalta, F.D.R., visibly wasted by his advancing illness, jokes with Churchill about his Russian-looking Astrakhan hat as Stalin and his interpreter (left) lean toward him to listen. Churchill removed the headgear.

O n the eve of the victory he had spent himself for, Franklin D. Roosevelt died. For as long as anyone could remember, nothing had seemed to daunt him, not even the heavy braces on his useless legs, crippled by polio so long ago. For a fortnight the ailing 63-year-old Commander in Chief had got away from the rigors of the war in his favorite restorative hideaway, a frame cottage on Pine Mountain, at the health resort of Warm Springs, Georgia. On the afternoon of April 12, as his Third Army entered Buchenwald, his Fifth Army took up positions for the final offensive in northern Italy and his Sixth Marine Division moved in for the capture of the northern tip of Okinawa, he murmured, "I have a terrific headache," and died. Within two hours Harry S. Truman was President.

On its editorial page LIFE expressed the nation's loss:

The most striking thing about Roosevelt's death was that millions and millions of people felt a personal sense of loss and found tears for it. "I'd been depending on him in such a personal way," they said; or, "I feel as though I'd lost my father."

That is how Walt Whitman expressed the country's grief at Lincoln's death; he called him "my father." Like great shafts driven into the national consciousness, these two deaths struck a stratum of grief that had lain untouched by any event in the 80 years between.

"My father!" It was more than a figure of speech. It was a confession of loving dependence. Even those who opposed Roosevelt, even some who hated him shared the abrupt sense of dizziness, as though a whole wall of the nation had been blown away. At the moment of his death he was the most important man in the world. He was the one American who knew, or seemed to know, where the world was going. The plans were all in his head. Whether one liked this or that policy or not, one knew that he would do what he would do. It was easier to let him worry for the whole country.

One of his "Young Guard" Democrats, Representative Lyndon Johnson of Texas, said, "There are plenty of us left here to try to block and run interference, as he had taught us, but the man who carried the ball is gone—gone . . . He was just like a daddy to me always; he always talked to me just that way. He was the one person I ever knew—anywhere—who was never afraid . . . God, how he could take it for us all!"

Epitomizing the nation's sorrow, a tear-streaked Navy musician, CPO Graham Jackson, plays "Goin' Home" as F.D.R.'s body is borne from his Warm Springs, Georgia, cottage.

Meeting in Potsdam in July to plan for victory over Japan and the peace beyond it, Churchill and Stalin flank a new partner, President Harry S. Truman.

1945
Return to the Good Old U.S.A.

Marlene Dietrich, boosted up to a troopship porthole by GIs at a New York pier, gives one of their buddies an athletic homecoming kiss.

In anticipation of possible peace, as the invasion of Japan looms, workers at the Moraine, Ohio, General Motors plant turn out shiny Frigidaires while airplane propeller blades move along an adjacent assembly line.

In a perfect landing, a jubilant airman home from Europe just after V-E Day kisses U.S. soil.

Also, Back in the States . . .

Christmas packages that could not be delivered to servicemen in combat pile up in New York City's General Post Office to be stamped RETURN TO SENDER—KILLED IN ACTION *or* MISSING IN ACTION.

With actress Lauren Bacall as a piano ornament, President Truman, an old World War I artillery captain, plays the "Missouri Waltz" for servicemen at the National Press Club canteen in Washington.

New Yorkers line up on Fulton Street to buy cigarettes. Each customer was allowed two packs. GIs in combat got all they wanted free.

One-armed Pete Gray, a St. Louis Browns war replacement risen to starting center fielder, fields a ball. He could flip a caught ball in the air, drop his glove, recatch the ball and get off the long throw as fast as most other outfielders.

Bacall feeds wedding cake to Hollywood tough guy Humphrey Bogart after their nuptials in Mansfield, Ohio.

"General Ike," in town for a triumphal ticker-tape parade up Broadway, claps New York's Mayor Fiorello La Guardia on the shoulder. He flashed his grin at 4 million spectators, outdrawing Charles A. Lindbergh.

A model shows off the blouse that Anna Miller fashioned after the waist-length combat jacket favored by General Eisenhower. The Miller version features a drawstring waist, colors far removed from olive drab and shoulders fit for five stars.

A Plexiglas canopy, a spin-off from the transparent plastic domes, turrets, noses and cockpit enclosures of military aircraft, forms a clear-as-glass oxygen tent for a hospital patient.

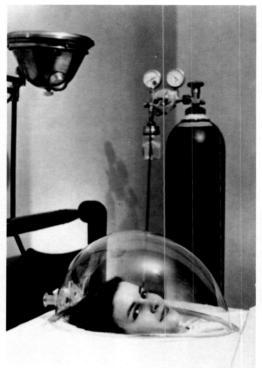

Singing sweater girl Janet Blair, in a well-publicized sacrifice for the clothing collection drive of war relief agencies, prepares to strip off her most becoming garment.

Alger Hiss, secretary general of the San Francisco conference that crafted the Charter of the United Nations, counts the final vote of the steering committee, composed of the chief delegates of the participating nations.

In Pride of the Marines, the Hollywood filming of the life of Guadalcanal hero Marine Sgt. Al Schmid, the blinded sergeant, played by John Garfield, returns to his Philadelphia home with his wife, portrayed by Eleanor Parker.

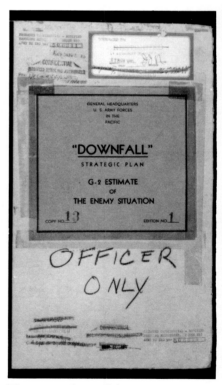

The cover sheet of the strategic plan for Operation Downfall, the invasion of Japan's home islands that was averted by the explosion of the A-bomb, is stamped with numerous warnings of its secrecy.

Climax in the Pacific

The fall of Saipan, the capital of Japan's South Seas empire, had marked the breaching of Japan's inner defense line. Taking it set the stage for the landing on perhaps the only island whose capture was unavoidably necessary. If B-29s were to succeed in blasting the Nipponese home islands sufficiently to soften them up for invasion, they required the terra firma of Iwo Jima, an eight-square-mile volcanic island halfway between Saipan and Tokyo, as a base for long-range fighters and a haven for crippled Superfortresses. Iwo was known to the strategians of both sides as the Pacific's toughest nut. Because the absolutely essential high ground, 556-foot Mount Suribachi, was on the extreme southwestern tip of the island, only a frontal attack could be made. The final staff briefing, on Saipan, was in the nature of a *Morituri salutamus* to men about to die. The Third, Fourth and Fifth Marine divisions got the job. As the first waves hit the beaches, 22,817 dug-in defenders opened up with artillery and mortars, including 320-mm monsters. For a hellish month after the attackers were fully engaged, in the scrubby banyan jungle of the lower plateau and the sulfur-laden steam of the volcano's steep sides, Iwo was one of the most densely populated places on earth, with 10,000 battling men to the square mile. And once again, in the painful struggle up the Pacific, a battle became that blackest of statistics: the costliest in Marine history. Indeed, only one other U.S. offensive action of any service, Pickett's charge at Gettysburg in the Civil War, had so great a percentage of casualties. More than 6,800 Marines were killed and 18,200 wounded. Of the island's defenders more than 20,000 died.

General MacArthur wades ashore on Luzon. He had made good his famous I-shall-return pledge two months earlier, on Leyte, but the dramatic symbolism of recapturing the Philippines' main island was not lost on him—or on LIFE photographer Carl Mydans, who had been with him when Manila fell and had been taken prisoner—so he got wet again.

Waves of landing craft churn toward the shore of Iwo Jima, dominated by sulfur-breathing, 556-foot Mount Suribachi.

1945
Up the Bloody Sands of Iwo Jima

Keeping flat despite a lull in withering fire from the dug-in defenders, Marines of the 28th Regiment struggle up a steep slope of soft volcanic sand on Iwo's shore. U.S. naval fire adds dust and gunsmoke to clouds of sulfurous steam from the extinct volcano's fumaroles.

On the Volcano, A Man-Made Eruption and a Classic Flag Raising

*Forming an image like a relief on a heroic frieze, five Marines and a
Navy medical corpsman plant the Stars and Stripes on Suribachi's summit.*

**Amid the charred trunks of a clump of banyans, a Marine demolition team blasts
a cave that held a blockhouse and Japanese infantrymen who refused to budge.**

1945
An Epic Linking: Okinawa and the 'Divine Wind'

The last island step to Japan, Okinawa, only 240 miles south of the home islands (and 550 miles from Tokyo) was Tojo's last chance to keep the foot of the avenging enemy off Nippon's sacred soil. Accordingly, all the elements of the greatest seaborne war the world has ever seen came together at Okinawa—with the frightening addition of Kamikaze, the "Divine Wind." The aircraft carrier had long since replaced the battleship as queen of the seas in warfare. Since 1942, when the *Enterprise* was the single serviceable U.S. carrier in the Pacific, the carrier fleet had grown to more than 100, capable of launching some 5,000 planes. Of these, 28 were not slow escort vessels but

the fast carriers of Task Forces 38 and 58, there were 18 of the 27,000-ton Essex class and the balance of the light Independence class, converted from cruiser hulls. As more carriers than ever before softened Okinawa for invasion, the Japanese hurled at them not only conventional bombers but also their last-ditch weapon, the pilot who rode his plane as a guided missile straight into his target.

Two of the most spectacular victims of the Japanese navy's death throes were the carriers *Franklin (right)* and *Bunker Hill (below)*. The *Franklin*, with most of her planes on the flight deck for a strike at the naval base of Kure prior to the Okinawa invasion, was hit by two 500-pound bombs, which set off huge fires

fed by high-octane gasoline, on both the flight deck and the hangar deck below. She lost 724 of her complement of some 2,400. (Her twisted hull eventually made it back to the Brooklyn Navy Yard). The *Bunker Hill*, flagship of Vice Admiral Marc A. Mitscher's Task Force 58, was readying a strike at Okinawa when two fighter planes, one low and one in a vertical dive, came screaming out of the clouds and exploded on her flight deck, igniting her planes like a string of giant firecrackers and turning her into a floating furnace. For six hours her crew battled the flames. When the fire was under control, 396 men were dead or missing. Two were Japanese. The *Bunker Hill* was out of the war.

Firefighters with a fog nozzle move in on a wall of flame on the hangar deck of the Bunker Hill, *staggered by the impacts of two Kamikazes off Okinawa.*

The carrier Franklin, *after taking two bombs on her deck, wallows in the sea between Okinawa and Japan's coast.*

A fusillade of rockets roars from LSMs (Landing Ships, Missile) at Tokashiki Shima, an island near Okinawa, five days before the invasion of the big island.

1945

Out of the Clouds, a Hybrid Guided Missile

Okinawa was not the debut of the Kamikaze. In the battles for the Philippines the Japanese flew 650 suicide missions; 174 were successful. But the implications of the one-life-for-many melding of theology and combat weapon, a hybridization of man and missile, were so awesome that censorship forbade mention of Kamikazes for six months, lest Tokyo find out how effective they had been.

Japanese legend has it that Vice Admiral Masabumi Arima made the first Kamikaze attack, off the Philippines, in October 1944. His kill was never identified, but his act, said the Japanese, lighted "the fuse of the ardent wishes" of his fanatically courageous pilots, and they were soon crashing regularly on U.S. flight decks. At a sacrifice of his single life a suicide pilot could take hundreds of American lives and destroy valuable military hardware. At Okinawa 279 ships were hit in 1,900 tries. Among some 13,000 U.S. sailors killed in the war's last year, Kamikazes accounted for nearly three fourths. For the whole war, the record shows 474 hits for 2,550 planes expended.

A Kamikaze, coming in low across splashes of diving fighters' machine-gun fire and through antiaircraft bursts, makes a run at the battleship Texas. *This one did not take out his intended victims.* Texas *gunners scored a direct hit just in time.*

The Epic Amphibious Operation: Okinawa

A mortar shell's near miss causes two GIs to flatten themselves against the volcanic rock of a steep Okinawan ridge.

As was expected, after the gory struggle at Iwo, Okinawa proved to be the epic amphibious operation. From the landing on April Fool's Day—which was also Easter Sunday—to its ending 81 days later, the fighting was just as hellish, per man, per acre, per whatever historians like to measure, as on any of the previously bloodied stepping-stones to Tokyo. In one 53-day period U.S. gains averaged 163 yards a day. But Okinawa's epic proportions tempt chroniclers to sum it up in statistics. Some 183,000 Army and Marine troops and 747,000 tons of cargo were loaded onto 430 assault transports and landing ships. Just in the three hours before the landing, the offshore craft fired 44,825 rounds of five-inch to 16-inch shells, 33,000 rockets and 22,500 mortar shells. In 36 hours beginning April 6, 355 Kamikaze pilots sank six ships and damaged 22 others. Among the 4,155 aircraft Japan lost in the battle, 1,900 were Kamikazes. This time the great negative statistic was the Navy's. Its 4,907 killed and 4,824 wounded were the greatest number of casualties it had ever suffered in a similar length of time. At the same time 36 of its ships were sunk and 368 were damaged. The 10th Army's seven divisions lost 7,604 dead, 31,816 wounded. The Marines' totals were 2,957 killed and 15,723 wounded. The Japanese counted 100,000 dead, with possibly 20,000 sealed in caves.

A U.S. tank, its standard 75-mm gun replaced by a flamethrower, scorches the face of a natural fortress as another gets set to fire. Many defenders, dug in deep, shrugged off such assaults and waited for the infantry.

Marines flush out an Okinawa civilian, his head swathed in a wet towel to protect him from the heat.

1945
Japan's Gorgeous Nightmare

B-29s over Fujiyama! Three and a half years after Pearl Harbor, the once impossible dream becomes real as Superforts skirt Japan's 12,389-foot sacred volcano on their way to bomb Tokyo, less than 15 minutes away.

1945

Forecast by the Bomber Command: Firestorm

Even before the capture of Iwo Jima and Okinawa, B-29s had been making high-altitude precision bombing runs on Tokyo. An immense one on March 10, by more than 250 of the Superforts, killed 100,000. From then on, increasingly as airfields became operational on the two islands, other cities came to share the capital's punishment. General Curtis LeMay, chief of the 21st Bomber Command, decided to hit industrial centers with incendiaries from bombers at normal altitudes. Japan's use of wood and paper for most nonindustrial structures made its cities particularly vulnerable. Even in industrial centers, blazes would race through entire sections, setting up the huge upwellings of convection called firestorms. By mid-August 602 military and industrial installations had been destroyed or badly damaged and nearly half the area of 66 cities, a total of 178 square miles, had been razed.

Antiaircraft searchlights in Sakai pin a B-29 in their crossed beams.

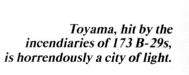

Toyama, hit by the incendiaries of 173 B-29s, is horrendously a city of light.

406

Wooden structures in downtown Osaka are devoured by a firestorm set off by 274 Superforts. Some wood frames remain in place, but not for long.

1945
Amid the Ruins, the Will to Fight On

Charred corpses lie in a Tokyo street after the catastrophic March 10 raid. It took almost a month to dispose of the bodies of the victims.

Like tombstones in a cemetery, buildings of concrete and brick stand amid acres of ashes in Tokyo's industrial section along the Sumida River. Estimates at this time were that a million of the city's structures had been destroyed, leaving only 380,000 standing, many of them but hulks.

A homeless Yokohama family trudges out of the city to a center for displaced persons. Yokohama had been a haven for DPs until it was blasted May 29. By August the year's raids had displaced 10 million.

As the hour of the long-dreaded American invasion nears, an army officer instructs Japanese housewives in handling bamboo spears. The samurai code forbade surrender, even in the face of inevitable defeat.

After the fire storm, nothing remains of downtown Osaka but a huge scatter of rubble. Even streets are barely discernible in the wasteland.

The Atom Bomb

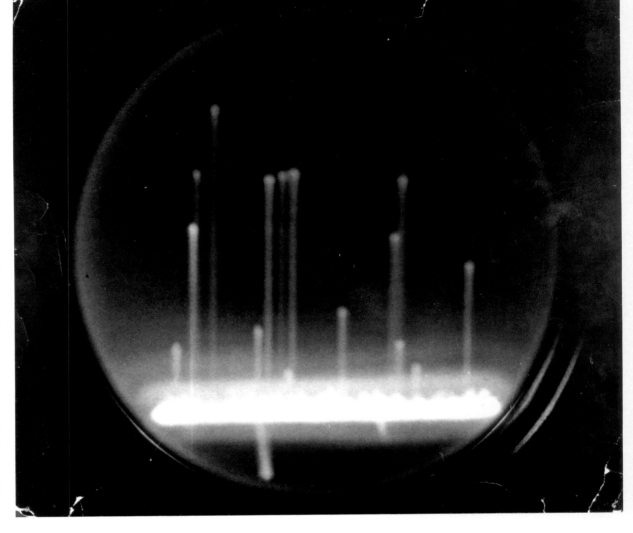

The start of it all is recorded in this epochal LIFE picture, which ran in the magazine in April 1939, eight months before Pearl Harbor and four months before Albert Einstein informed President Roosevelt (opposite page) of the awesome possibility of an atomic bomb. It shows the historic splitting of an atom of uranium 235 in Columbia University's cyclotron. A voltage meter indicated peaks of 200 million electron volts discharged at the instant of fission.

The chain of logic that led ineluctably to the Bomb was forged by scientists of many countries, over many years. When President Roosevelt received a letter from Albert Einstein informing him that the atom had been split and that it might be possible to use the energy of the atomic nucleus to explode a bomb on an order of magnitude previously unimaginable, he set in motion an operation, code-named the Manhattan Project, that brought together the most powerful aggregation of sheer intellect in the history of science.

The father of the atomic theory, Democritus, posited in the 5th century B.C.

that elementary matter was not continuous but was made up of infinitely tiny particles, atoms, that were constantly in motion and were indivisible. The English scientist John Dalton, who revived the theory around 1808, also believed atoms were indivisible.

Over the years after Dalton reawakened interest, investigators discovered that the atom was made up of even more infinitesimal particles, a dense nucleus of positively charged protons surrounded by a vaporous cloud of negative electrons, and that the elements, from the lightest, hydrogen, with only one electron rotating around its nucleus, to

the heaviest metal, uranium, with 92, differ from one another in the number and arrangement of these particles. Dmitri Mendeleev formulated a table of the elements according to their atomic weights and their valences, or the bonding forces that hold their subatomic particles together.

In 1932 another Englishman fascinated by the invisible world of the atom, Sir James Chadwick, proved that another particle, neither negative nor positive, existed in the atom's nucleus along with the proton. He named it the neutron. Two years later the French couple Irène Joliot-Curie and Jean Frédéric Joliot

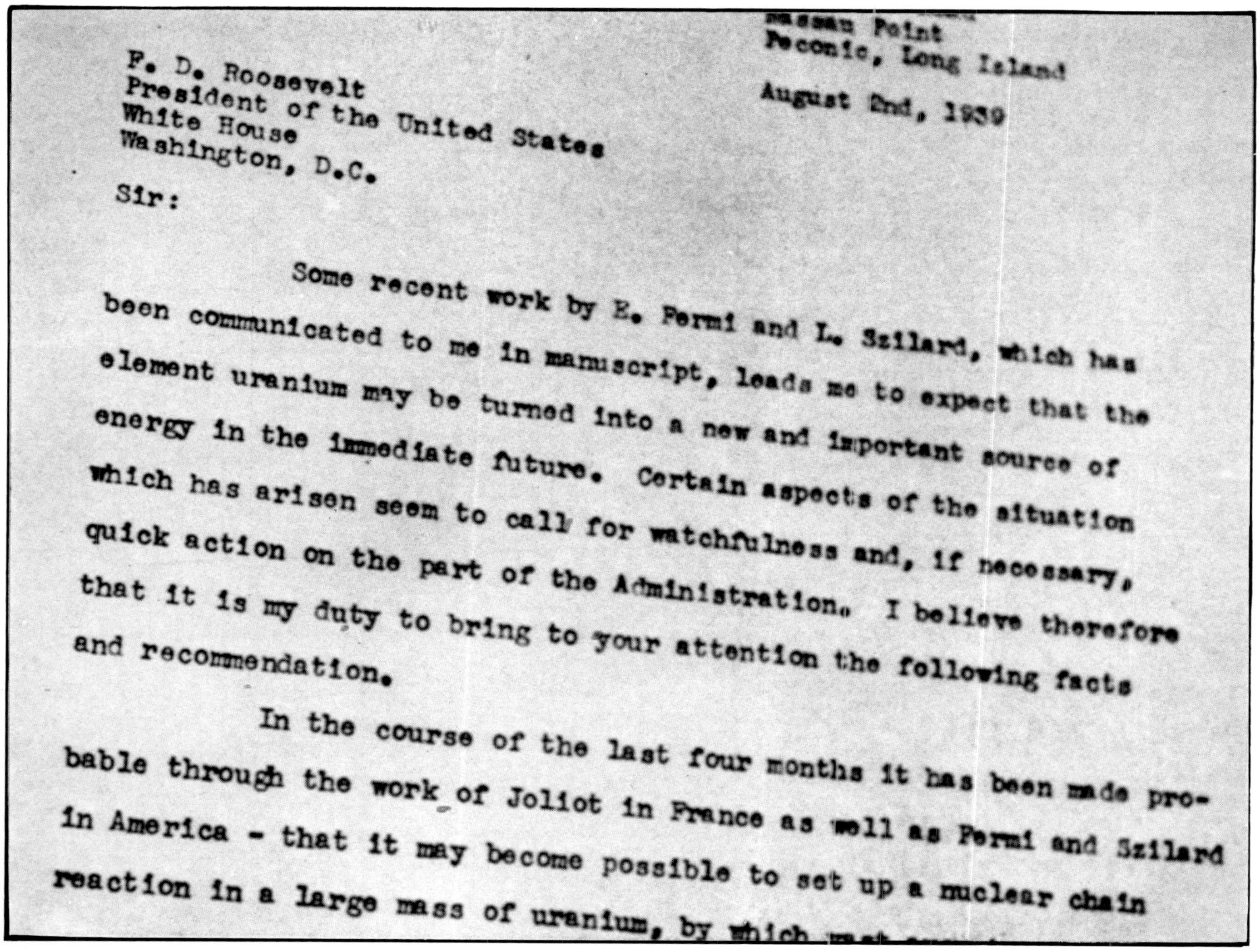

F. D. Roosevelt
President of the United States
White House
Washington, D.C.

Nassau Point
Peconic, Long Island
August 2nd, 1939

Sir:

Some recent work by E. Fermi and L. Szilard, which has been communicated to me in manuscript, leads me to expect that the element uranium may be turned into a new and important source of energy in the immediate future. Certain aspects of the situation which has arisen seem to call for watchfulness and, if necessary, quick action on the part of the Administration. I believe therefore that it is my duty to bring to your attention the following facts and recommendation.

In the course of the last four months it has been made probable through the work of Joliot in France as well as Fermi and Szilard in America - that it may become possible to set up a nuclear chain reaction in a large mass of uranium, by which

This is the letter from Albert Einstein that alerted the President to the unprecedented levels of energy bound in atoms such as uranium's. The scientist urged Roosevelt to investigate the possibilities of nuclear energy. An ardent pacifist, he underscored the moral questions that would attend its use in a superbomb.

found that certain elements could be made artificially radioactive. A few months later Enrico Fermi at the University of Rome produced the same effect in uranium, the heaviest element, by bombarding it with Chadwick's neutrons, thus creating what he thought was a new element, heavier than uranium.

The next development was achieved thanks to Adolf Hitler. Dr. Lise Meitner, exiled from Germany because of her Jewish ancestry and working in Copenhagen with Dr. O. R. Frisch, concluded that bombarding uranium with neutrons was not producing a new element but was splitting the uranium nucleus in two.

Another gift of Hitler to the Allies, Leo Szilard, a refugee Hungarian physicist who gravitated, like Einstein, to Princeton University, had postulated that an atom split by the hammering of neutrons would in turn release more neutrons, which under certain conditions would split the nuclei of other atoms, resulting in a proliferating chain reaction. It was Denmark's great physicist Niels Bohr who, while working at Princeton, suggested that the nucleus not of ordinary uranium but of its rare isotope U-235 was the easiest to split. By the time that isotope was isolated in 1939, a critical mass of the world's greatest physicists, including Bohr, Fermi, the distinguished German refugee Hans Bethe, Szilard and Szilard's colleague from Hungary, Edward Teller, had come together in and around New York.

At Columbia University's cyclotron in New York City, then the jewel of Professor Isidor I. Rabi's nuclear modernized physics department, Fermi, aided by Teller and others, put Szilard's thesis to the test. The result was the reaction shown above. About three months later, Einstein, at the urging of Szilard, wrote F.D.R. his fateful letter.

411

1945
In the Desert, the Shatterer of Worlds

Einstein had written his letter to F.D.R. on August 2, 1939. Two weeks shy of six years, and $2 billion, later, the world's first atomic bomb was exploded, at the Alamogordo Bombing Range, some 200 miles south of Los Alamos, in the New Mexico desert. The Manhattan Project, with its expanding core of savants and technicians, its growing atomic pile, plants to produce fissionable materials for the pile and a remote fastness to assemble and test the bomb, had spread, in top secrecy, to the University of Chicago; Oak Ridge, Tennessee; Hanford, Washington; and here.

The test, at a point in the sand named Trinity, was conducted in the predawn darkness of July 16, observed from concrete bunkers five miles away by Fermi, most of the other physicists who had brought this moment about, and Leslie R. Groves, the Army general who had overseen the project for the War Department, which had footed the bill. The countdown started at 5:10 a.m., Mountain Daylight Time. At 5:29 the counter shouted "Zero" and Fat Man, its designers' name for the bomb, turned night to noon. Its fireball, its sand-melting circumference rushing outward faster than any race car, its light and its heat exceeding those of its parent the sun, struck all its observers dumb. After it rose into its false noon and filled the sky with a mushroom cloud of gas, smoke and debris, they found their voices. But they struggled for words to describe this eruption 20,000 times as powerful as TNT. The project's official chronicler, William Laurence, the science reporter of *The New York Times*, wrote, "On that moment hung eternity. Time stood still. Space contracted to a pinpoint. It was as if the earth had opened and the skies split. One felt as though he had been privileged to witness the birth of the world." Oppenheimer, who had been the project's director, said later that his thought, unuttered, was a passage from the Bhagavad Gita:

> If the radiance of a thousand suns
> Were to burst at once in the sky,
> That would be like the splendor of
> the Mighty One . . .
> I am become Death,
> The shatterer of worlds.

One twentieth of a second after the world's first nuclear detonation, the expanding fireball, brighter than the noontime sun and, at its core, four times as hot, is a huge, incredibly fast-expanding hemisphere of burning gas, dust, debris and molten New Mexico sand.

A crater 25 feet deep at its center and a quarter of a mile across, surrounded by scorched earth and filled with green glass alchemized from sand, marks the site of the detonation. The 100-foot steel tower that held the bomb was atomized instantly.

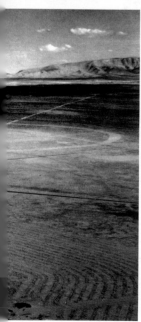

To conceal the size and shape of top-secret Little Boy, Fat Man's operational counterpart, ground crewmen on Tinian adjust a canvas screen beneath the bomb bay of the Enola Gay, the B-29 that the pilot, Colonel Paul W. Tibbets Jr., named for his mother.

Just 21 days after Fat Man turned part of the New Mexico desert into green glass, its counterpart explodes over Hiroshima (inset). Seen from an altitude of more than 20,000 feet, the head of its mushroom cloud has separated from the stem. The stem rises from an immense and still growing pillow of gas and smoke grayed with debris. Pictured three weeks after the explosion, only a scattering of concrete walls can be seen rising from the carpet of powdered rubble across the entire panorama of the incinerated area.

1945

In the Aftershock of a Great Wound

Following the blast came fire and it proved to be Hiroshima's greatest killer. The thermal wave sweeping out over the flat countryside left an enormous vacuum in its wake into which roared hurricane winds. The thousands of little fires that had been set almost everywhere were now suddenly whipped by the torrents of wind into one big one—a firestorm that raged through the city for hours.

Someone in Hiroshima when the bomb was dropped aimed a camera skyward and took this picture of the atomic cloud mushrooming 40,000 feet above the city.

Those close enough to the blast were simply vaporized. Others, like this person who was about half a mile from ground zero, was burned to death by the thermal wave. Less lucky were the thousands who died of agonizing internal hemorrhages from radiation.

In 1945 passionate, opinionated James Agee was the movie critic for LIFE's sister publication, Time. To write the cover story on the Hiroshima bomb, Time's managing editor called upon his finest writer, regardless of his specialty. A future Pulitzer Prize winner for his moving and memorable novel A Death in the Family, Agee responded with these words.

The greatest and most terrible of wars ended, this week, in the echoes of an enormous event—an event so much more enormous that, relative to it, the war itself shrank to minor significance. The knowledge of victory was as charged with sorrow and doubt as with joy and gratitude. More fearful responsibilities, more crucial liabilities rested on the victors even than on the vanquished.

In what they said and did, men were still, as in the aftershock of a great wound, bemused and only semi-articulate, whether they were soldiers or scientists, or great statesmen, or the simplest of men. But in the dark depths of their minds and hearts, huge forms moved and silently arrayed themselves: Titans, arranging out of the chaos an age in which victory was already only the shout of a child in the street.

With the controlled splitting of the atom, humanity, already profoundly perplexed and disunified, was brought inescapably into a new age in which all thoughts and things were split—and far from controlled. As most men realized, the first atomic bomb was a merely pregnant threat, a merely infinitesimal promise.

All thoughts and things were split. The sudden achievement of victory was a mercy, to the Japanese no less than to the United Nations; but mercy born of a ruthless force beyond anything in human chronicle. The race had been won, the weapon had been used by those on whom civilization

could best hope to depend; but the demonstration of power against living creatures instead of dead matter created a bottomless wound in the living conscience of the race. The rational mind had won the most Promethean of its conquests over nature, and had put into the hands of common man the fire and force of the sun itself.

Was man equal to the challenge? In an instant, without warning, the present had become the unthinkable future. Was there hope in that future, and if so, where did hope lie?

Even as men saluted the greatest and most grimly Pyrrhic of victories in all the gratitude and good spirit they could muster, they recognized that the discovery which had done most to end the worst of wars might also, quite conceivably, end all wars—if only man could learn its control and use.

The promise of good and of evil bordered alike on the infinite—with this further, terrible split in the fact: that upon a people already so heavily drowned in materialism even in peacetime, the good uses of this power might easily bring disaster as prodigious as the evil. The bomb rendered all decisions made so far, at Yalta and at Potsdam, mere trivial dams across tributary rivulets. When the bomb split open the universe and revealed the prospect of the infinitely extraordinary, it also revealed the oldest, simplest, commonest, most neglected and most important of facts: that each man is eternally and above all else responsible for his own soul, and, in the terrible words of the Psalmist, that no man may deliver his brother, nor make agreement unto God for him.

Man's fate has forever been shaped between the hands of reason and spirit, now in collaboration, again in conflict. Now reason and spirit meet on final ground. If either or anything is to survive, they must find a way to create an indissoluble partnership.

Twenty-four hours after the industrial and shipbuilding center was destroyed by the second bomb, survivors walk by a landscape of shards and bodies.

In the light of dawn a lone tree stands with incongruous grace over a sea of rubble as two rescuers search for the living.

1945
Appalling Sights as the Atomic Dust Settles

The morning after the bomb went off, a young Nagasaki woman, her body depleted of water by the blast, gets her first drink. Shortly afterward she, and the other victims around her, died.

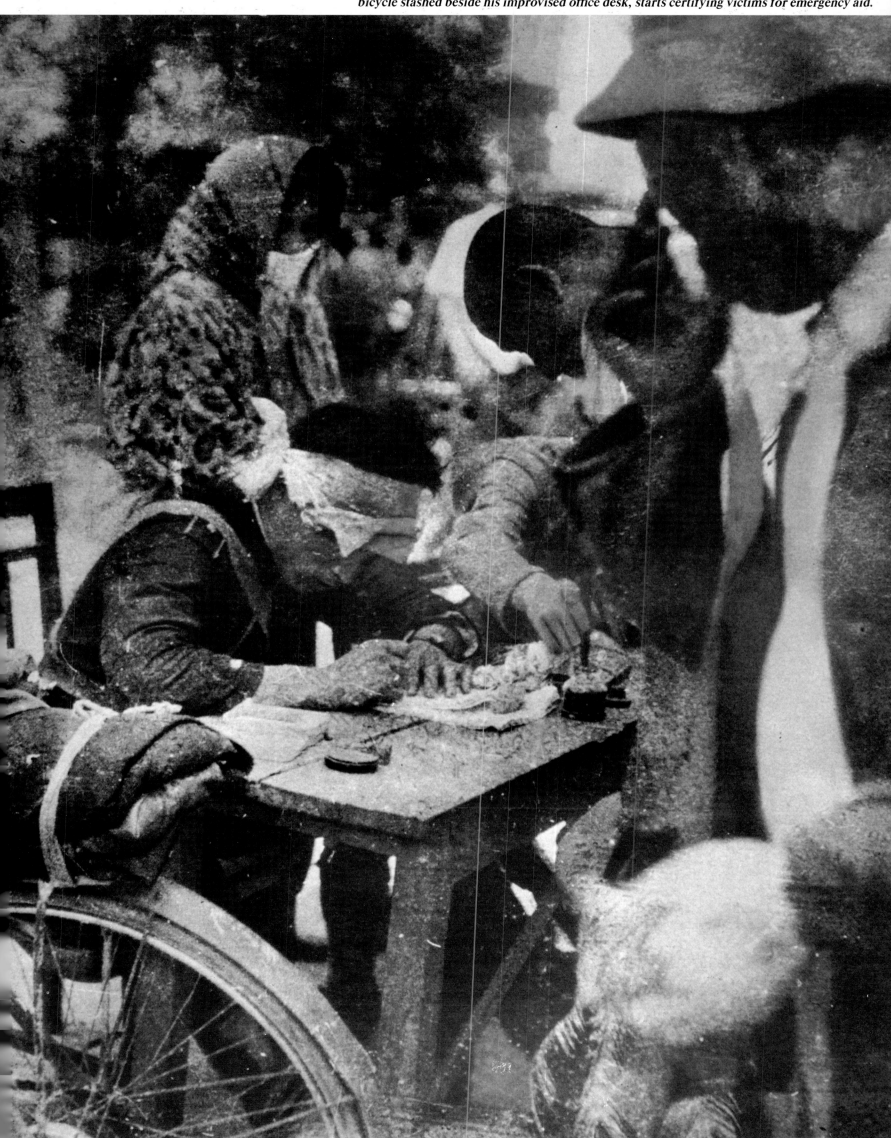

Disregarding his own hastily bandaged wounds shortly after the explosion, a Hiroshima policeman, his bicycle stashed beside his improvised office desk, starts certifying victims for emergency aid.

How the Surrender Was Decided

At a meeting so secret that no artist or photographer was admitted, Emperor Hirohito meets with his ministers in an underground room on August 14. This painting was executed after the fact by Ichiro Shirakawa, guided by Prime Minister Kantaro Suzuki (at left, front row).

With bowed heads and tears, citizens in a Tokyo suburb, who have never before heard their Emperor's voice, listen to a radio broadcast in which he announces Japan's surrender.

The Son of Heaven, shed of his godhead, stands with General MacArthur, shed of his ribbons (and his tie) in the U.S. embassy, where he called for his first talk with his new boss.

Surrender did not follow immediately on the two explosions. Hirohito's ministers and his top generals were not all ready to go along with the Emperor's desire, expressed at a meeting with his ministers *(upper left)*, to end the war on the terms of the joint resolution the Allies had issued at Potsdam. Between the two bombings, the U.S.S.R. joined the Pacific war by invading Manchuria. Amid a storm of rumors and misleading broadcasts, Foreign Minister Togo beamed directly to Washington the statement that emerged from that meeting.

"The Japanese government is ready to accept the terms enumerated in the joint declaration issued at Potsdam on July 26, 1945," it read, "with an understanding that the said declaration does not comprise any demand which prejudices the prerogatives of His Majesty as a sovereign ruler." President Truman saw that wording as contradictory to unconditional surrender. At a Cabinet meeting called to discuss a reply, Secretary of War Stimson suggested that "Something like this use of the Emperor must be made to save us from a score of bloody Iwo Jimas." After the discussion Secretary of State Byrnes wrote the U.S. response.

"From the moment of surrender," it read, "the authority of the Emperor and the Japanese Government to rule shall be subject to the Supreme Commander of the Allied powers, who will take such steps as he deems necessary to effectuate the surrender terms." It said further that "the ultimate form of government of Japan will be established by the freely expressed will of the Japanese people"

This last provision assured the preservation of *kokutai*, Nippon's essence as embodied by the Emperor. Truman approved the message. All the Allies but the U.S.S.R. signed off on it. Russia wanted a share in the high command and veto power over the choice of the commander. "Utterly out of the question," Ambassador Harriman told Foreign Minister Molotov. A few hours later the Soviets backed down and signed. On August 15 Japan surrendered.

A Japanese soldier guarding route to Yokahama fo conquerors stands facing awa Japanese always did whe Emperor passed. Peop doorways also turned their f away. It took some time fo Americans to convince themse that this was a sign of res

Two Faces of Surrender: Pandemonium and Protocol

*Navy men at Pearl Harbor, where for America the who[le]
thing began, cheer at the broadcast of the surren[der]
ceremonies in Tokyo Bay. At right, seen from the yardarm [of]
Admiral Nimitz's flagship the Missouri, the world's larg[est]
battleship, General MacArthur stands at the surrender tab[le]
awaiting the Japanese delegation grouped stiffly befo[re]
him. Behind MacArthur are signers for the victorious n[ine]
nations and dominions; lined up at his left are a score [of]
two- to four-star Allied admirals and genera[ls.]*

1945
On the 'Big Mo'

Standing expressionless before the baize-covered GI chow table with its burden of fateful documents, Mamoru Shigemitsu, Japan's new foreign minister, leans heavily on his cane to support the artificial leg he wears as a result of a bomb thrown at him years before by a Korean in Shanghai. Beside him stands the beribboned chief of the general staff, General Yoshijiro Umezu. When the Japanese contingent boarded the Missouri they were greeted by a silence broken only by the sound of the boatswain's pipe.

On Broadway

In New York's Times Square, a sailor grabs a passing nurse for a celebratory kiss and makes her, or at least her figure, an icon of the joy of peace.

THE WAR'S STATISTICS

BATTLE DEAD

15,000,000

he greatest tragedy the world has ever known was over, but the immensity of
the death and broken lives that World War II left behind can never be counted with complete
accuracy, nor truly comprehended. A half-century later, with the world rebuilt, the
staggering costs of the trillion-dollar conflict at first sound meaningless, too large to grasp—50 million
dead, 60 million left starving. It is only after contemplation and comparison that the size
of the horror begins to take on reality. The gigantic, rounded-off numbers that appear on
these final pages are based on the best statistics available. Still, a few are approximations. For in some
devastated places, the counting process was incomplete. Either that, or nobody bothered to take
the toll or measure the consequences of all that insane slaughter.

At an American military cemetery near Anzio, Italy, marble crosses mark the
graves of some of the 85 million who served in uniform during the war.

CIVILIAN DEAD
AND MISSING
40,000,000

Bodies from the fire-bombing of Dresden smolder in a makeshift pyre.

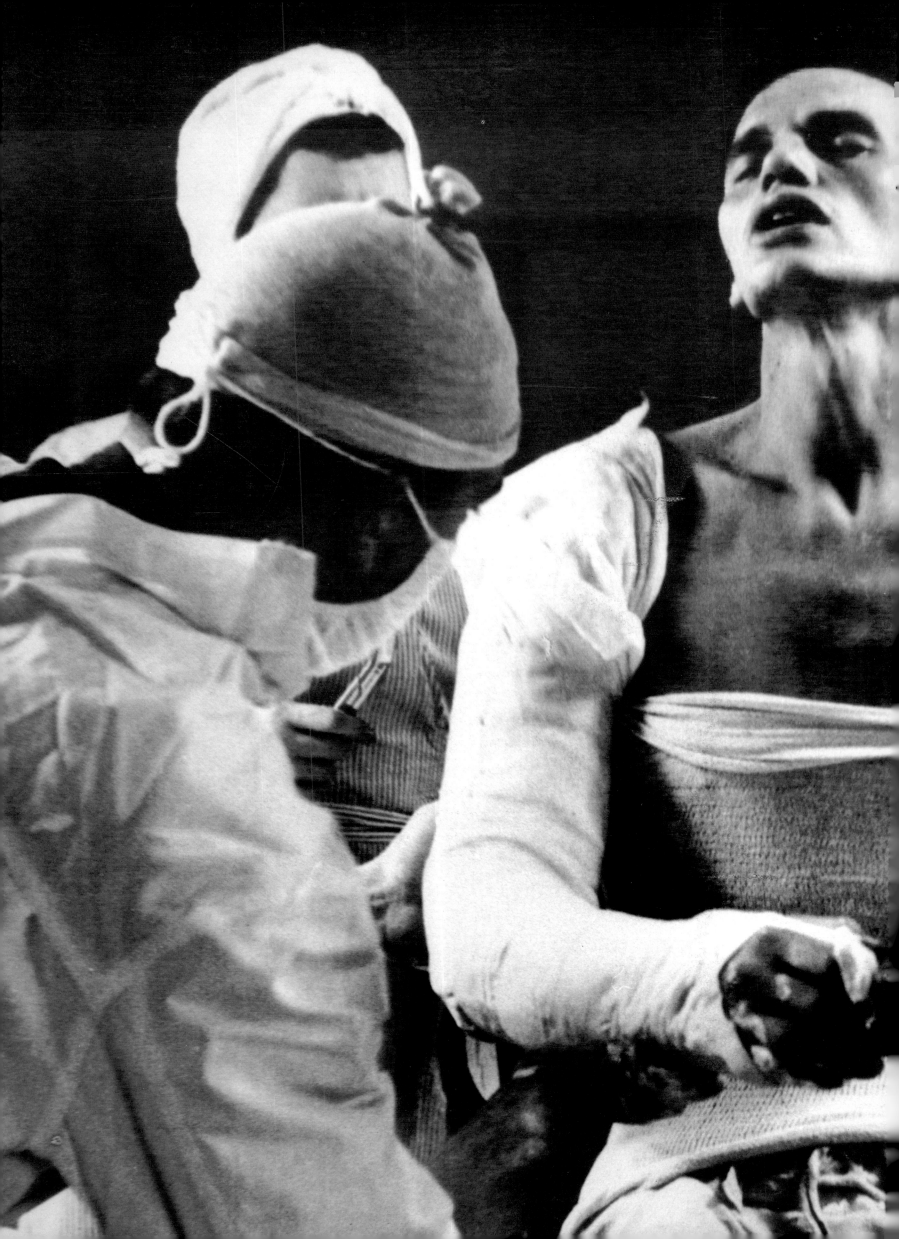

WOUNDED
Military
and Civilian
35,000,000

A plaster cast is painfully molded to the body of a GI hit by mortar fire.

Carrying her baby, a quilt and several pots, one of the 10 million displaced people of Europe leads her daughter across a field to nowhere.

HOMELESS
28,000,000

Their city still smoking, a stunned Nagasaki mother and son join 10 million Asian homeless.

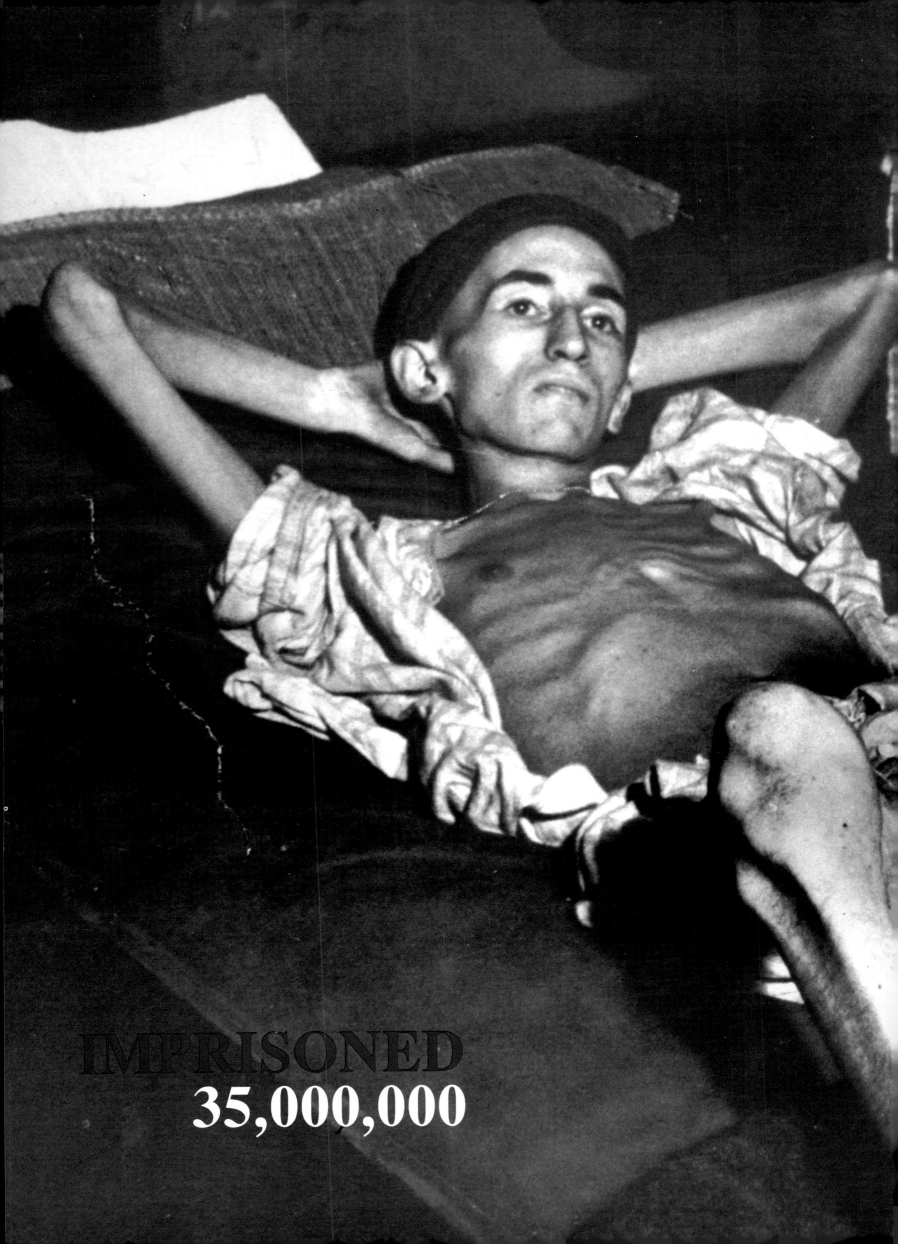

IMPRISONED
35,000,000

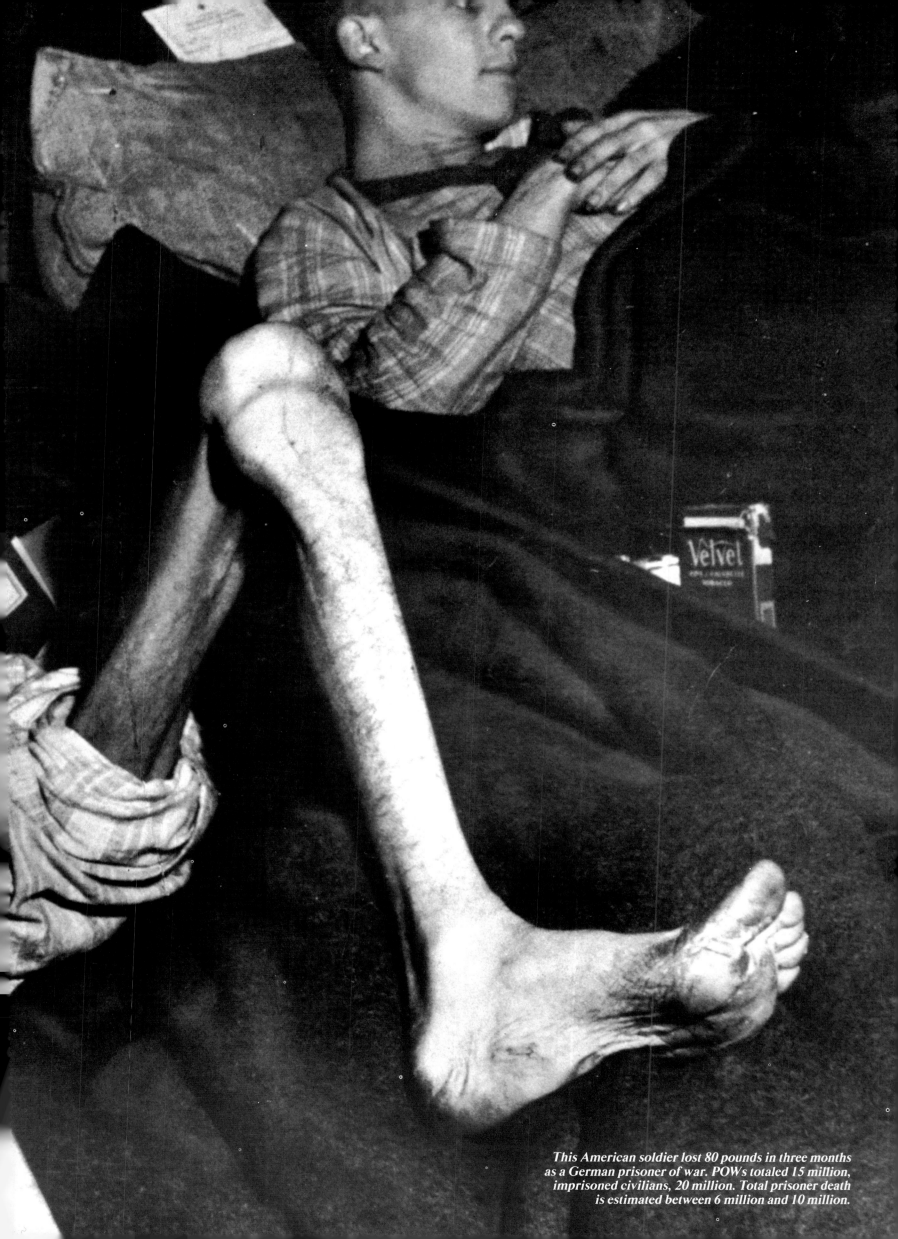

This American soldier lost 80 pounds in three months as a German prisoner of war. POWs totaled 15 million, imprisoned civilians, 20 million. Total prisoner death is estimated between 6 million and 10 million.

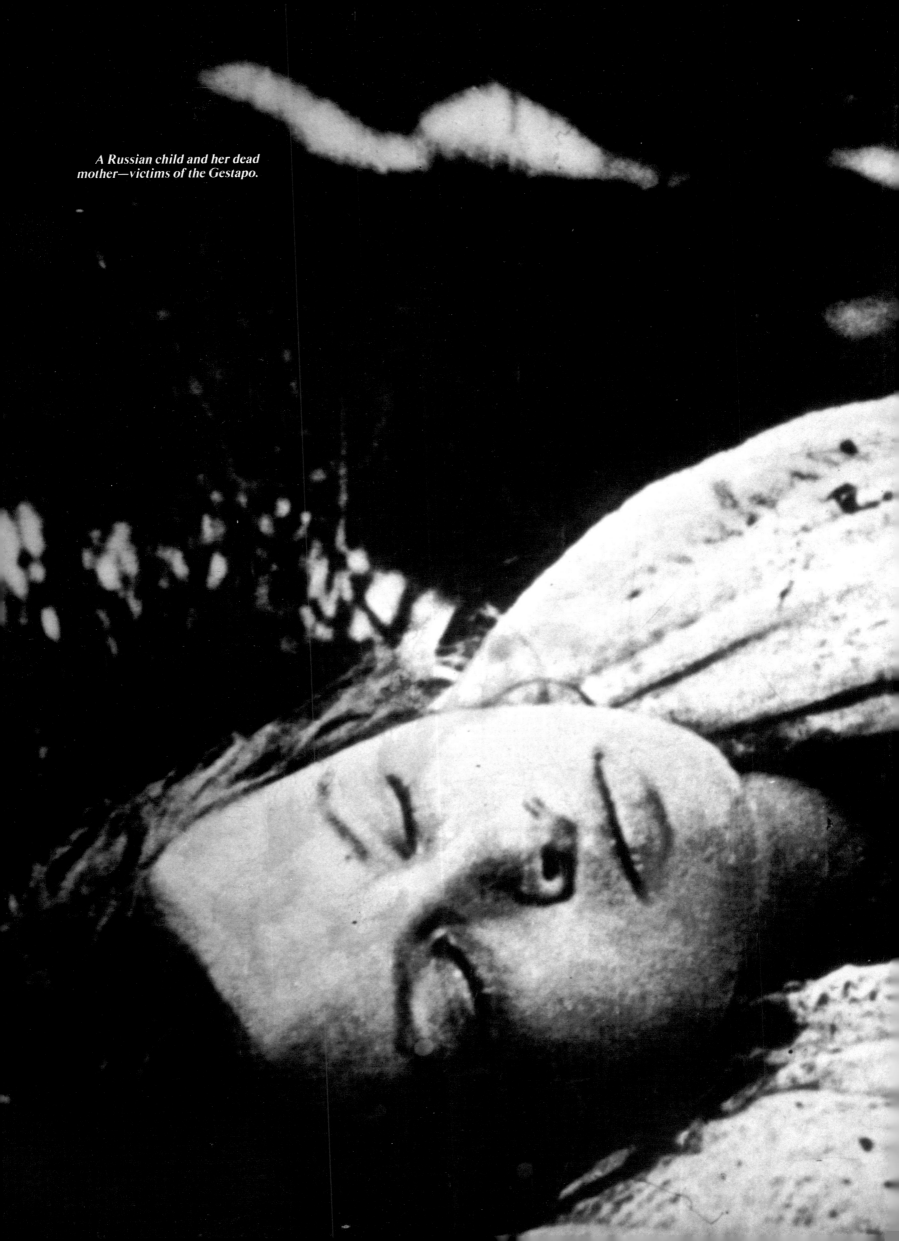

A Russian child and her dead mother—victims of the Gestapo.

5,000,000

EXTERMINATED
11,000,000

A Jewish prisoner dying of starvation at Bergen-Belsen mourns those he soon will join.

However much they had suffered, most of the world lived. These women were prisoners in a German concentration camp. From a window of a train taking them home, their faces reflect a wide range of war's emotions.

SURVIVORS

INDEX

PHOTO CREDITS

Photographers' credits are listed page by page and separated left to right by semicolons, from top to bottom by dashes.

1: W. Eugene Smith, LIFE. **2:** U.S. Army. **4:** U.S. Army. **6:** Bildarchiv Preussischer Kulturbesitz. **8:** Bettmann Archives. **10:** Bettmann/UPI (both). **12:** Popperfoto. **14:** Brown Brothers. **16:** Margaret Bourke-White—Robert Capa. **18:** Hugo Jaeger. **20:** Heinrich Hoffmann. **22:** Time Inc. **23:** Wide World. **24:** Bettmann/UPI. **25:** © Topham Picture Source/The Image Works. **26:** map by Richard Edes Harrison (both). **27:** Bildarchiv Preussischer Kulturbesitz. **28:** European. **30:** Sueddeutscher Verlag Bilderdienst. **32:** Centralna Agencia Fotograficzna. **34:** Wide World. **35:** Wide World—Camera Press. **36:** Bettmann-/UPI—Bettmann/UPI; U.S. Army. **37:** Wartime German Govt. Photo—Wide World. **38:** Wide World. **40:** Wartime German Govt. Photo—No Credit. **41:** Bundesarchiv Koblenz—Bettmann/UPI—No Credit. **42:** Dever, Black Star. **43:** Julien Bryan. **44:** Bettmann/UPI; Combine—LIFE; Wide World. **45:** William Davis for LIFE. **46:** Bettmann/UPI—Bettmann/UPI—Dever, Black Star; Bettmann/UPI. **47:** Finnish Defense Forces—Wide World. **48:** Carl Mydans, LIFE. **49:** Visii Sodon Vuotta; Dever, Black Star **50:** Bettmann/UPI; George Strock—Carl Mydans, LIFE—Alfred Eisenstaedt; Wide World. **51:** Thomas D. McAvoy, LIFE. **52:** Bettmann/UPI.—Paul Dorsey, LIFE. **53:** Service Cinematographique de l'Armee. **54:** Wide World. **55:** Wartime German Govt. Photo. **56:** C.P. Detloff. **57:** map by Richard Edes Harrison. **58:** European **60:** Wide World. **61:** The Keystone Collection. **62:** Wartime German Govt. Photo. **63:** Hans Bredewold Collection, Leiden, Netherlands **64:** Wartime German Govt. Photo (both). **65:** Wartime German Govt. Photo (both). **66:** Keystone Press Agency—Wartime German Govt. Photo. **67:** Wartime German Govt. Photo—Service Cinematographique de l'Armee. **68:** Wartime German Govt. Photo. **69:** Wartime German Govt. Photo, **70:** Wide World—LIFE. **71:** Pathe News. **72:** No Credit: **74:** Topix; LIFE—The Times, London. **75:** Service Cinematographique de la Marine. **76:** Estate of Martin Munkacsi; Martin Harris; Wide World—Walter Sanders; George Karger; Arthur Griffin; Edmund Bert Gerard. **77:** Robert Capa; Peter Stackpole, LIFE; Paul Dorsey—No Credit; Otto Hagel; W.Eugene Smith. **78:** J. B. Cabell. **79:** LIFE cover by Underwood & Underwood—Bettmann/UPI—Interphoto. **80:** Pathe News (4 pictures). **81:** Wartime German Govt. Photo. **82:** Wartime German Govt. Photo. **83:** No Credit. **84:** Wartime German Govt. Photo. **85:** No Credit. **86:** No Credit. **88:** Popperfoto. **89:** William Vandivert, LIFE. **90:** Bettmann/UPI (3)—British Govt. Photo. **91:** map by Richard Edes Harrison—Bettmann/UPI. **92:** London News Chronicle; British Govt. Photo—British Govt. Photo; Wartime German Govt. Photo—Wide World. **93:** Combine; British Govt. Photo—Harris & Ewing—Combine. **94:** William Vandivert, LIFE. **96:** London Daily Mirror. **97:** Popperfoto. **98:** Bill Brandt. **99:** British Govt. Photo. **100:** London Daily Mirror—Bettmann/UPI. **101:** London News Chronicle. **102:** Graphic Photo Union; Robert Landry; Haensel Mieth, LIFE—Paul Dorsey; Peter Stackpole, LIFE; Charles E. Steinheimer. **103:** Wide World; Wide World—Thomas D. McAvoy, LIFE; George Strock, LIFE. **104:** U.S. Navy. **106:** map by Richard Edes Harrison—Heinrich Hoffmann. **110:** C.D. Hackett Collection. **111:** Ghetto Fighters' House, Israel. **112:** Sueddeutscher Verlag Bilderdienst. **113:** Vladimir Karpov (both). **114:** Wartime German Govt. Photo. **116:** Wartime German Govt. Photo (both). **117:** Bibliothek fuer Zeitgeschichte, Stuttgart. **118:** Vladimir Karpov. **120:** Margaret Bourke-White. **121:** Vladimir Karpov. **122:** Novosti Press Agency—Wartime German Govt. Photo. **124:** Novosti Press Agency. **126:** Dever, Black Star. **127:** map by Time Inc. **128:** Bundesarchiv, Koblenz. **129:** Wartime German Govt. Photo. **130:** London Daily Mirror—News Syndicate Inc.—Bettmann/UPI(5). **131:** Bettmann/UPI—Lothar Guenther Buchheim Collection. **132:** British Govt. Photo.—British Govt. Photo; William Vandivert, LIFE. **133:** Topical Press. **134:** British Govt. Photo; art by A. Leydenfrost for LIFE—Wide World. **135:** art by A. Leydenfrost for LIFE—Janusz Piekalkiewicz. **136:** Wide World. **137:** Wide World. **138:** Wide World—Margaret Bourke-White; Bettmann/UPI. **139:** Wartime German Govt. Photo—Bettmann/UPI. **140:** Bettmann/UPI—map by Richard Edes Harrison—Geoffrey Landesman. **141:** No Credit. **142:** Robert Landry; Ron Partridge, Black Star; Robert Landry—Bettmann/UPI; Fritz Goro; Bettmann/UPI. **143:** William C. Shrout, LIFE; Thomas D. McAvoy, LIFE—Alfred Eisenstaedt; Thomas D. McAvoy, LIFE. **144:** Pix. **145:** Robert Landry. **146:** Novosti Press Agency. **147:** U.S. Navy. **148:** Novosti Press Agency—British Govt. Photo. **149:** United States Information Agency (inset). **150:** U.S. Navy (all). **151:** map Time Inc.; U.S. Navy (all). **152:** U.S. Navy. **153:** U.S. Navy. **154:** U.S. Navy. **156:** Wartime Japanese Govt. Photo. **157:** Robert Landry, LIFE—Robert Landry, LIFE—U.S. Navy. **158:** U.S. Army. **159:** Wartime Japanese Govt. Photo. **160:** map by Richard Edes Harrison. **161:** map by Richard Edes Harrison. **164:** Wartime Japanese Govt. Photo (both). **165:** Bettmann-/UPI. **166:** Bettmann/UPI—Tsuguichi Koyanagi. **167:** map by Time Inc.—Tsuguichi Koyanagi. **168:** Tsuguichi Koyanagi—Bettmann/UPI. **169:** U.S. Marine Corps. **170:** U.S. Navy; U.S. Army Air Force—Ralph Morse, LIFE—Wide World. **171:** Wartime Japanese Govt. Photo—U.S. Army Air Force—Wide World. **172:** U.S. Navy (both). **174:** U.S. Navy. **175:** U.S. Army Air Force (inset). **176:** Alfred Eisenstaedt—George Baker. **177:** Library of Congress—Myron H. Davis, LIFE **178:** George Karger; Wide World; Eliot Elisofon—Wide World(2). **179:** Wide World; Bettmann/UPI; Library of Congress—Myron H. Davis, LIFE; Bettmann/UPI; Nina Leen—Ed Clark; Nina Leen; John Phillips, LIFE. **180:** Milwaukee Journal. **181:** Gordon Coster—Philip Gendreau/Bettmann Archives. **182:** Bettmann/UPI—New York Daily News; Eliot Elisofon. **183:** Wide World. **184:** art by A. Leydenfrost for LIFE. **185:** Nelson Morris. **186:** Bettmann/UPI. **187:** British Govt. Photo (both)—British Govt. Photo.—Robert Landry, LIFE. **188:** Wide World; National Archives—map by Time Inc. **190:** Wartime German Govt. Photo—No Credit. **191:** Map by Time Inc.—Imperial War Museum. **192:** British Govt. Photo.; Wide World(inset). **194:** U.S. Coast Guard (both). **195:** Lothar Guenther Buchheim Collection—U.S. Coast Guard. **196:** U.S. Navy. **198:** Farabola. **200:** Bettmann/UPI; Culver Pictures—J.C. Patel, Keystone Press Agency; U.S. Navy. **201:** Combine—Wide World. **202:** Wartime Japanese Govt. Photo. **203:** George Karger. **204:** Mark Kauffman—John Florea—Mark Kauffman. **205:** Wide World. **206:** Peter Stackpole, LIFE. **207:** John Florea. **208:** U.S. Marine Corps; Norman Bel Geddes for LIFE—Bettmann/UPI. **210:** Ralph Morse, LIFE (all). **211:** Ralph Morse, LIFE. **212:** Sovfoto. **213:** Bettmann/UPI—Georgi Zelma. **214:** Sovfoto. **215:** U.S. Marine Corps. **216:** Wide World. **217:** George Strock, LIFE. **218:** map by Richard Edes Harrison. **219:** U.S. Navy. **222:** Polonia Publishing House. **223:** United Israel Appeal. **224:** Glavnoye Arkavnoye Upravlenine. **225:** Bildarchiv Preussischer Kulturbesitz. **226:** No Credit. **227:** No Credit. **228:** Archive Amicale de Mauthausen, Paris. **229:** No Credit. **230:** No Credit. **231:** ADN—Tass Photo. **232:** British Govt. Photo—Norman Bel Geddes for LIFE. **233:** Margaret Bourke-White. **234:** Frank Scherschel, LIFE. **236:** U.S. Army **238:** Imperial War Museum. **240:** U.S. Coast Guard. **241:** Robert Capa; Wartime German Govt. Newsreel. **242:** George Rodger, LIFE—Sandro Aurisicchio De Val; Robert Capa. **243:** Robert Capa. **244:** U.S. Army Air Force (both). **245:** U.S. Army Air Force (both). **246:** Heinrich Hoffmann—Bettmann/UPI. **247:** Georgi Zelma. **248:** Wartime German Govt. Photo. **249:** Novosti Press Agency. **250:** Novosti Press Agency. **251:** Novosti Press Agency. **252:** Library of Congress. **253:** Georgije Skrigin—No Credit—Wide World. **254:** U.S. Army Air Force—Wide World. **255:** Wide World—U.S. Army Air Force. **256:** Black Star. **257:** Keystone Press Agency. **258:** Edmund B. Gerard; Seattle Times—Alfred Eisenstaedt; Charles E. Steinheimer; Walter Sanders; Wide World. **259:** Library of Congress; Carol Eyerman; Bernard Hoffman, LIFE—Charles E. Steinheimer; Gjon Mili; Wide World. **260:** Ralph Vincent for Portland Journal. **261:** Ewing Krainin; Movie Star News; Bud Fraker, Paramount Pictures—Margaret Bourke-White. **262:** U.S. Army Air Force (both). **263:** map by Time Inc. **264:** William Vandivert, LIFE. **265:** William Vandivert, LIFE. **266:** G.P. Adams Collection, London. **268:** U.S. Army Signal Corps. **270:** Wide World. **272:** U.S. Marine Corps (both). **273:** Map by Time Inc (inset): Wide World. **274:** U.S. Army, courtesy Col. Eugene C. Jacobs. **275:** George Silk, LIFE. **276:** Robert Capa. **278:** map by Richard Edes Harrison. **279:** W. Eugene Smith, LIFE. **280:** U.S. Navy. **282:** U.S. Army—Robert Landry, LIFE. **283:** Bundesarchiv, Koblenz (both). **285:** Frank Scherschel, LIFE . **286:** Frank Scherschel, LIFE—Wide World. **287:** U.S. Army. **288:** U.S. Coast Guard; Royal Canadian Navy (inset). **290:** Robert Capa. **291:** Robert Capa (all). **292:** British Govt. Photo—U.S. Army—Robert Capa. **293:** U.S. Coast Guard—Robert Capa. **294:** Frank Scherschel, LIFE—Wartime German Govt. Photo. **295:** Wartime German Govt. Photo; Bildarchiv Preussischer Kulturbesitz. **296:** U.S. Army Signal Corps—Robert Capa. **298:** George Silk, LIFE. **299:** U.S. Army Air Force, courtesy Nino Arena—Fotolocchi, Florence. **300:** Novosti Press Agency (both). **301:** N. Petrov. **302:** Jerzy Tomaszewski (all). **303:** Jerzy Tomaszewski. **304:** Bundesarchiv Koblenz. **305:** Imperial War Museum; George Rodger, LIFE—Bettmann/UPI. **306:** Ralph Morse, LIFE. **307:** Ralph Morse, LIFE. **308:** Ralph Morse, LIFE—Collection Roger-Viollet. **309:** Robert Capa, LIFE. **310:** Robert Landry, LIFE. **312:** U.S. Army—Robert Landry, LIFE. **313:** Robert Capa, LIFE—U.S. Army. **314:** map by Time Inc.—U.S. Army. **315:** John Florea, LIFE. **316:** Imperial War Museum. **317:** U.S. Army. **318:** Robert Capa, LIFE. **319:** Robert Capa, LIFE. **320:** Bundesarchiv Koblenz—Hans Brunswig. **321:** © Dr. Wolf Strache. **322:** John Phillips, LIFE; George Skadding, LIFE—Popperfoto. **323:** Frank Scherschel, LIFE—Wide World; Bettmann/UPI. **324:** Andreas Feininger, LIFE. **325:** © Eileen Darby. **326:** Marie Hansen, LIFE; Harold Trudeau—William David Bell; Bettmann/UPI. **327:** Carl Mydans, LIFE; Ralph Crane—Thomas D. McAvoy, LIFE; George Skadding, LIFE. **328:** W. Eugene Smith, LIFE. **329:** No Credit. **330:** U.S. Naval Historical Center. **332:** Bettmann/UPI; Australian War Memorial—Nihon Hoso Kyokai. **333:** Peter Stackpole, LIFE—LIFE—Wartime Japanese Govt. Photo. **334:** U.S. Navy. **335:** U.S. Navy. **336:** U.S. Navy. **337:** U.S. Navy. **338:** George Strock, LIFE—map by Time Inc. **339:** George Strock, LIFE. **340:** U.S. Marine Corps. **341:** W. Eugene Smith, LIFE. **342:** Peter Stackpole, LIFE. **343:** Peter Stackpole, LIFE. **344:** Painting by Tom Lea for LIFE. **345:** Painting by Tom Lea for LIFE. **346:** U.S. Army; map by Time Inc. (inset). **347:** Bettmann/UPI—Frank Cancellone, Bettmann/UPI. **348:** Naval Historial Center—U.S. Navy. **349:** U.S. Navy. **350:** U.S. Navy. **351:** U.S. Navy (inset). **352:** Yoshito Matsushige. **353:** Brian Brake. **354:** Map by Richard Edes Harrison. **355:** Map by Richard Edes Harrison. **356:** U.S. Navy. **358:** George Silk, LIFE. **360:** George Silk, LIFE. **361:** Robert Capa, LIFE. **362:** U.S. Army. **364:** George Silk, LIFE. **365:** Robert Capa, LIFE. **366:** John Florea, LIFE. **367:** Ullstein Bilderdienst. **368:** Hanns Hubmann, Bildarchiv Preussischer Kulturbesitz. **369:** Sueddeutscher Verlag Bilderdienst—ADN-Zentralbild. **370:** Yevgeni Khaldei. **372:** U.S. Army Signal Corps. **373:** Margaret Bourke-White. **374:** art by A. Leydenfrost for LIFE. **375:** No Credit. **376:** William Vandivert, LIFE. **377:** No Credit; William Vandivert, LIFE - Bettmann/UPI. **378:** courtesy David Pollak. **379:** George Rodger, LIFE. **380:** George Rodger, LIFE—William Vandivert, LIFE. **381:** John Florea, LIFE—Margaret Bourke-White. **382:** Margaret Bourke-White. **383:** Bettmann/UPI. **384:** London News Chronicle—Sovfoto. **385:** Vladimir Karpov. **386:** U.S. Signal Corps. **387:** U.S. Army—Ed Clark, LIFE. **388:** P.M. Photo—George Lyons, Wide World. **389:** James M. Keen. **390:** Frank Scherschel, LIFE; Charles Cort, Bettmann/UPI; N.Y. Daily News—Wide World; Ed Clark, LIFE; Sam Shere, LIFE. **391:** Philippe Halsman 1945, © Yvonne Halsman 1990; Marie Hansen, LIFE; Martha Holmes, LIFE—Gjon Mili; Walter Sanders, LIFE; National Archives. **392:** U.S. Navy—Carl Mydans, LIFE. **394:** Lou Lowery. **396:** Wide World. **397:** W. Eugene Smith, LIFE. **398:** U.S. Navy. **399:** U.S. Navy (all). **400:** U.S. Navy. **402:** W. Eugene Smith, LIFE. **403:** W. Eugene Smith, LIFE—U.S. Marine Corps. **404:** U.S. Army Air Force. **406:** Wartime Japanese Govt. Photo. **407:** Wartime Japanese Govt. Photo— U.S. Army Air Force. **408:** Koyo Ishikawa; George Silk, LIFE—Mainichi Shinbun. **409:** Shunkichi Kikuchi—Wartime Japanese Govt. Photo. **410:** Fritz Goro, LIFE. **411:** U.S. Army Signal Corps. **412:** Los Alamos National Laboratories—Fritz Goro, LIFE. **413:** U.S. Dept. of Defense. **414:** George Silk, LIFE; U.S. Army Air Force (inset). **416:** No Credit; Satsuo Nakada, Hiroshima Heiwa Bunka Center Foundation. **417:** Photoworld/FPG International. **418:** Yosuke Yamahata. **419:** Yosuke Yamahata. **420:** Yosuke Yamahata. **421:** Yoshito Matsushige. **422:** Ichiro Shirakawa, Japan Artists Assn. Inc.—Mainichi Shinbun—U.S. Army Signal Corps. **423:** Carl Mydans, LIFE. **424:** Wide World. **425:** John Florea, LIFE. **426:** Carl Mydans, LIFE. **427:** Alfred Eisenstaedt. **428:** N.R. Farbman, LIFE. **430:** ADN-Zentralbild. **432:** Ralph Morse, LIFE. **434:** Georgije Skrigin. **435:** Yosuke Yamahata. **436:** John Florea, LIFE. **438:** U.S. Army. **440:** Margaret Bourke-White. **441:** Imperial War Museum. **442:** AB Text & Bilder. **Endpapers:** U.S. Army.